cj LIM | STUDIO 8 ARCHITECTS

images Publishing

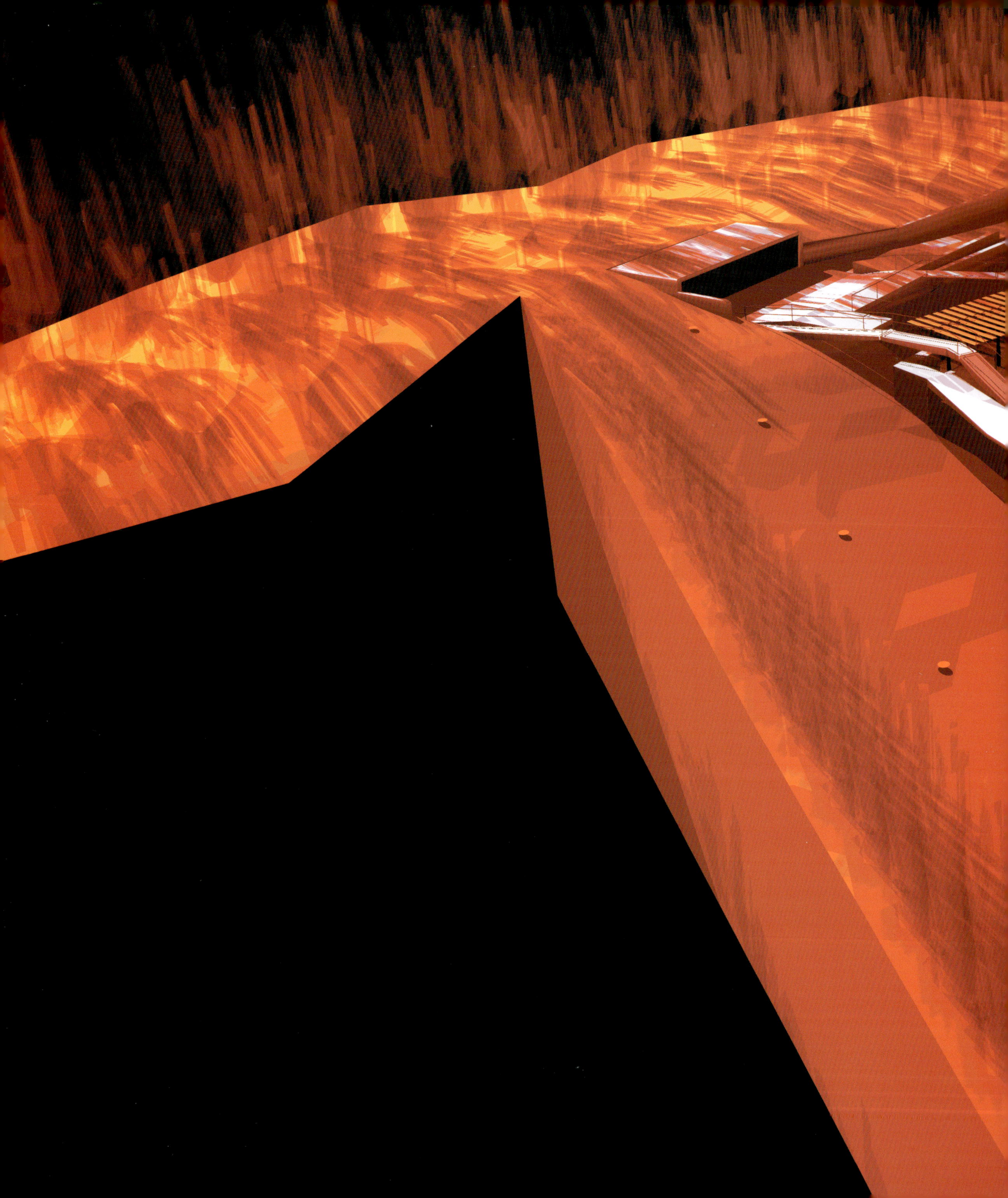

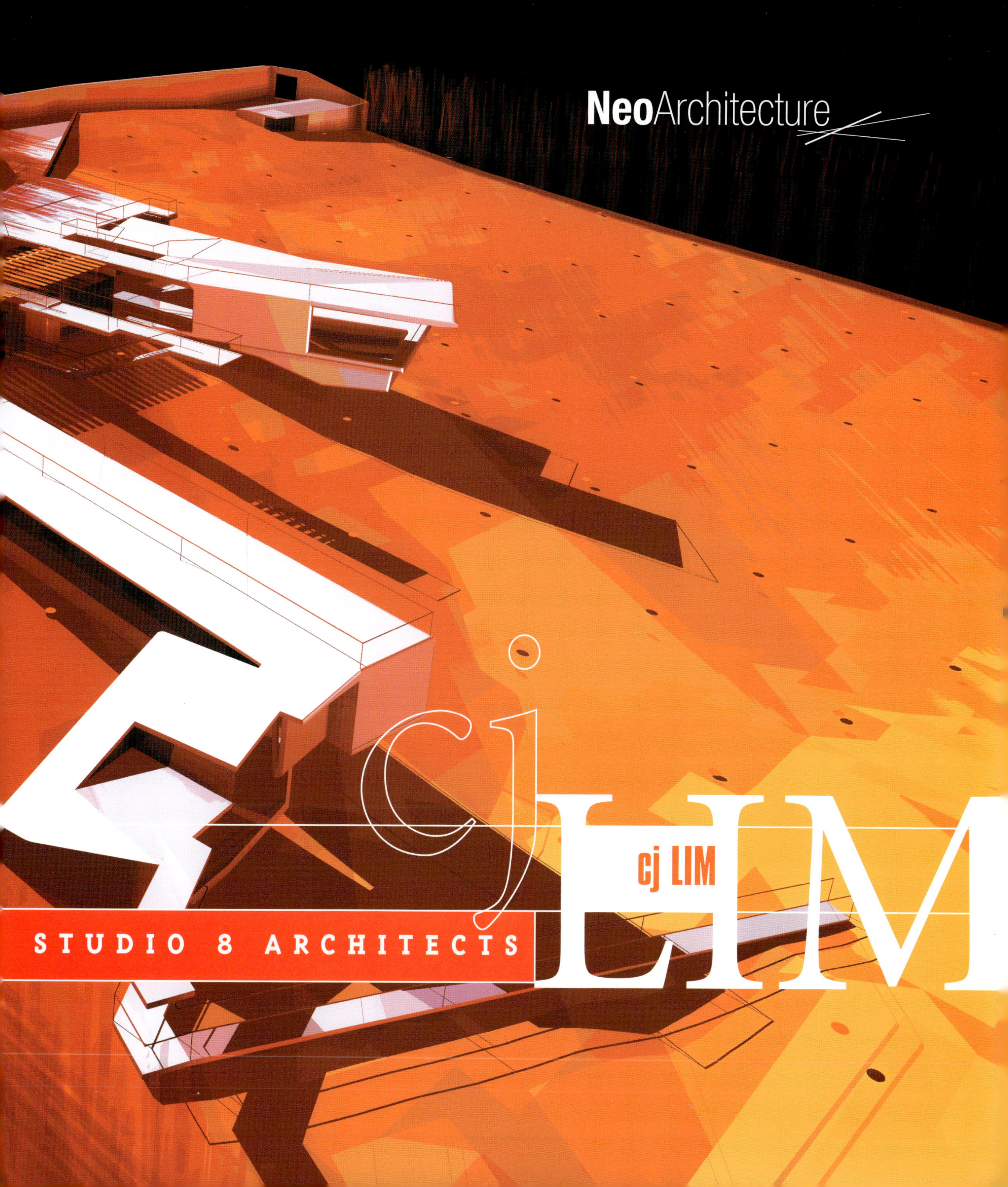

NeoArchitecture

cj LIM

cj LIM

STUDIO 8 ARCHITECTS

Published in Australia in 2005 by
The Images Publishing Group Pty Ltd
ABN 89 059 734 431
6 Bastow Place, Mulgrave, Victoria 3170, Australia
Tel: +61 3 9561 5544 Fax: +61 3 9561 4860
books@images.com.au
www.imagespublishing.com

The Images Publishing Group Reference Number: 627

National Library of Australia
Cataloguing-in-Publication entry:
cj Lim – Studio 8 Architects.

Bibliography.
ISBN 1 920744 80 0.

1. Lim, cj, 1964–. 2. Studio 8 Architects (Firm).
3. Architects – Great Britain – Biography.
4. Architectural firms – Great Britain – London – History.
5. Architecture, Modern – 20th century – Great Britain.
6. Architecture, Modern – 21st century – Great Britain.
I. Pavlovits, Daniel. (Series: Neo architecture series).

720.92

Designed by The Graphic Image Studio Pty Ltd, Mulgrave, Australia
www.tgis.com.au

Digital production and printing by Everbest Printing Co. Ltd in Hong Kong/China

CONTENTS

cj Lim established Studio 8 Architects in London in 1994. In parallel with practice, he is an educator and researcher, and is currently a director at the Bartlett, University College London. He spent his teenage years in Malaysia and has lived in London since 1982.

He was educated at the Architectural Association, London in the 1980s at the zenith of theory and experimentation in deconstructivist architecture. This early exposure to radical teachings and liberal thinking has since inspired a challenging of the status quo in his pursuit of new architectural territories. Innovation has been the hallmark of his work ever since.

Another marked facet of cj Lim is that he has continually maintained an unabashed affinity with the fusion of Eastern values and Western popular cultures, being fiercely British but ever mindful of his roots. More so than any of his contemporaries, he fully understands his cultural background's implications for design and architectural practice; something to be exploited as the very substance and palette of contemporary creativity. As cj Lim refuses to separate the world, its cultural content and the product of architecture into high culture and low culture, he does not take architecture too seriously, and in doing so, snubs the perhaps more elite or highbrow proponents of the profession into ridicule. He wants his architecture to be intelligent but mainly fun and eccentric, his inspirational hero being Heath Robinson rather than Le Corbusier

The love of the narrative form often provides the catalyst for the creative momentum of his work. His sharp observations of life and all its tales have led cj to capture the subtle nuances of space making. His architecture is much more than just elegant and sometimes complex forms; it is embedded with spatial tales and has soul. One should savour and experience his projects through the multi-layered architectural narratives. All these qualities and sensibilities have produced an architectural oeuvre that addresses our consumer reality and daily participation in capitalism head on. Such is the conceptualisation of his architecture, which is applied equally in his work to interiors as it is to museums, building commissions or research projects. The result is a range of pop-culture buildings and products, ranging from the incorporation of insect cuisine with gardening culture through to the deconstruction of Hollywood blockbusters.

Having initially focused on projects in the UK, Studio 8 Architects has become increasingly international in its outlook, with a portfolio covering Asia, North America and Western Europe. Whatever and wherever projects may emerge in the future, we can assume that cj Lim will continue to pursue the practice of architectural design through a witty and contemporary take on the world. Such conceptualisation of architecture and design sensibility is one marked by a youthful vigour, ready to embrace and interpret the cultural affects of globalisation. It is thus fitting that as the 21st century dawns, an architectural practice also emerges which is not ashamed of the times, sensibility and contexts within which it practises.

Daniel Pavlovits
Series Editor

››› *cj Lim comes from a quiet part of Malaysia but is a very London-centric character.*

A long time ago he became much more comfortable in the world of the academic hothouse with its implicit (but tantalising) threat that some bright student might fly past towards the new architecture. Nervousness created by the surmise that down the corridor might be some equally talented and equally investigative designer. A situation particular to a few cities – London and New York certainly, Los Angeles and Tokyo maybe and possibly one or two more. With their essential ingredients of competitiveness, gossip, proximity and myriad available mannerisms that demand that you develop a sophisticated – and eventually a distinctive – language, you can retain the attention of your peer group but continue to evolve as well. So as you contemplate his work of the period from 2000 to 2005, you realise that the creative response to this discomfort is manifest in a series of quizzical proposals: the eavesdropping, the glimpsing, the sly confrontation of machine with nature that results in a series of inventions that are more than just hybrids. The shafts, machines, gliding planes – all are enlivened, but also threatened by the implicit critique of their parasitic butterflies and plants. Both need each other – the tectonic elements and the parasites, both.

Undoubtedly, he has acquired that particular brand of wry commentary upon the commonplace: combining the seemingly ordinary with the quaintly absurd: very much part of the British culture of Monty Python, *Fawlty Towers* or the current crop of stand-up comedians. That gentle confrontation of the acceptable by the possible: listening to the late Cedric Price – quite probably and listening to any number of fellow-critics of student presentations – certainly, with the conversation perversely avoiding the directness of academic conversations in the United States or mainland Europe. How else to explain the programme of the Arena with its invocation – in a famous public place – of 'sofa therapy' (a form of 'confessional'), or the creative encouragement of screaming, or explain the delight in 'half-heard dialogues' in the Clone House, the titling of 'Chummy's' seafood pavilion at Folkestone, or the sight of twenty or more figures lying on the pavement with one ear downwards ... listening ... listening?

He is the quintessential draw-er designer, but has become a happy and relaxed lecturer.

It's curious isn't it, that as soon as an architect's work becomes interesting to other architects, he or she is dragged onto a series of platforms where there is the obligation to explain or define what all those lines were about. cj was as tongue-tied as most of the others at first, typically full of jargon and awkward pauses, but as his formal fluency developed, so did his recognition of the processes involved. Undoubtedly, teaching helped this: the constant practice of working your mind through *other peoples'* creative process edged itself towards that weird (but ultimately legitimate) state of post-rationalisation.

Nowadays, his projects transfer seamlessly to the lecture hall: organised into séances of not more than three or four sections. Clearly prefaced by a description of what they are about, a sequence of consecutive and constructive diagrams and at least one or two key images that seduce the memory. The insistence of colour too: it is no accident that whole books of his work can be in red, whole sequences can be of tantalising little figures doing things, whole formations of land and architecture seemingly constructed of endless paper aeroplanes. If the work of the late 1990s delighted in the juxtaposition of intriguing little coloured objects insinuating their way amongst great screens of surface – in projects such as the UCL Museum – and if it resulted in delicious paintings of the phases of the insinuation, the later work is more puritan, in a sense. Each work of the new Millennium establishes a central theme and a clearly poised aesthetic: each of them insists. The Country House totally reinterprets the tradition of landscaped surface with its planar insistence whereas the Hanging Gardens establish a landscape of captive racks without concerning themselves too much with surface. In such a way, this more recent work identifies a means of expression with which to clarify its statement.

Yet the motivating force remains the act of placement, followed swiftly – even seamlessly – by the integrity of the linkages of that placement. How perfectly, how elegantly does a drawing enable that to happen. In a drawing there can be a recognisable device – a door, a window, an enclosing arm perhaps – then a sudden and unexpected swing of the arm to suggest the act of exposure or explosion. cj has the dexterity to put the unexpected together with the expected. A group of jagged outcrops will suddenly (but deftly) turn and reveal a counter-movement. In the same way that a composer will cheekily drop the hints of counterpoint into a melodic line, Lim uses the essential linearity of drawing to ensnare the predictable. His language of form, enlarged and enjoyed, sets a series of palliatives, re-quotations and then surprises: but then the lines move on.

As time goes by, he starts to preface these moves by a series of titles, headlines, statements or provocative captions: the designer becomes rhetorical. Encouraged, no doubt, by the atmosphere of the academy.

He is happiest when perfecting a piece of hand-drawn eccentricity, yet his finished sheets absorb the photographic and the computer-generated as apparent essentials.

Maybe he's stopped worrying whether his drawings are too seductive, too controlled, too intricate, too clever. It seems so: of course they have been accused of all four characteristics, but Lim knows that his creativity has pretty well outlasted the bleatings of those critics who anyway possessed little ability themselves. Amongst young architects there is little charity and only grudging admiration for exceptional talent. Everyone secretly wants the others to slip on a banana skin: manipulation is suspect, dexterity is suspect, complexity is suspect and – heaven forbid sophistication.

Now he is openly delighting in the magic of current technologies: they interweave with all his other themes so that the plates of the Folkestone Pavilion indulge in 'periodic unfurlings of protective skin', the Arena delights in the potential of LEDs, the Country House enjoys its 'air-lift technology' and the Nam June Paik Museum twists its light catchers in a variety of magic movements.

He is shy outside his circle, but intrigues newcomers.

So he has, like many others of high talent, ways of insulating himself from the tedium of most architecture – new and old. He creates a series of pieces of a curious, quizzical world. A world resting on a fragile bed of irony, but structured by a continuing dependence on the benefits of architectural composition. He might gossip with ›››

Zaha Hadid, he might share students and ideas with Christine Hawley and undoubtedly refine his thoughts in collaboration with Ed Liu – a former student. Yet as time passes, we see cj becoming more and more determined to coerce the very refinement, the particularity of his work towards inevitability. The arguments take no prisoners, the designs allow for few modifications.

It is as if his finesse is its own provocation.

That oh-so-informed train of viewers who glide around the Venice Biennale of Architecture were puzzled and shocked by his exhibit in the British Pavilion last year. There were the fragile models, the birds and butterflies, the shadows, the filigree dances: but then, on the surrounding walls some tough, well-diagrammed and essentially *informational* stuff. The curators from Paris and New York had pigeonholed him as an elegant delineator, but now they had to catch up to the fact that his developed sure-footedness led into the narrative and even the atmospheric.

They were intrigued – and just a little scared. Unprepared for the 21st-century architect – who can glide from the digitally precise to the fey and back again. The world of architectural dreams no longer dependent upon those old jerky, scribbly, hairy, imprecise hints of the *other*.

His work is intensely stylish, but flirts with dangerous and even unfashionable ideas.

Such work threatens the moralist wing of architectural thought that is still bedded in some amalgam of northern Calvinist 'correctness' and its Modernist expression. Simultaneously it threatens the dictum that drawings are only a means to an end (and by implication should certainly *not* be enjoyed). And again, it threatens the comfortable assumption that architecture just creeps forward by way of modest, uncontentious scenarios.

There is no cj Lim building, but you seem to remember the ambience of his projects so well that you feel that you have been in them.

The early Lim building would have been a sharply profiled composition of containers.

Later it would have been layered-over with screens and trellises. Later still it would start acquiring gadgetry.

Now it clears the air, perhaps laying a ground of such stark abstractness that while you are getting over the shock, the fact that some parts of the construct are beginning to quiver comes, almost, as a release. Nonetheless, there will be beautifully fashioned enclosures, the working parts sleeved and tucked as precisely as any Swiss watch.

Remember the story of Bernard Tschumi? Just before the Parc de la Villette he was 'somebody seen in exhibitions'. Remember Neil Denari before the Tokyo room or the L.A Eyeworks? Just beautiful compositions and drawings, they said. cj is in that band of talent and his building will come?

Must come!

A hothouse product perhaps?

The hothouse propagates the rare hybrid, the plant that needs a rarefied territory in which to breed. Cleverly, cj has also constructed his own hothouse around himself as he has gone along: with 44/10, 'Sins', 'How Green is your Garden?' and several others: in these he has created a sounding board listened to by the young architects who buy them. They are for him the equivalent of Tschumi's New York exhibitions or Denari's dynamic sheets.

More fundamentally, we can regard this particular hothouse as a portent of the 21st-century architect. Working obsessively – with whatever materials are necessary – any and every computer programme, a small coterie of followers/friends, thrush's feathers, imported Venezuelan glue, chemists' tubes, 2000 digitalised faces, cow's bums, memories (somewhere) of Malaysian rubber plantations as a hiding-place: seen through an English mist.

Peter Cook
London, March 2005

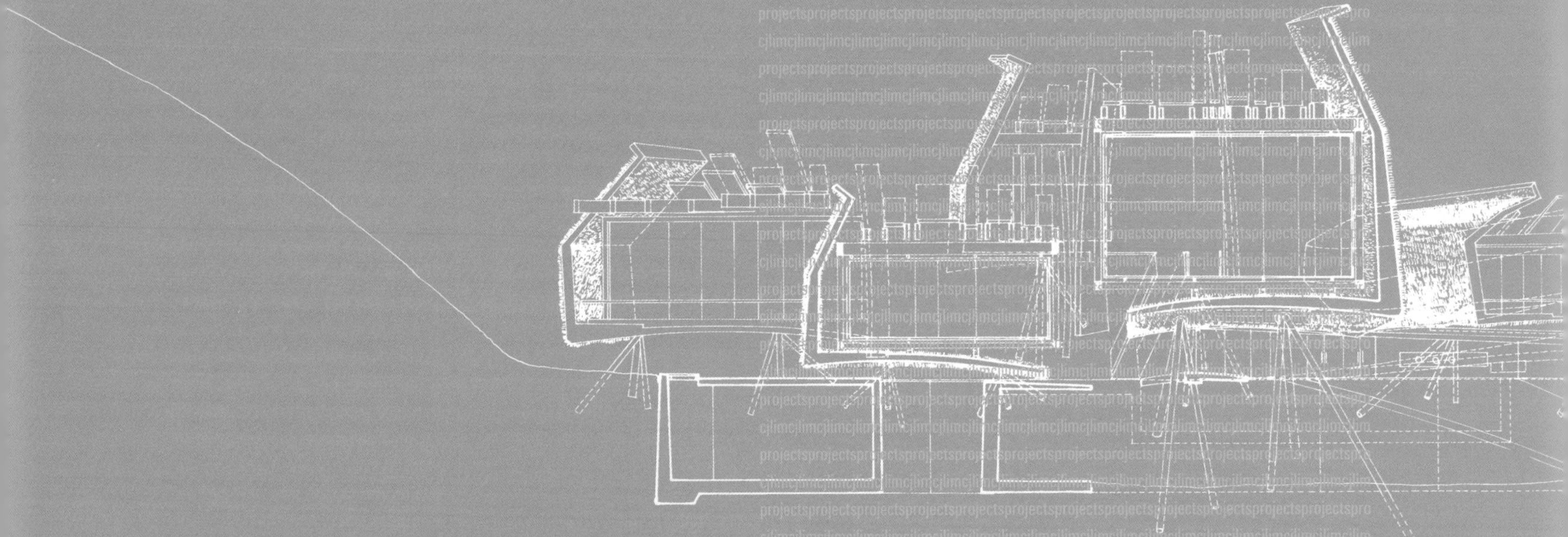

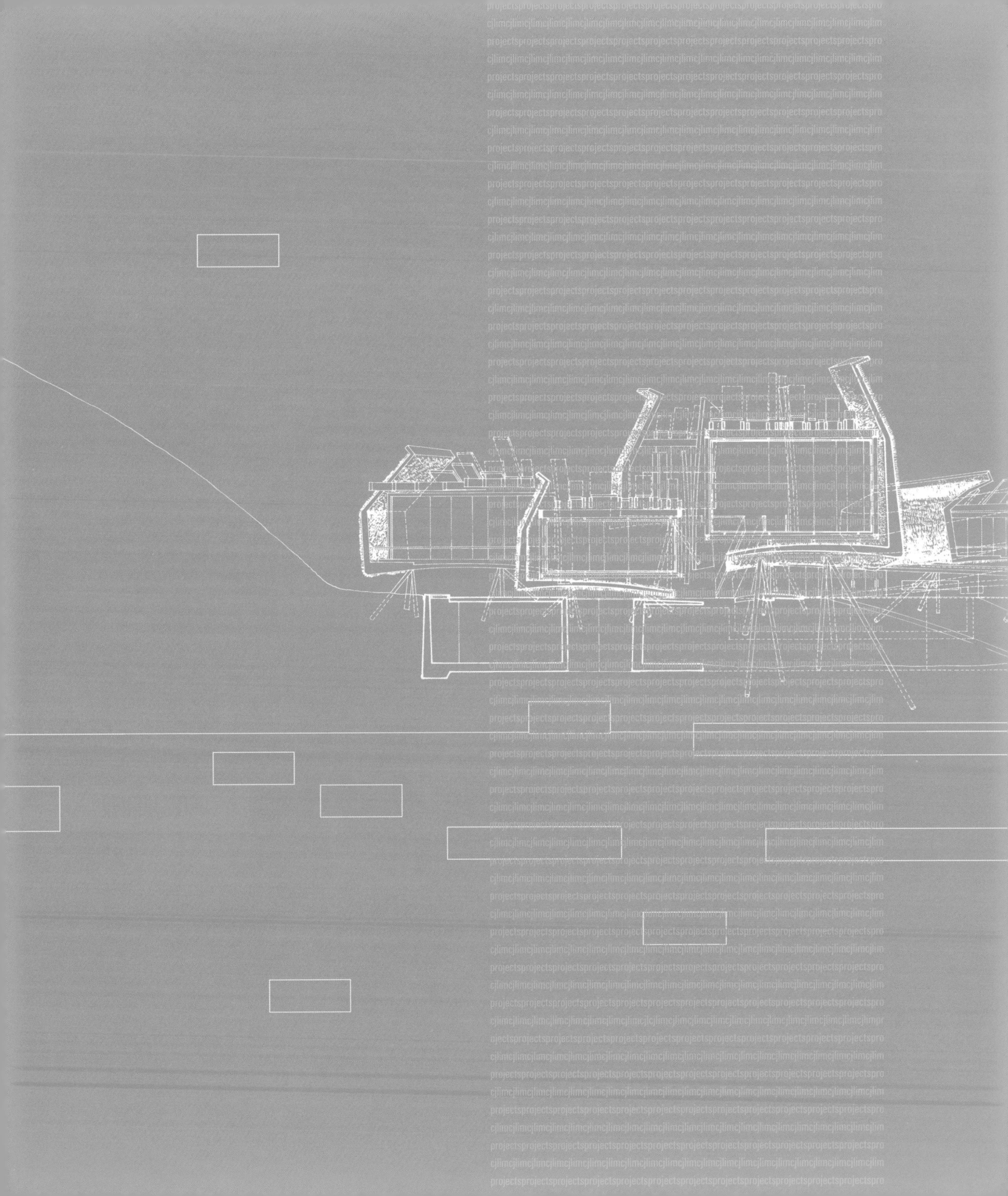

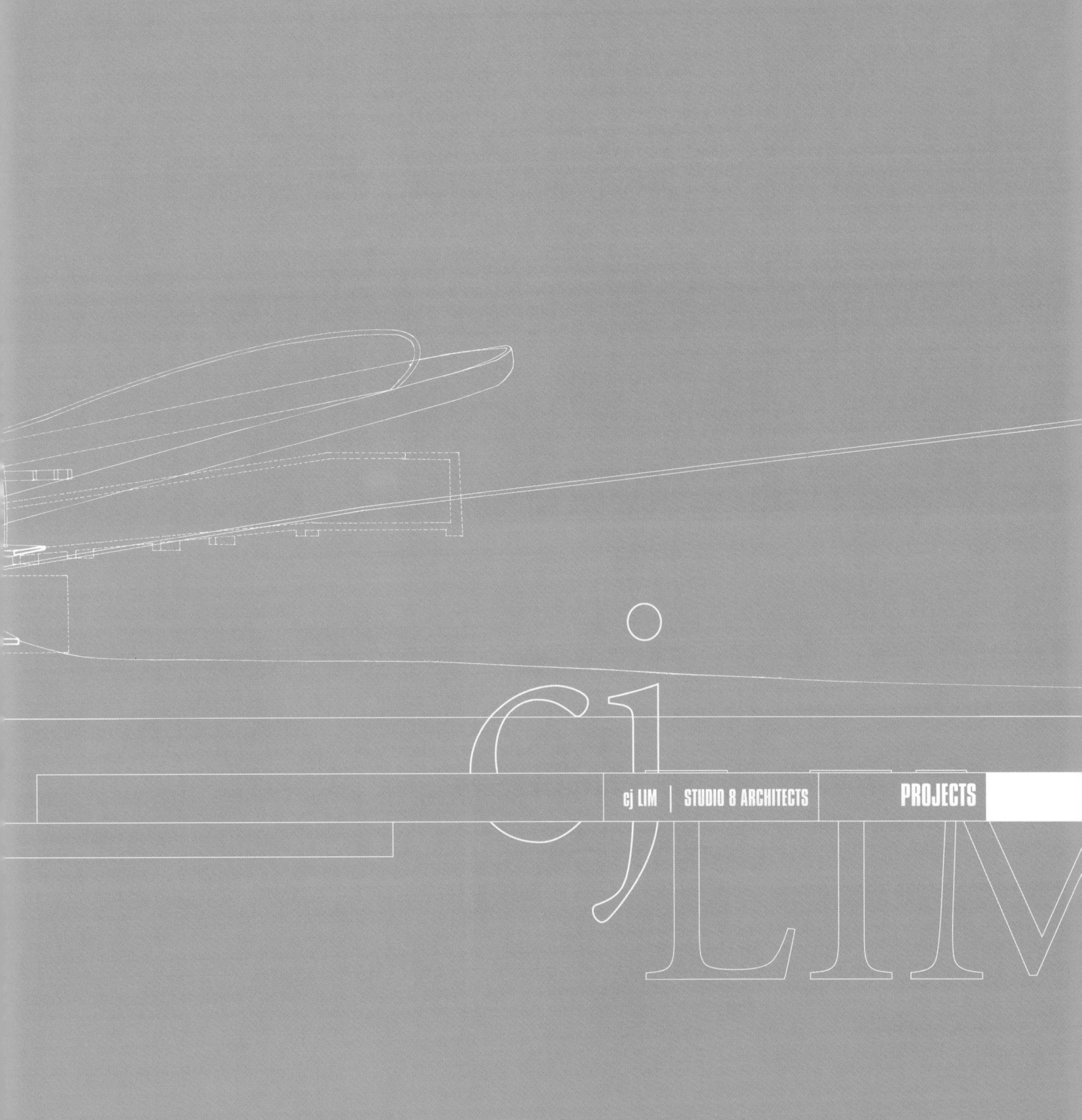

cj LIM | STUDIO 8 ARCHITECTS

PROJECTS

›››

'It's a wonderful world, if you'll only take the time to go around it!'
Around the World in Eighty Days,
Jules Verne

Inspired by the adventure story of French author Jules Verne, the project presents a flotilla of thirty red, blue and white hot-air balloons appearing to have fetched guests from all the participating countries to this site of the 30th Olympic Games. Tethered to the ground, these floating vessels are located 20 to 28 metres off the ground in mid-air. Suspended below the balloons are 'dancing' periscopes of various lengths to tease visitors, while a chorus of digital displays animates the ground surface with images of Paris's 2012 Olympic proposals.

The double life-size papier mâché guest figures can be seen doing acrobatic acts and waving from the wicker baskets. Sculpted and clad with 'chicken wire' and newspapers (with waterproof varnish) from their individual countries, these figures illustrate the importance of diversity of language and culture. To add to the fanfare, rudders of national flags from all participating countries wave in the wind while seemingly guiding the flight path of these vessels. These live hot-air balloons are remote-controlled. Their perpetual movement will tug and pull the periscopes, leading them to dance and float in mid-air.

With elements either floating above ground or embedded in ground, the entire allocated tarmac ground surface is left free for circulation and other temporary events. There are two spatial connection moments between air and ground:

- shadows from the floating hot-air balloons stroking and layering the ground and hence activating the digital displays via a 'shadow switch';
- visitors to this landmark physically forming a link between ground and floating elements, eagerly peering into the elegantly hovering periscopes, hoping to catch glimpses of surrounding Paris. The vast balloon envelope also forms an animated canopy providing shade for visitors.

At night, the flames from within these vessels will illuminate the hot-air balloons, thus enhancing the French colours. This will light the site and allow the landmark and the Olympic site to be seen from all over Paris and possibly beyond.

1

2

These figures illustrate the importance of diversity of language and culture.

These figures illustrate the importance of diversity of language and culture.

1 *Aerial view with periscopes peering through*
2 *Overall ground level view of landmark*
3 *Aerial view showing shadows from the floating hot-air balloons layering the ground*
4&5 *Papier-mâché figure above hot-air balloons* **6** *Aerial view of landmark*

3

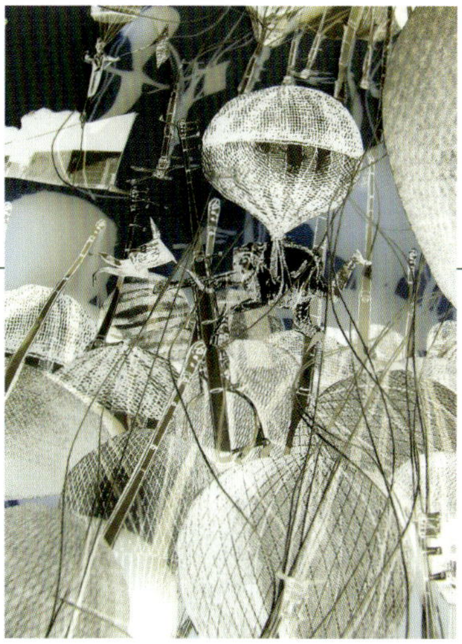

4

5

6

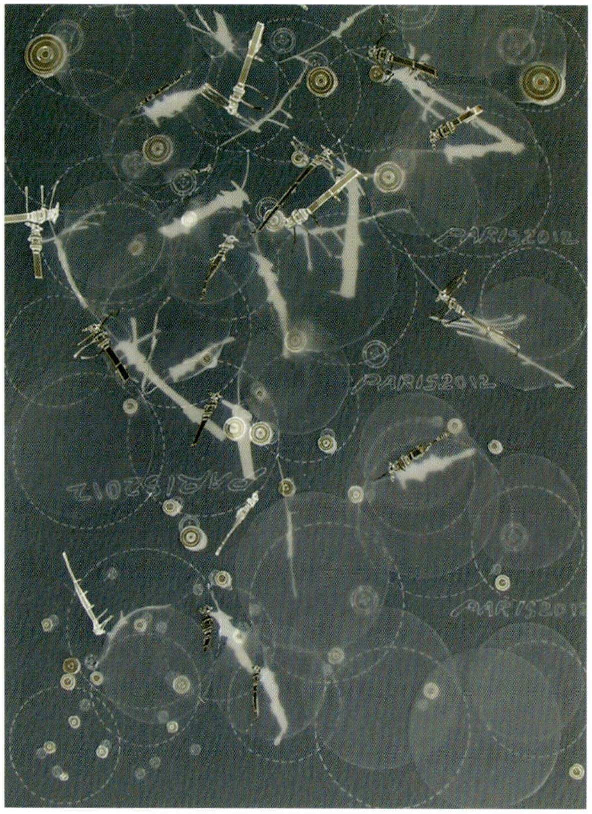

7

8

9

7 *Plan: digital display units performing with hovering periscopes and hot-air balloons above* **8** *The double life-size papier-mâché figures doing acrobatic acts and waving from the wicker baskets* **9** *Aerial view with periscopes peering through* **10** *Spectators peering into the hovering periscopes, hoping to catch glimpses of Paris* **11** *Overall elevation*

10

11

1

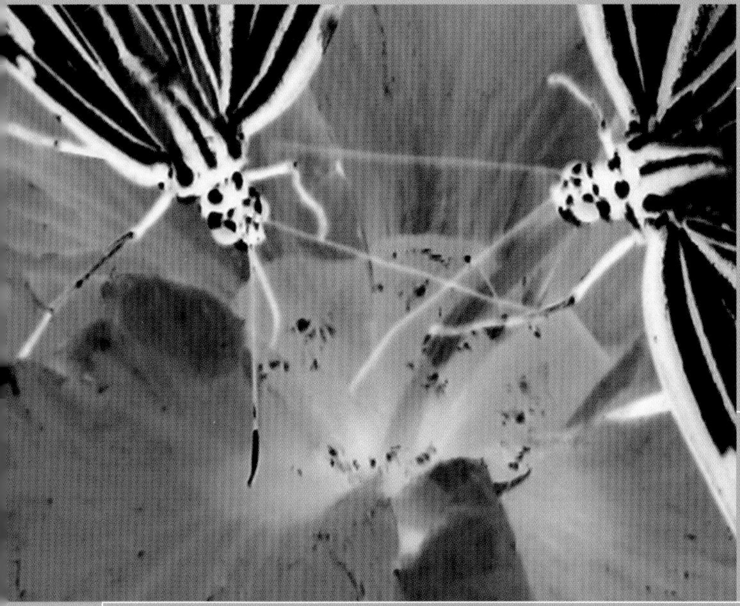

1 *Reference image of butterflies controlled by sugar-water* **2&3** *Front elevations* **4&5** *Building in context* **6** *Conceptual diagrams*

2

3

The first seed of inspiration for the proposed Nam June Paik museum, nestled within the pine forest setting of Sanggal National Park, derives from one of Paik's most celebrated works, *One Candle*. The second comes from the equally seminal 'TV Garden' (1974), a work where 120 television monitors flicker in a verdant garden of 600 plants, projecting filmic compositions onto leafy beds of foliage. This seemingly symbiotic insinuation of nature around a man-made artefact, which hints at a merged cybernetic entity, forms the basis for the section of the building. A moss and timber clad skin envelops a concrete shell, within which the TV garden is in turn housed. Object is transcribed into space; art is transcribed into architecture.

The building begins to evolve through a simultaneous proliferation of graphite lines, planes and ray-traced volumes. The entrance hall and main permanent galleries, concrete and immovable, are buried into the undulating landscape. Dark masses of earth fold over the exhibition spaces in waves, creating a hermetic chamber excluding all extraneous sound, light, and air to create the still environment so crucial to the experience of Nam June Paik's work. Branching off the main space like a many-headed hydra are storage and ticketing wings and three linear galleries, the easternmost of which slowly erupts from its concrete encasement and metamorphoses into a cluster of cantilevered glass pavilions housing the travelling exhibitions. Supported on slender tripodal frames and sheltered by a lattice of timber louvres, the volumes lighten in weight and transparency. The upper exposed surfaces of the louvres are of self-finished pine, claimed from the trees that were felled to make way for the building. Belying their natural exterior, the undersides are faced in a synthetic red fabric, casting a warm glow into the spaces below. Suspended high above the gallery floor, an illuminated ribbon mirroring the contours of the earth serves the two-fold purpose of reinforcing the concrete shell and directing visitors around the exhibits.

During the course of the design process, *One Candle* surreptitiously becomes more of a brief than the space programme, and *TV Garden* a far more demanding client than the Kyonggi Cultural Foundation. Taking a cue from the narrative conceit of choreographing simultaneous projections of the same object, the earthworks around the building synchronise and overlap with the surrounding gardens over the course of the year. From November to March, a blaze of cobalt, azure and delphinium flowers merge with the crushed blue glass of the hard landscaping. Between the months of April and July, a planting of green nicotiana and verdant sage merges with the moss-covered concrete escarpment. And from August to October, crimson and vermilion hues of tulips and astilbes amalgamate with the hard red terracotta pathways.

First vignette

A skein of butterflies form on the surface of the moss screens. They flicker and dart, attracted to the liquid sugar being slowly secreted by a matrix of capillary tubes implanted into the building's skin. The butterfly wall is a visual metaphor for the white noise on an untuned television set, an unusual incidence of nature designed and constructed to mimic the electronic rather than the reverse.

Second vignette

The Buddha sits unmoving, a serene and knowing smile crossing his imperturbable countenance. Partially buried in earth behind a sheer curtain of glass that truncates the building at its entrance, the statue contemplates itself and its place in the world on closed-circuit video. Inadvertently captured within the monitor screen across the glass veil, new arrivals to

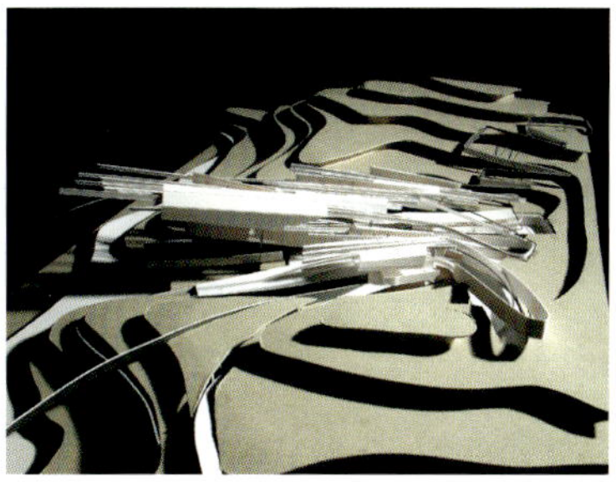

4

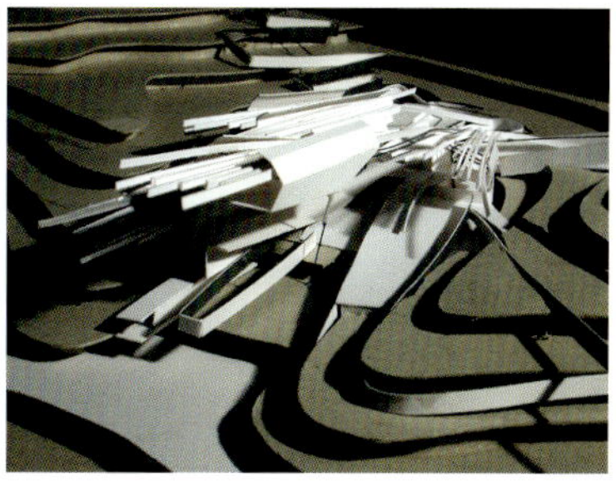

5

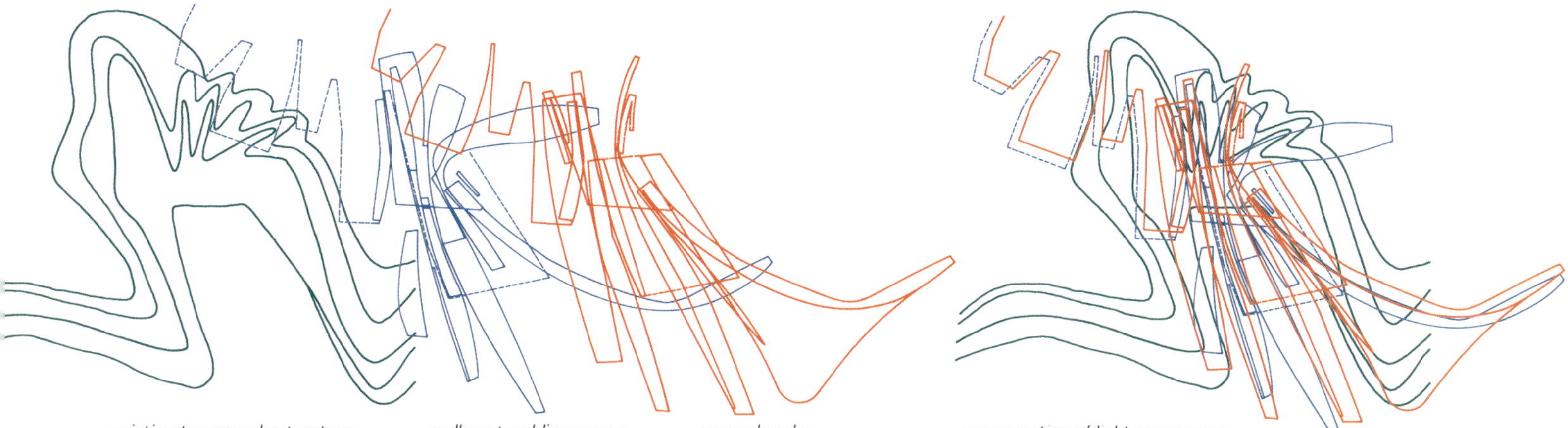

6

YONG-IN, PROVINCE OF KYONGGI, KOREA

NAM JUNE PAIK MUSEUM

competition entry

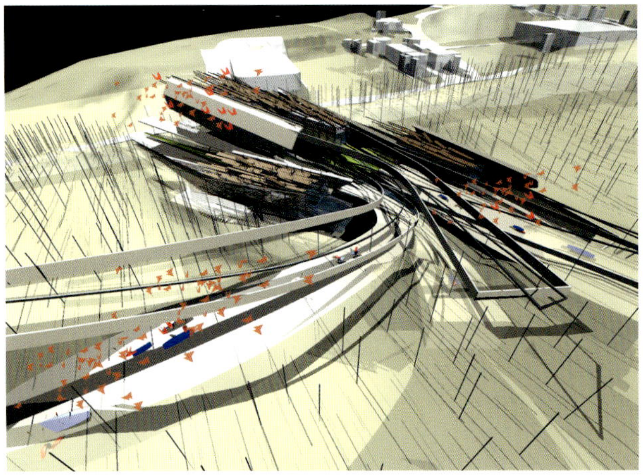

7

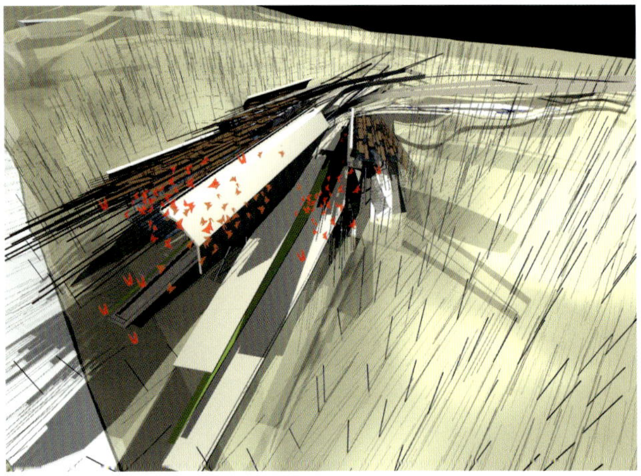

8

»› the gallery regard their disembodied selves encountering Paik's *TV Buddha* as they enter. A virtual link fashioned through light and electronic media creates a natural synthesis between the architecture and the artefacts that it protects and houses.

Third vignette

Circle, Paik's piece from 1997 composed of lasers, mirrors, prisms, smoke and motors, is positioned at the far end of the ramped gallery. Glowing like a red ember, light from the sphere spills onto the fluid elongated arc of the room. The asymmetric sweep of illumination forms a striking backdrop for the play of distorted shadows discarded by visitors as they walk through the space.

Fourth vignette

Suspended over the entrance lobby and courtyard is a replica of Paik's studio. Constructed out of liquid crystal glass, it hovers over the light garden as a frosted box. The eccentric interment of Paik's original studio, such that only a third of it appears above ground, is reflected in its new lofty location. As a visitor engages with the studio via a gantry, sensors trigger a flow of electric current through the lower third of the glass enclosure, manifesting the room's contents through clear glass for observation from below.

Fifth vignette

The three gallery roof lights perform the perverse function of excluding natural light from entering the building during the day while encouraging the leakage of artificial light into the forest at night. As evening falls, the strategically positioned black boxes focus the light emitted from laser installation pieces in the exhibition rooms below through one-way glass into a halo of light on the roof. Mobile 'light-catchers' swaying in the wind scatter the collected light into the mantle of surrounding pine trees. The net of light cast into the forest marks an intangible and ephemeral territory for the museum.

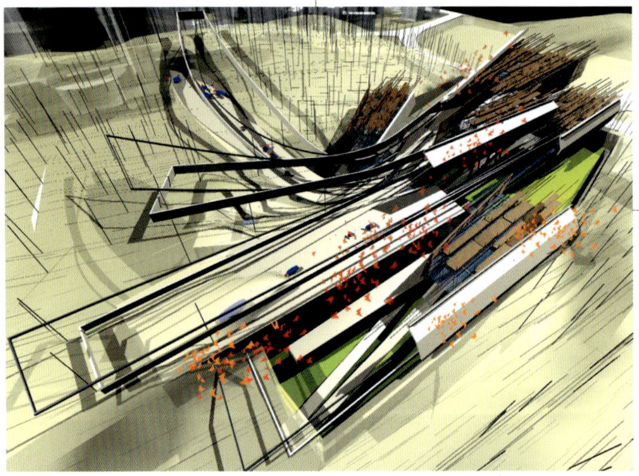

9

7-9 *A skein of butterflies form on the surface of the moss screens; a visual metaphor for the white noise on an untuned television set*

10 *Planting and colour concepts for landscape*

following pages *Composite plan*

Glory of snow

Squills

Iris missouriensis

Green nicotiana

Euphoria characias

Sage

Lychnis

Tulipa apeldon

Astilbe

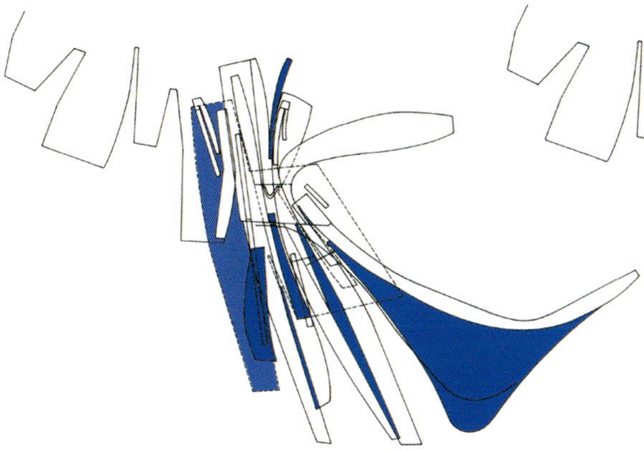
'Blue-light' garden (November - March)

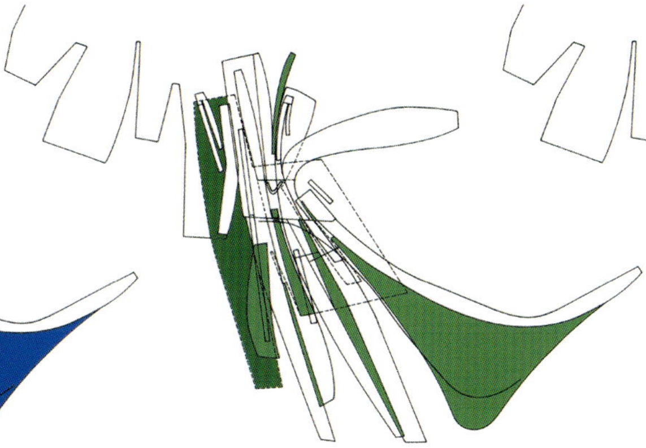
'Green-light' garden (April - July)

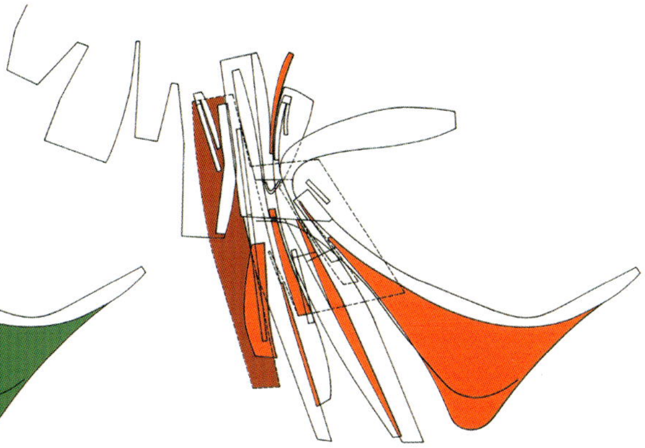
'Red-light' garden (August - October)

10

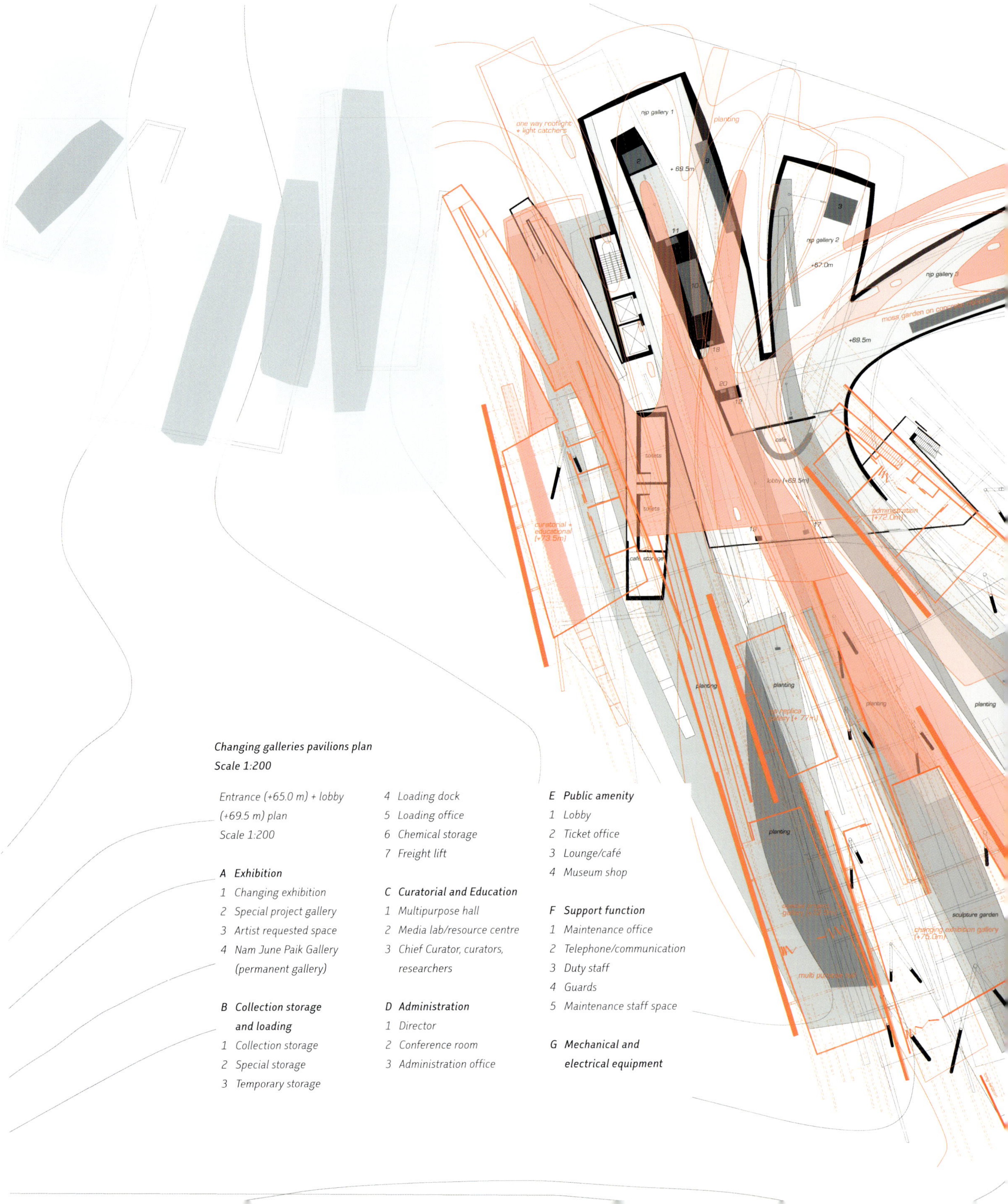

Changing galleries pavilions plan
Scale 1:200

Entrance (+65.0 m) + lobby (+69.5 m) plan
Scale 1:200

A Exhibition
1 Changing exhibition
2 Special project gallery
3 Artist requested space
4 Nam June Paik Gallery (permanent gallery)

B Collection storage and loading
1 Collection storage
2 Special storage
3 Temporary storage
4 Loading dock
5 Loading office
6 Chemical storage
7 Freight lift

C Curatorial and Education
1 Multipurpose hall
2 Media lab/resource centre
3 Chief Curator, curators, researchers

D Administration
1 Director
2 Conference room
3 Administration office

E Public amenity
1 Lobby
2 Ticket office
3 Lounge/café
4 Museum shop

F Support function
1 Maintenance office
2 Telephone/communication
3 Duty staff
4 Guards
5 Maintenance staff space

G Mechanical and electrical equipment

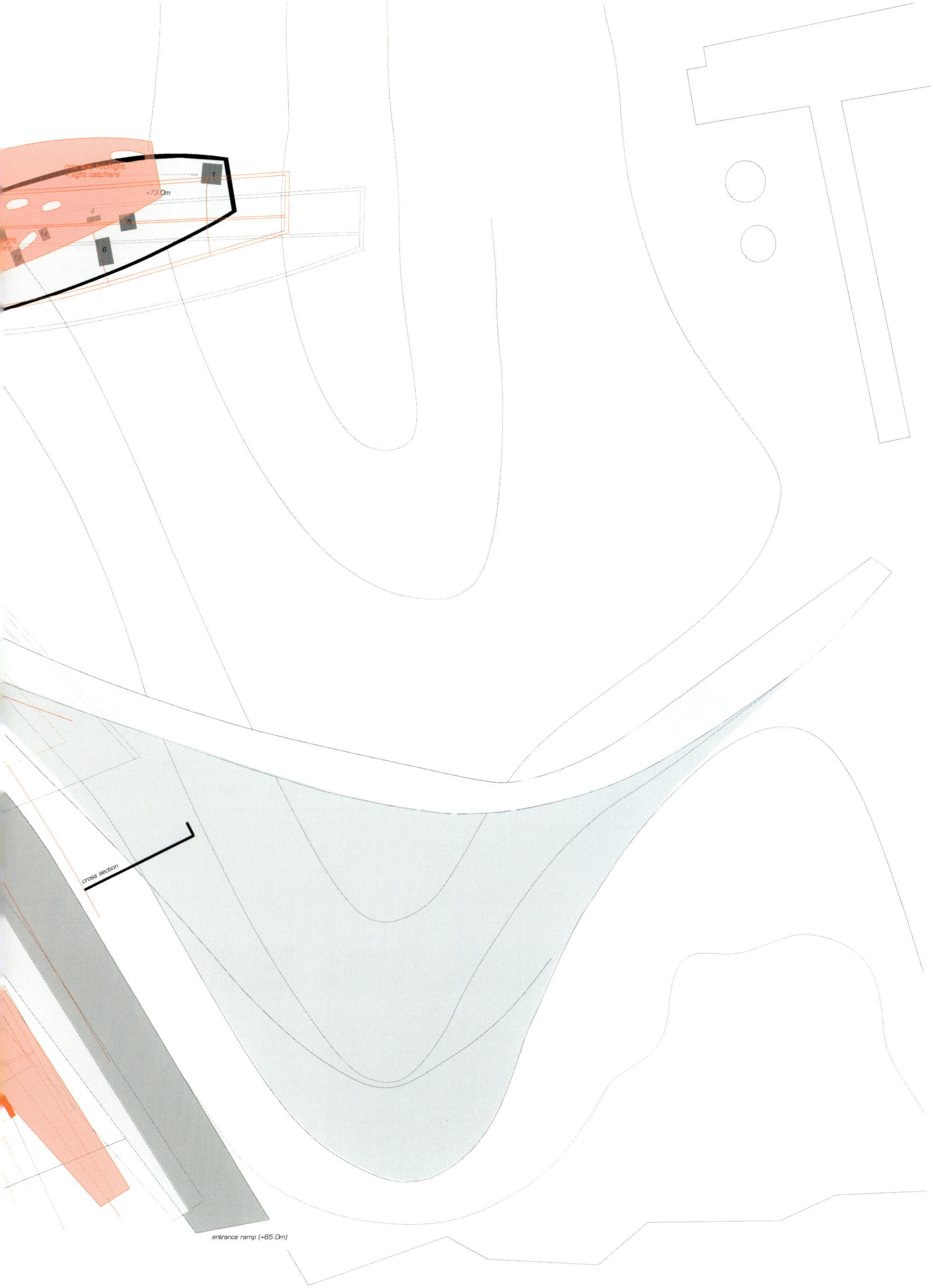
+ light catchers
+73.0m
1
4
5
6
13
cross section
entrance ramp (+65.0m)

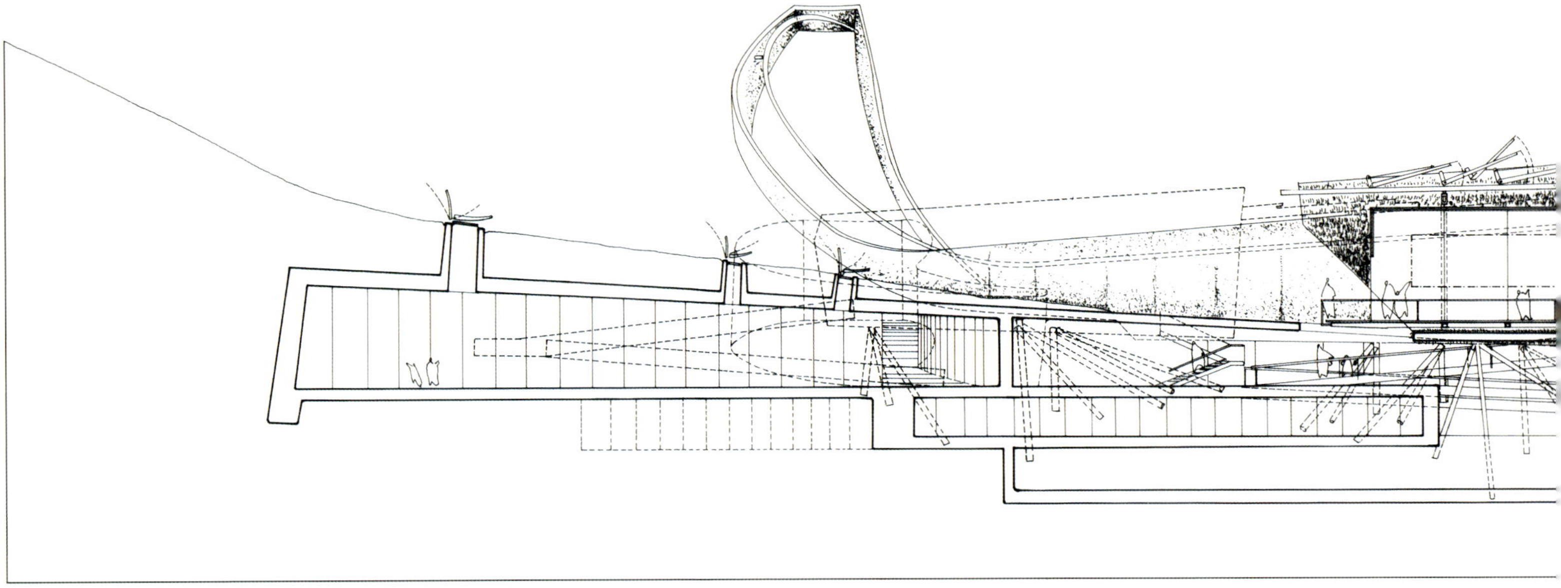

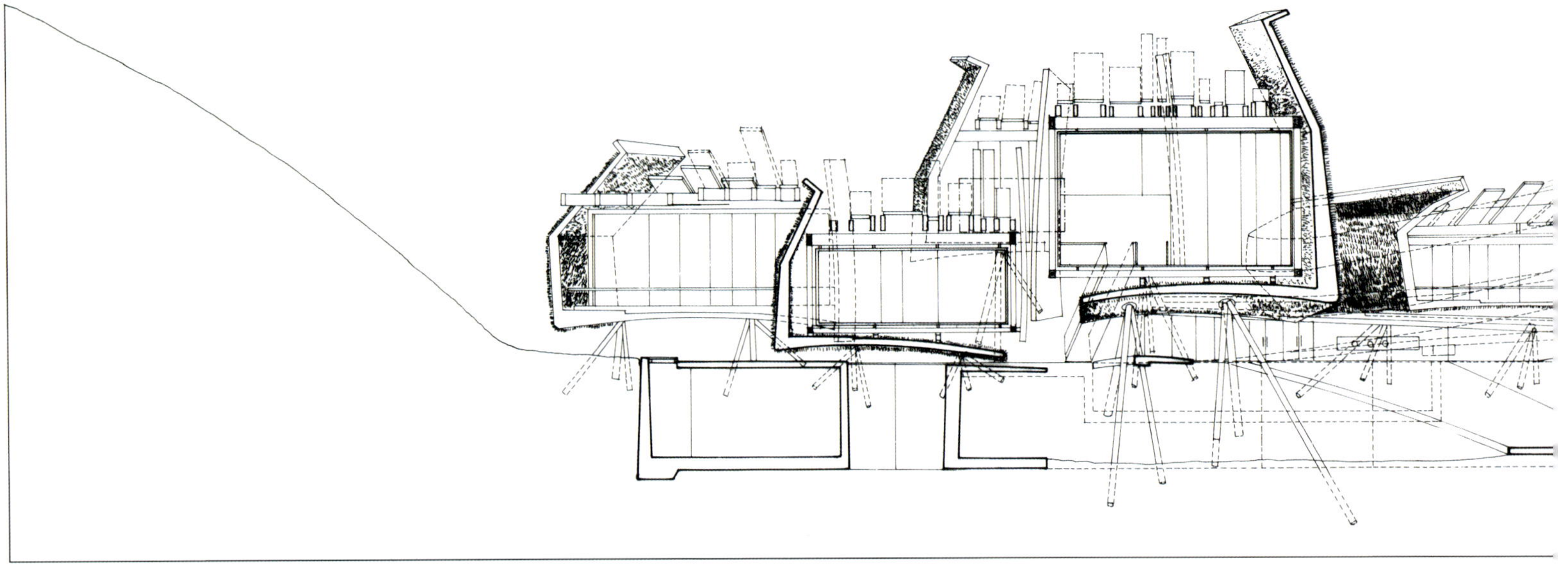

12

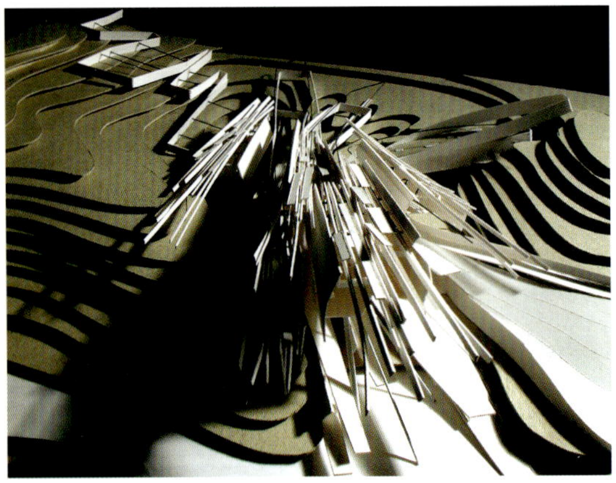

13

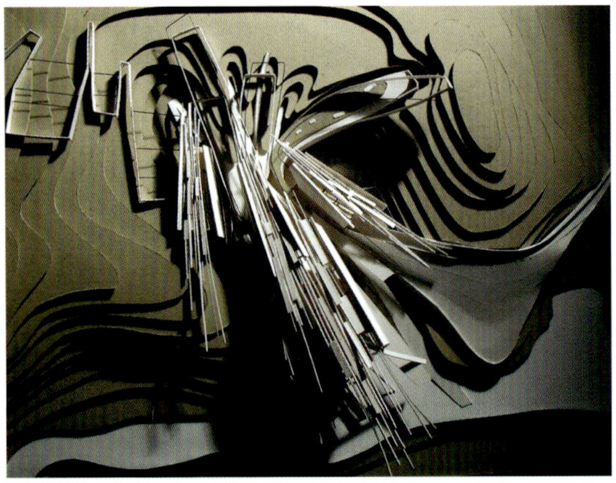

14

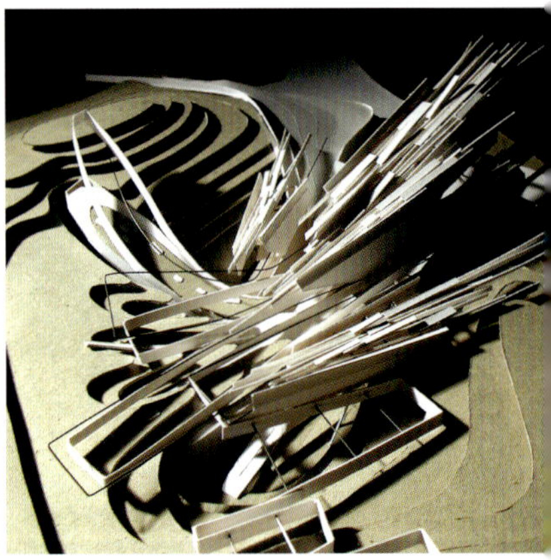

15

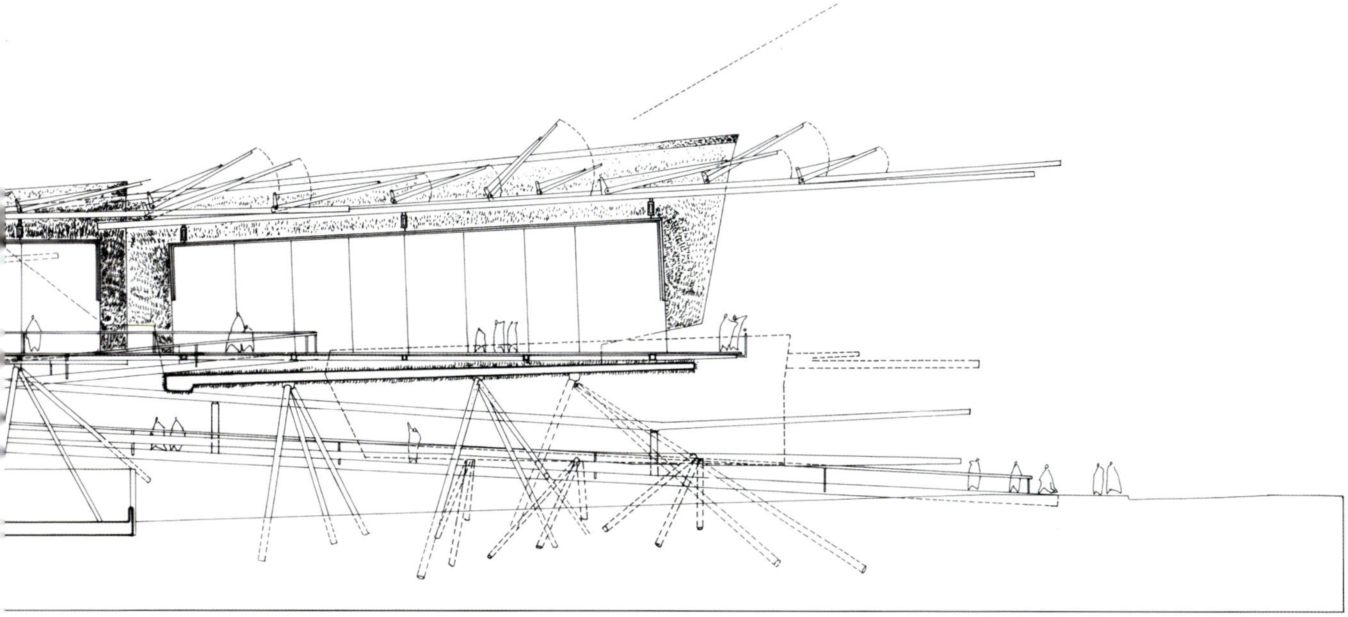

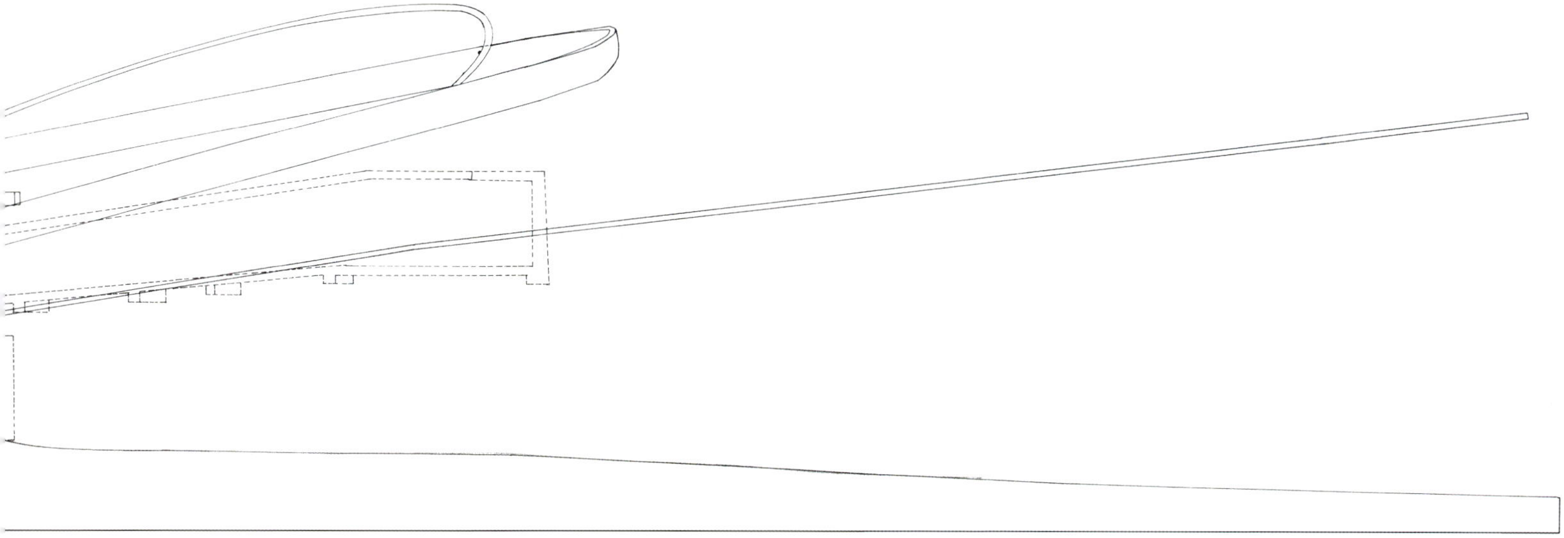

16

12 *Long section and cross section* **13** *Front elevation* **14** *Light lines are reconstituted as the framework for the museum* **15** *Buried spaces negotiating the undulating landscape before branching off like a many-headed hydra* **16** *Building in context* **following pages** *Overall image of building in landscape and context*

1

1&2 *Mobile glass tatami dining tables*
3 *Catching your supper*

2

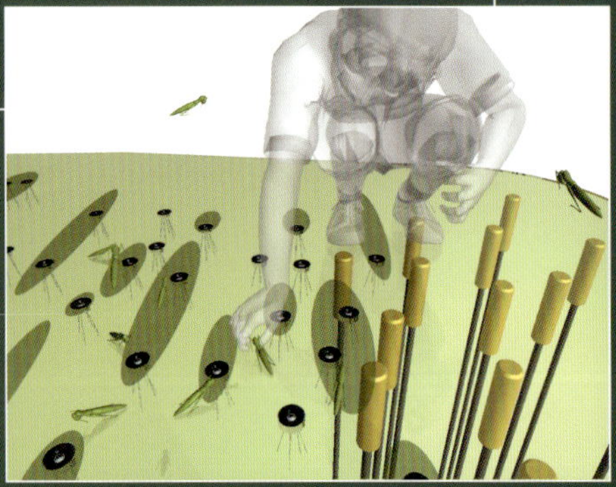

3

In the Far East, the grasshopper, along with termites and the large palm weevil grub, is prized as a great delicacy. The grasshopper is fit for consumption only in the imago phase, when it is sexually mature and newly emerged from metamorphosis.

In the Far East, the grasshopper, along with termites and the large palm weevil grub, is prized as a great delicacy. The grasshopper is fit for consumption only in the imago phase, when it is sexually mature and newly emerged from metamorphosis.

In the Far East, the grasshopper, along with termites and the large palm weevil grub, is prized as a great delicacy. The grasshopper is fit for consumption only in the imago phase, when it is sexually mature and newly emerged from metamorphosis.

There is a little-known eatery in the Japanese prefecture of Hokkaido where diners catch grasshoppers using insect mating calls, then cook and devour them on the premises. The restaurant is easy to miss, as it is located by an anonymous carriageway and nestled within a stretch of paddy fields, distinguished only by a neon sign bearing the katagana characters. The façade is made up of bales of straw and rammed earth, while the menu board consists of glass tubes containing different seasonal grasshoppers embedded into the hay screen.

As one approaches the building, strange will-o'-the-wisp-like lights bob across the black horizon. They flit and flock, at times congregating around a single spot, or dispersing to explore in seemingly random vectors, but always within some unseen, intangible boundary. The sight is quite bewitching. Similar to an octopus in appearance as well as size, the lanterns have gourd-shaped bodies that pulsate with a technicolour glow. In place of tentacles, however, they possess a miniature propeller and a long stick-like tail, with a rudder at the end, and make both a faint spluttering and a high-pitched clicking sound.

And as they rove over the undulating irrigated plains, the grasshopper-lanterns begin to gather suitors like a magnet, drawing grasshoppers by the light and call of their lascivious mate.

Dining tables carried by an ox may be located anywhere in the fields. Embedded into the glass surface are cooking elements, lighting tubes and loudspeakers. The speakers emit synthesised sounds of different grasshopper mating calls, luring the male grasshopper to flock onto the glass tatami. The vertical glass tatami rotates to a horizontal position, cantilevering over the crop plains to provide an area for relaxation while diners wait for their meal to appear. The grasshoppers are harvested off the glass surface, prepared, grilled and consumed on the glass tatami. In the evening, cooking fires define varying territories of the restaurant on the plain.

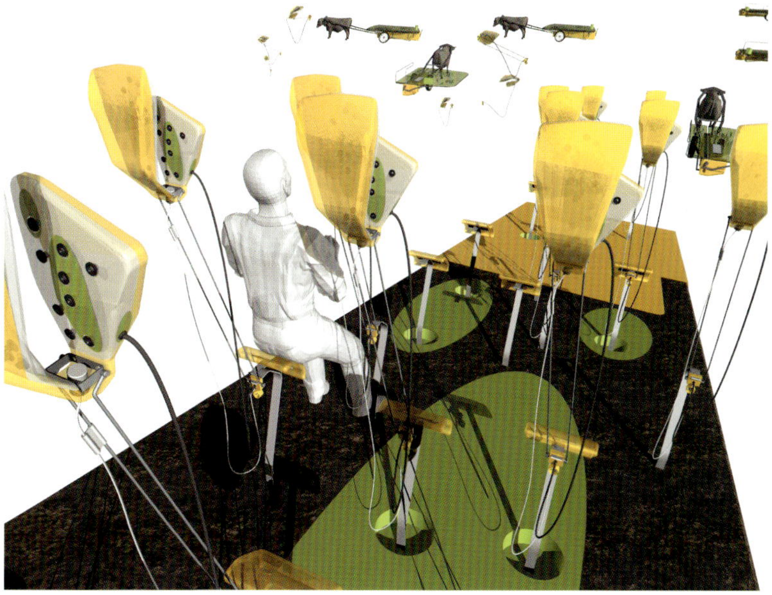

5

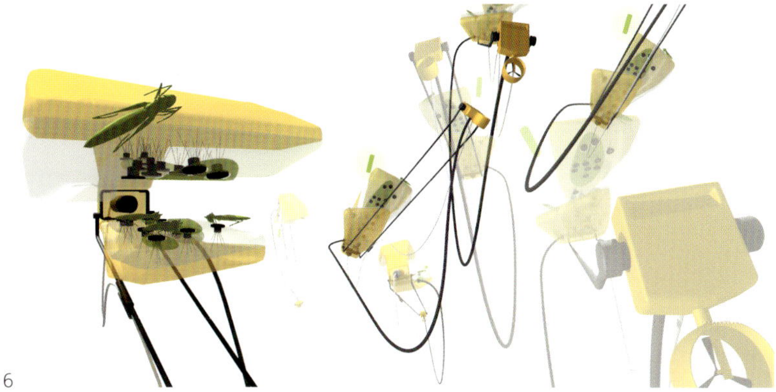

6

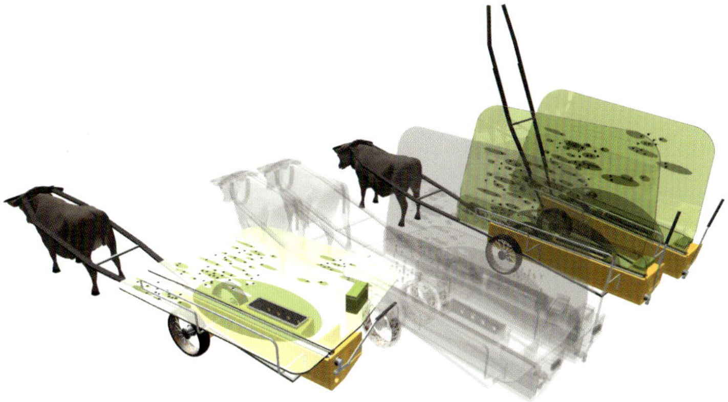

7

4 *Menu façade* **5** *Fields of grasshopper-lanterns flitting within unseen intangible boundary* **6** *Mobile grasshopper-lantern* **7** *Mobile glass tatami dining tables*

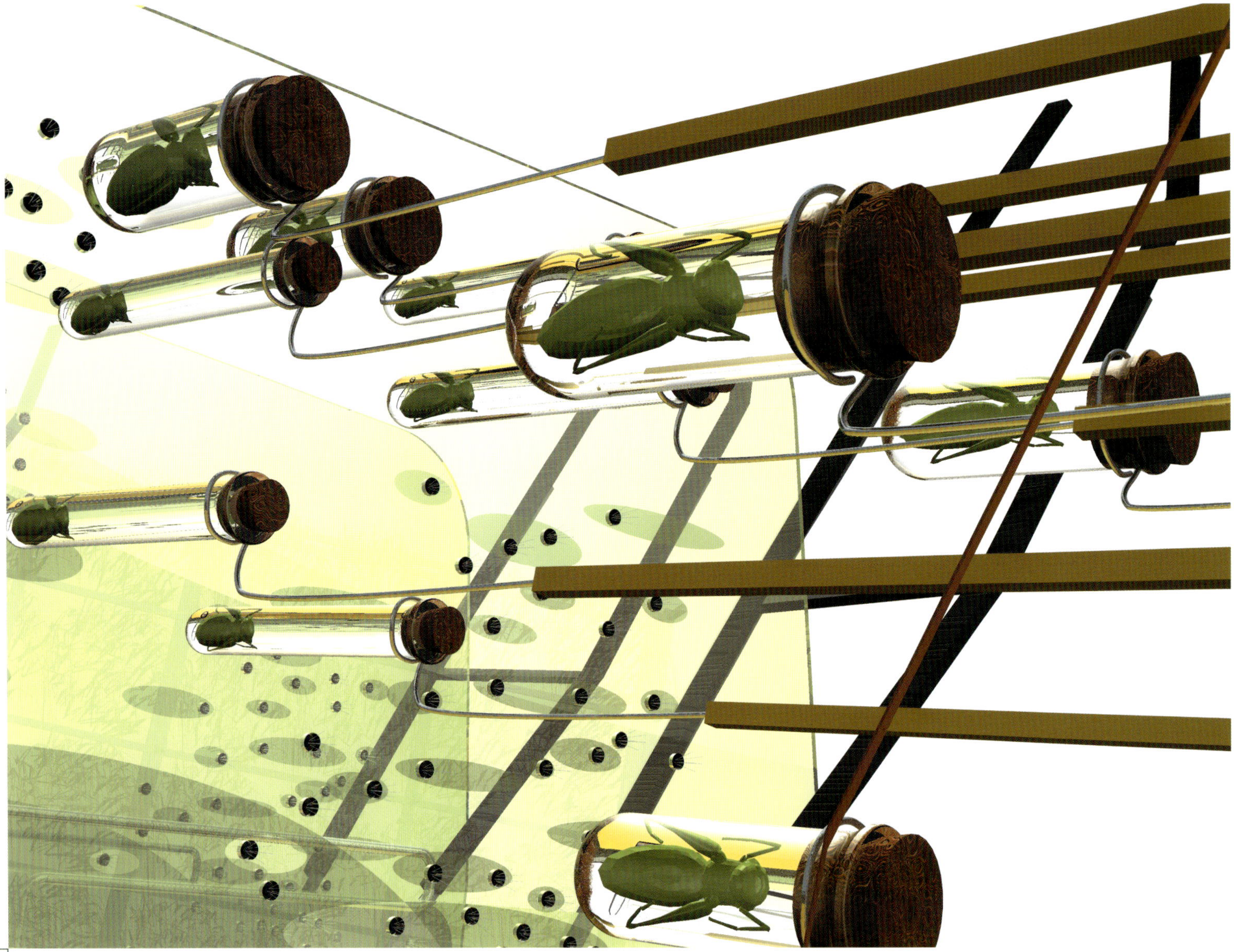

8

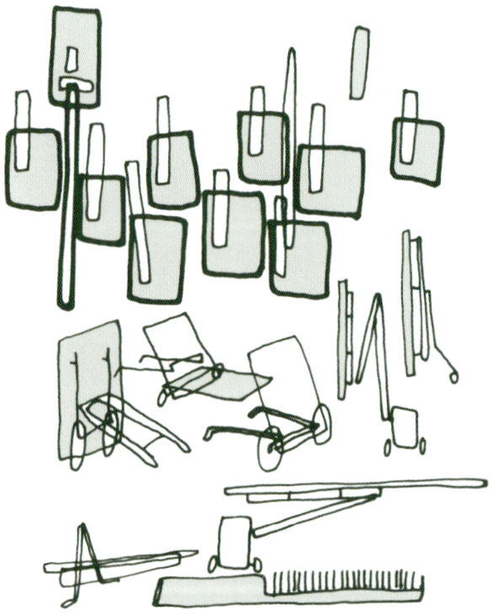

9

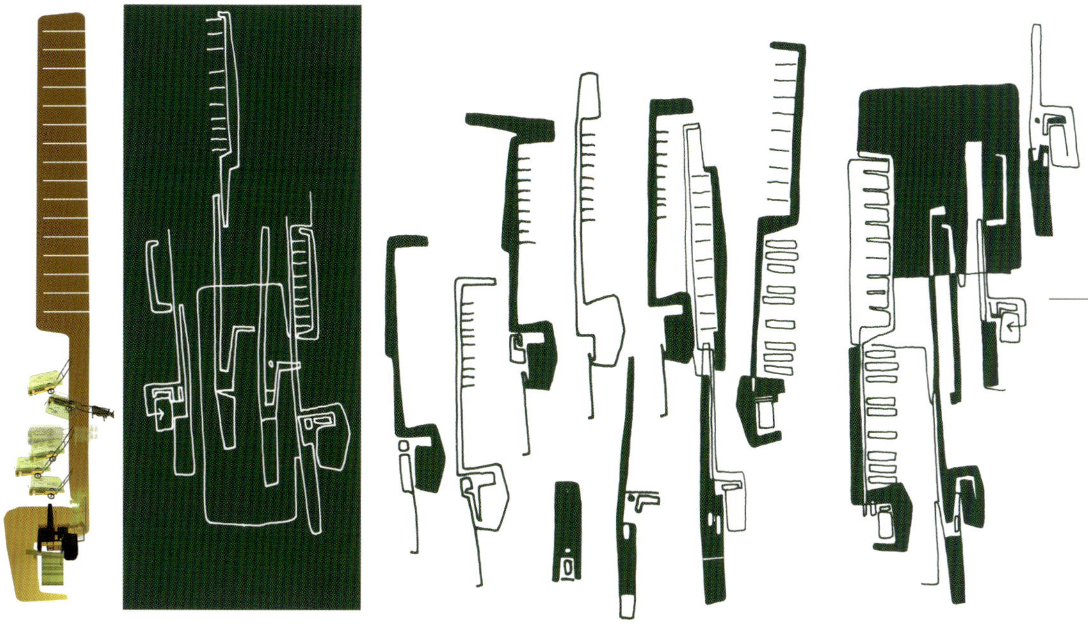

10

8 *Menu façade* **9** *Sketch studies of mobile glass tatami dining tables* **10** *Overall plan and studies of landscape* **11** *Fields of grasshopper-lanterns flitting within unseen intangible boundary*

11

12

12-15 *Fields of grasshopper-lanterns flitting within unseen intangible boundary* **16** *Sketch studies of grasshopper-lantern*

13

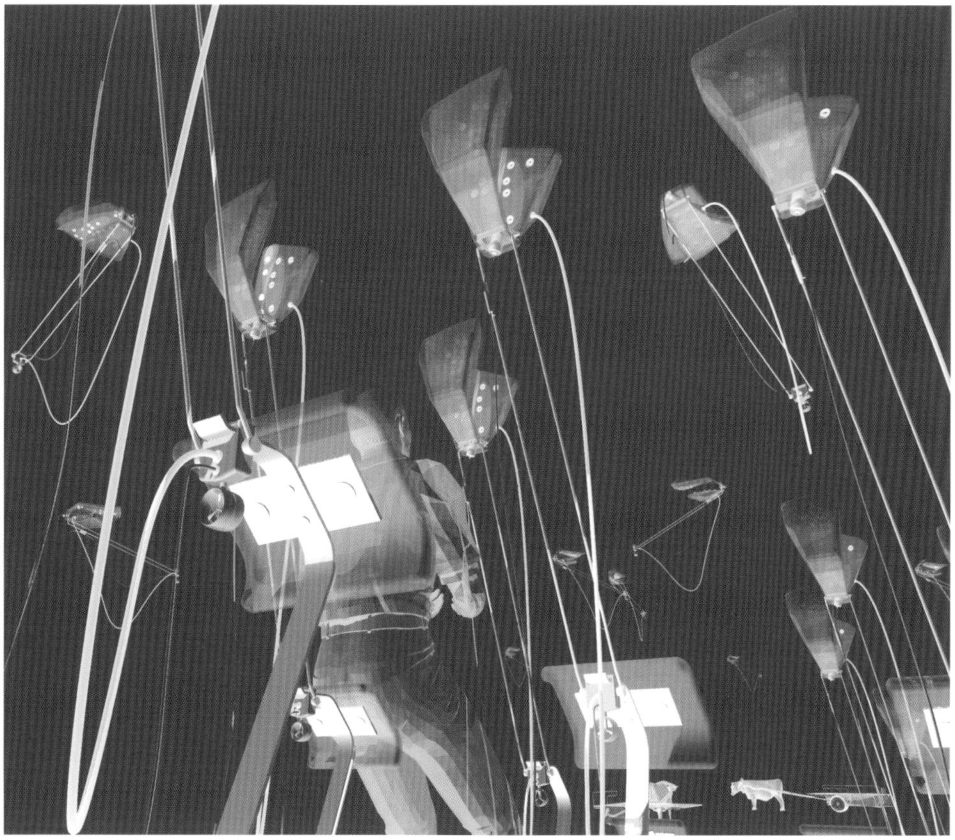

14

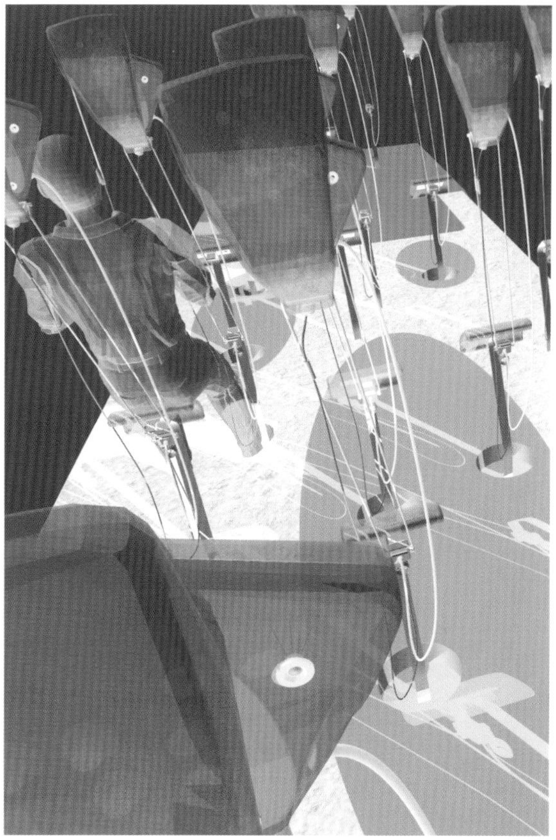

15

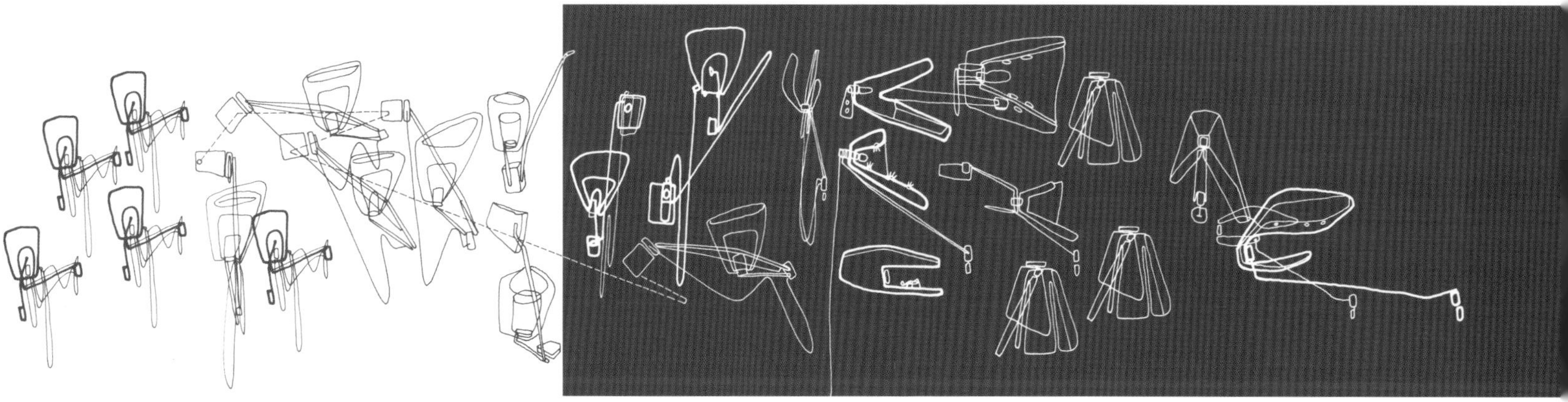

16

The sound of little children laughing and bold letters unfurling from the paving entice the public towards a surreal edifice consisting of processed paper. The entrance to the Sittingbourne Cultural Centre slopes gently into the structure's undercroft, the route peppered with whispered confidences, screened images and oblique glimpses into the garden's underbelly. The new cultural complex takes the form of an inverted landscape, its physical boundary extending up to the site perimeter. The conventional urban strategy of a building surrounded by a forecourt is subverted; the public forum appears as a semi-enclosed and raised interior courtyard redolent of a secret garden out of children's literature.

The monolithic 'garden wall' is embedded with colour, miniature speakers and video screens, relaying the paradoxical character of being simultaneously barrier and invitation while heightening the sense of community. The wall is a breathing entity, effecting an ethereal threshold between the civic and domestic, exterior and interior, urban and organic.

The informal and convivial nature of the den or secret garden extends into the interior: deckchairs, sofas and soft floors replace the staid uninviting furniture endemic of old municipal institutions. Fun replaces formality; oddity and delight are the order of the day.

The local and historic heritage of Sittingbourne forms an integral part of the architecture. In lieu of providing a building where objects are in frames or on plinths, paper, bricks and barges from the surrounding industries constitute the very fabric of the garden.

The wall of literature

The library follows the perimeter of the complex, forming a continuous ringed wall of knowledge. This is mirrored by the external envelope (the other side of the wall), which is clad in stacks of recycled literature – old newspapers and periodicals layered and sealed to withstand inclement weather. Inside, a glazed wall encloses the library, soundproofing the space from the museum and courtyard. At specific points, the library ring widens to form a children's story-telling area (with retractable headphones), and a bank of after-school study terminals.

The exterior recycled paper cladding is punctuated with miniature speakers and video screens, projecting the happenings within the garden out into the surrounding space. At any one time, one may hear the sound of children giggling from the crèche area, a story being read from an audiotape, or see tasters from the museum's current exhibition. Congregating around the garden wall, then, will be crowds of passersby, ears pressed to the speakers or eyes trained to the monitors – a human landscape made up of the community engaged with the community.

Enclosed by the perimeter library, the other principal elements of the Cultural Centre are zoned in long parallel strips, mimicking Sittingbourne's 'linear centre'. Floor surfaces, ranging from stone paving to grass and gravel reflect this organisation, providing auditory and tactile, as well as visual, indications of boundary.

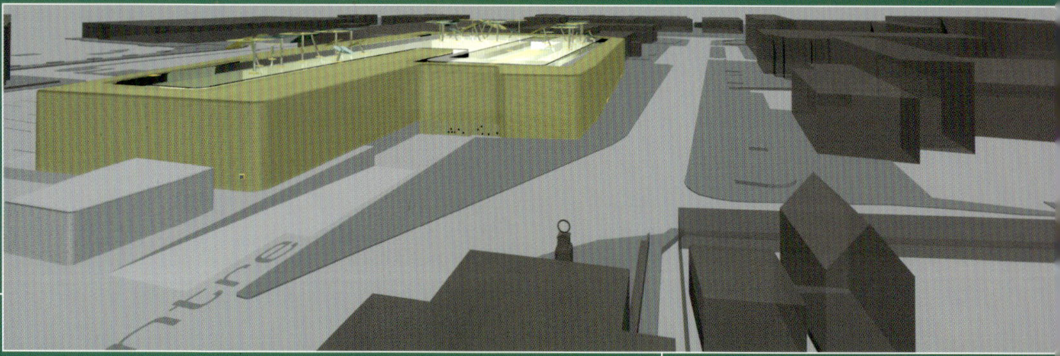

2

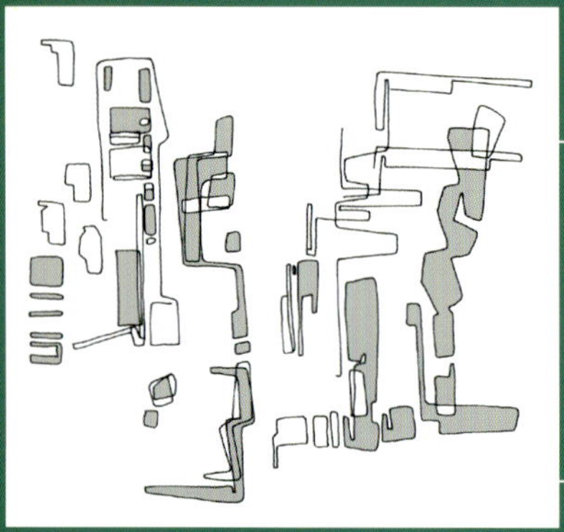

1

1 *Sketch of grassy hillocks in courtyard* **2** *View of main approach to building* **3** *Aerial view: building in context* **4** *Story-telling wall: side elevation*

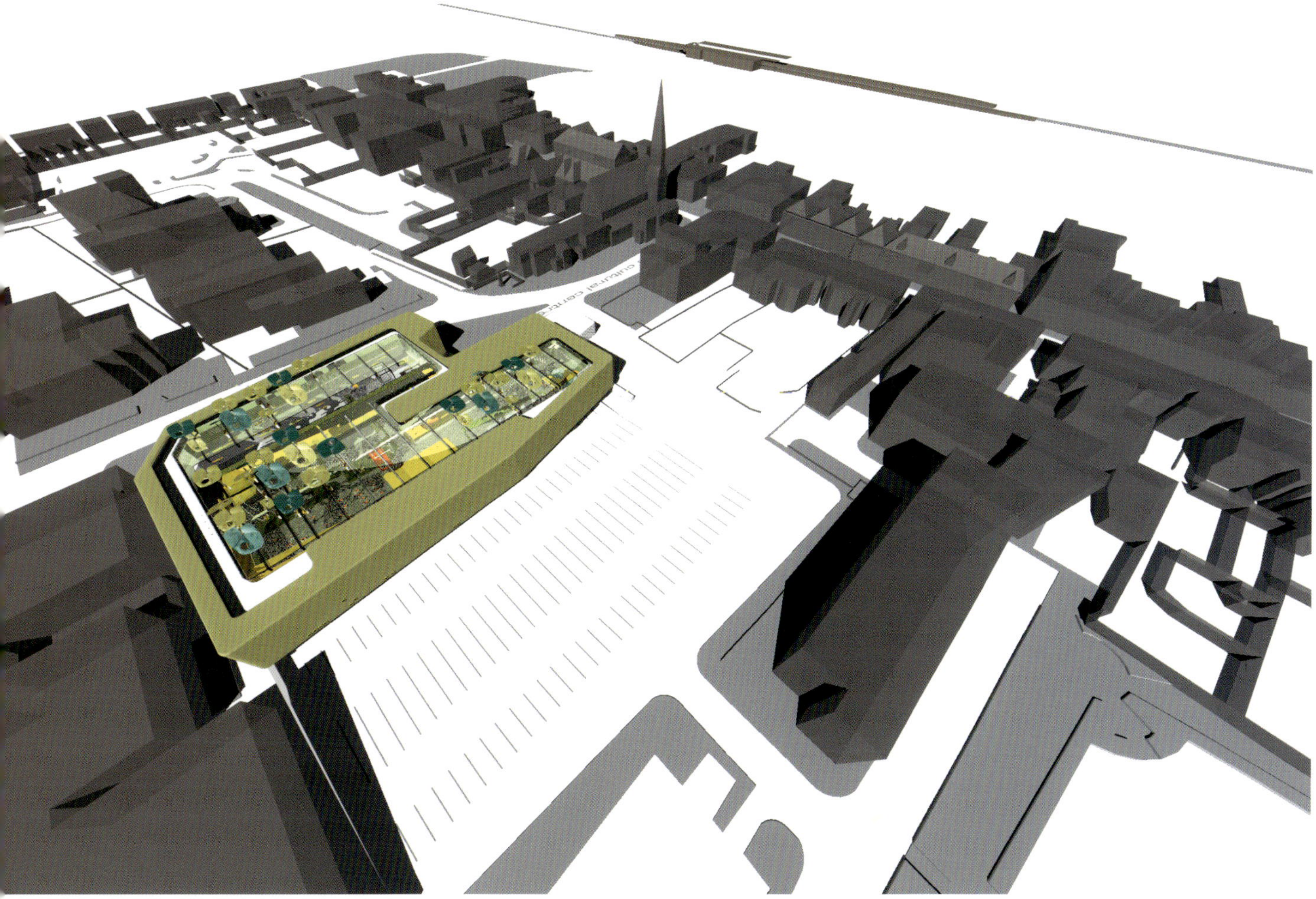

3

SITTINGBOURNE, KENT, UK

SITTINGBOURNE CULTURAL CENTRE

competition entry

4

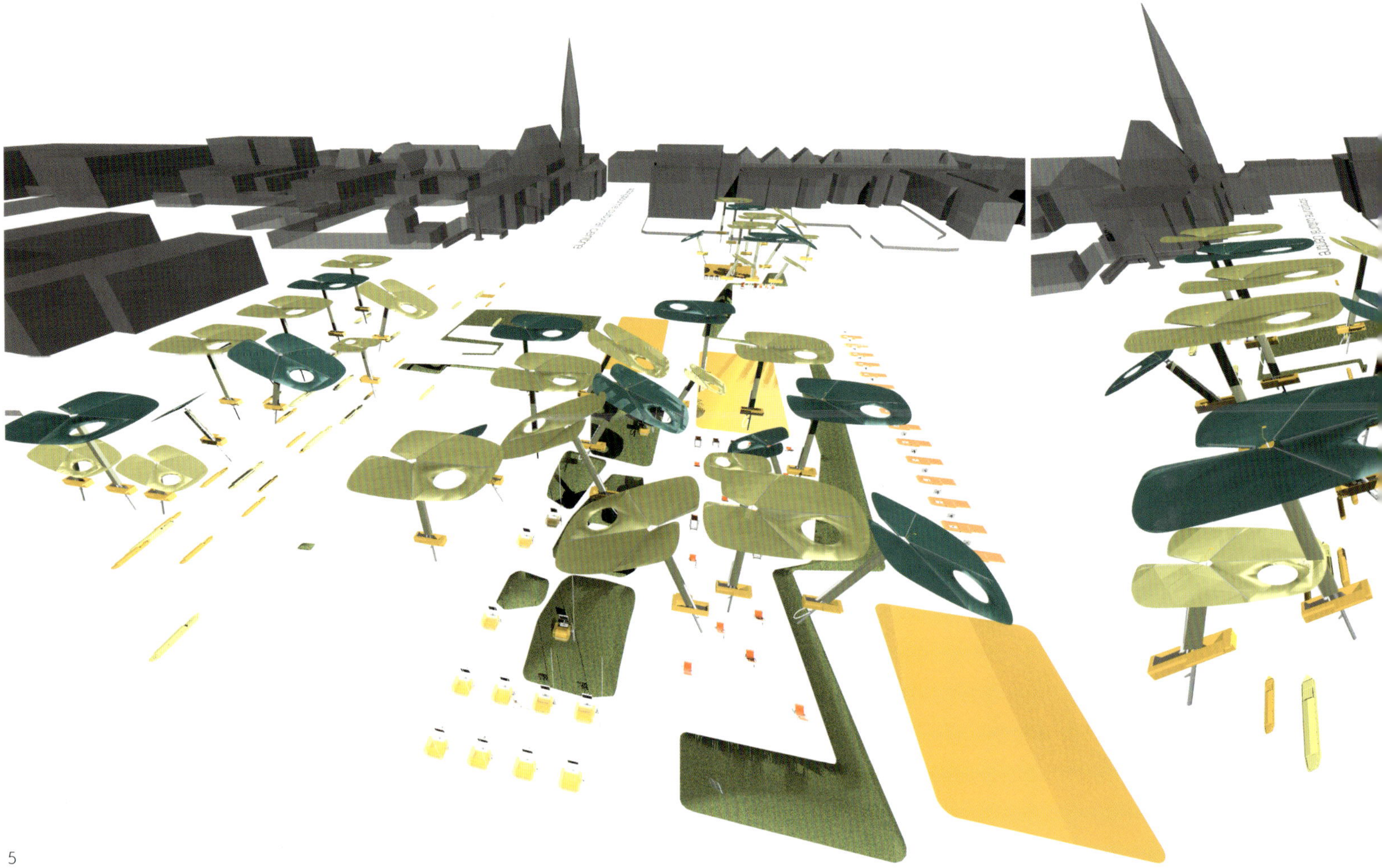

5

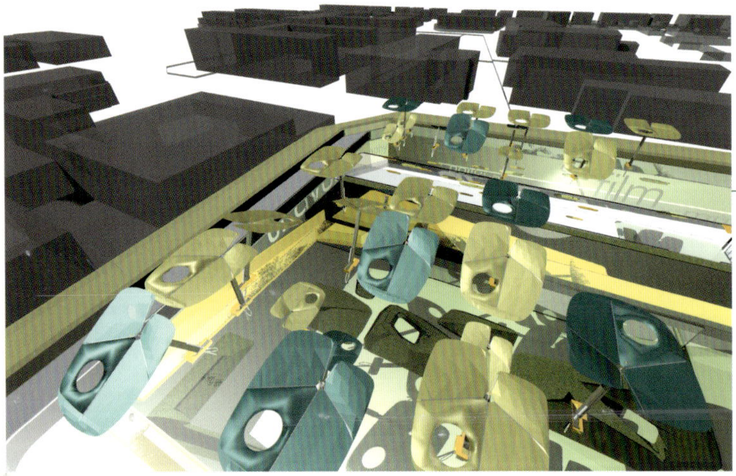

6

5 *Spatial elements in context* **6&7** *Panoramic view of roof with oversized flower shades*

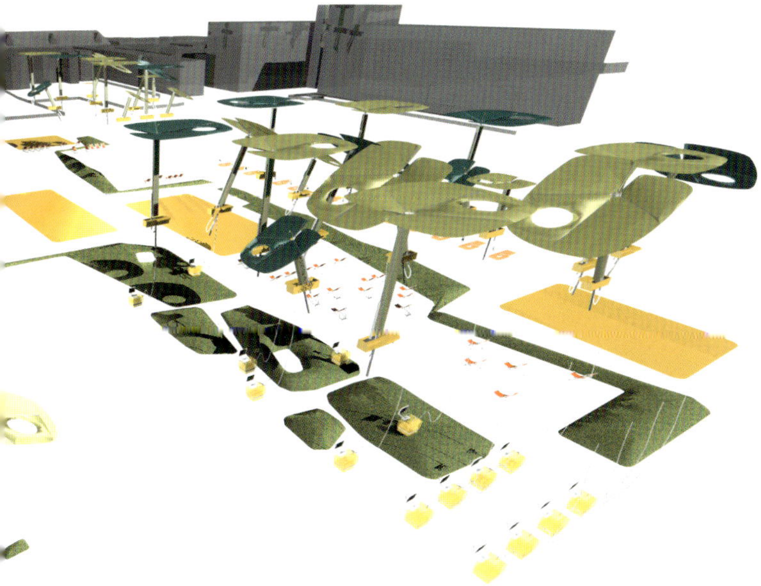

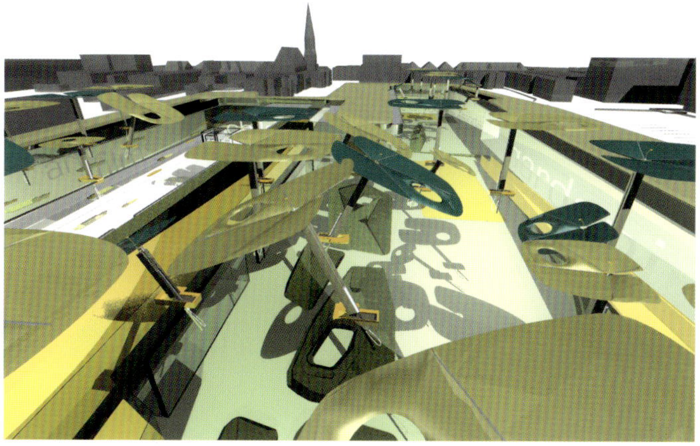

7

The sea of objects

On the west side, and directly adjacent to the reception lobby, the museum's spaces provide for three different display conditions: a brick-clad double-volume space for large objects such as the fire engine or stagecoach beneath a fleet of suspended scale-replica barges; a bay of semi-enclosed rooms affording protection from sunlight for drawings and paintings; and a blackout room next to the storage rooms for screening films and audiovisual presentations.

The trellis

A spine of offices and multipurpose meeting rooms along a north–south axis divides the museum from the courtyard. The east and west walls of the rooms are glazed (with retractable blinds for privacy), allowing visual access through the length of the building. Plantings above the office spine on the rooftop terrace complete the metaphor of a pergola within a country garden.

The courtyard

The strategy of employing a courtyard offers the flexibility of expansion or diminution pending changing requirements and finances. The courtyard may be open-air or enclosed by a glazed roof and comprises a series of dedicated and flexible spaces that offer varying degrees of habitation, tranquillity and landscaping. These include a picnic/café area with gently contoured grassy hillocks with sofas and internet facilities, a deckchair reading area, a crèche with inflatable flooring strips, and three multifunction spaces that may be used for temporary exhibitions, formal gatherings, rehearsals or meetings. When privacy is required, a paper pod-structure unfolds and inflates into a flower-like enclosure. A ramp leading up to the terrace provides views over the town's roofscape, and a mobile catering unit provides refreshments to each area.

The picnic pod

A mobile café/bar traverses the courtyard on an overhead track; function is dependent on position in the courtyard. The unit caters for formal gatherings as well as serving as a café, ice cream parlour, picnic supplier and wastebin.

Wind and flowers

The large span of the roof is broken up into strips, deep gutters allowing cross-ventilation though the main museum and courtyard spaces. Localised solar shading over the glazed roof is provided by gargantuan petals flowering above the skylight.

Light sensors above the roofline trigger heating elements within the flower's sealed cylinders of expanding gas. This mechanism causes the petals to open up when shading is required, and to retract as the temperature drops coinciding with evening's fall.

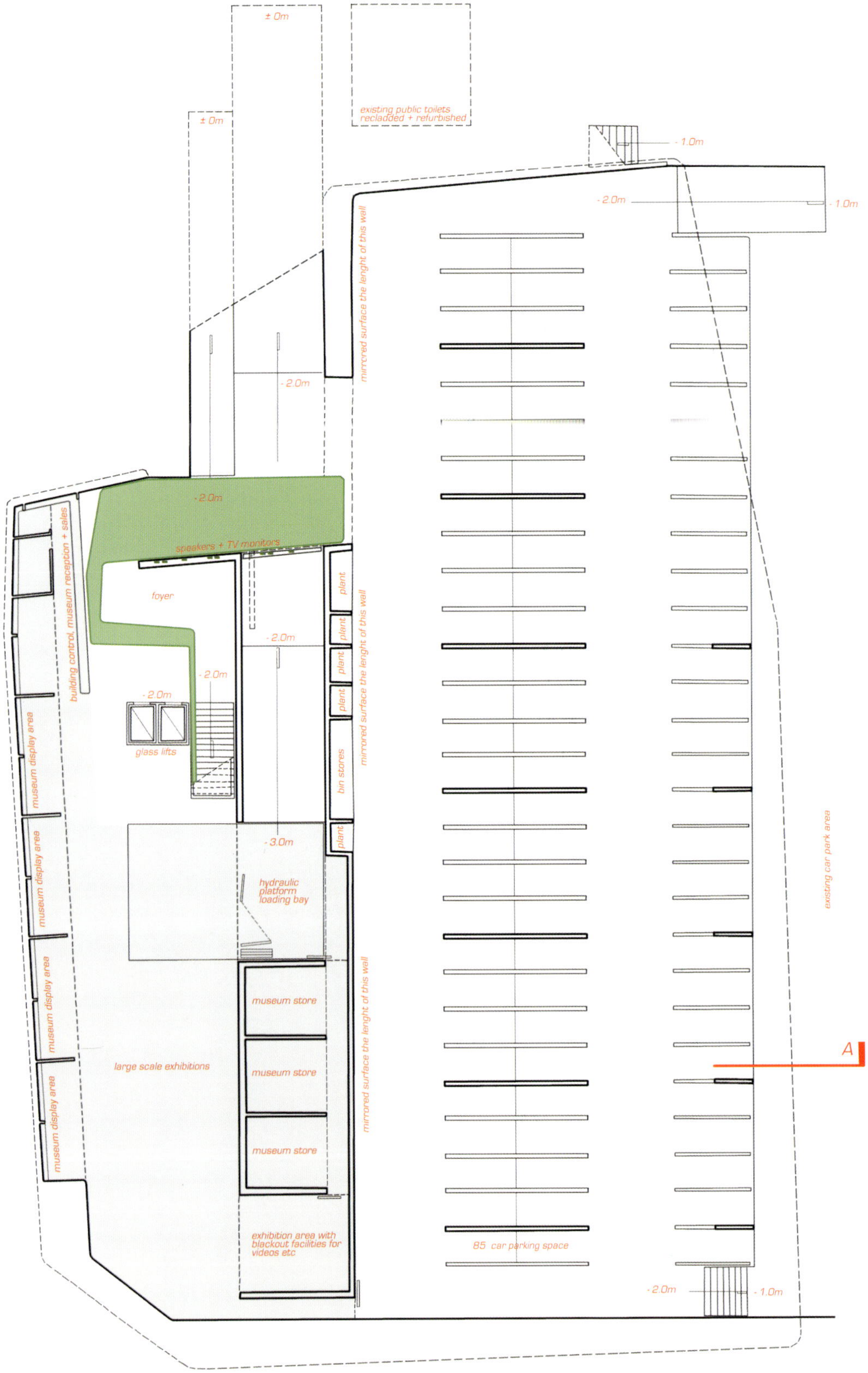

8

9

10

8 *Basement plan* **9** *Bird's-eye view of courtyard* **10** *View from book storage into entry/exhibition hall* **11** *Sea of miniature barges floats over entry hall, playfully questioning scale and natural order* **12** *Ground floor plan*

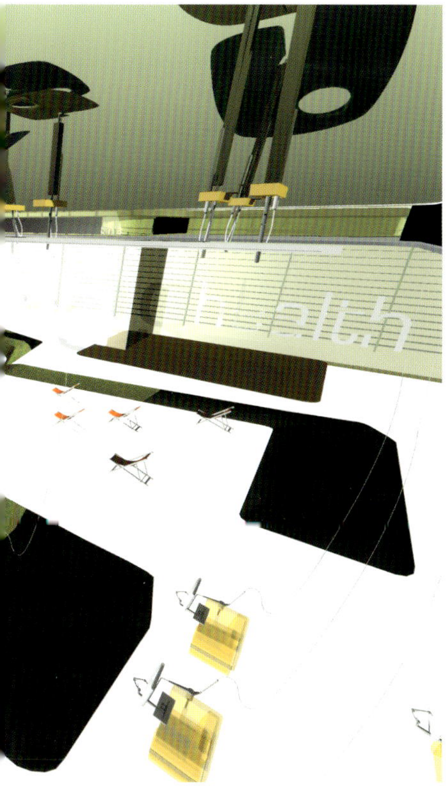
health

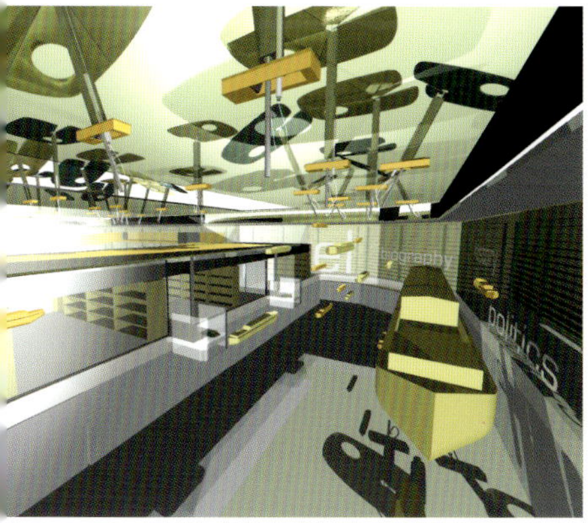
politics

11

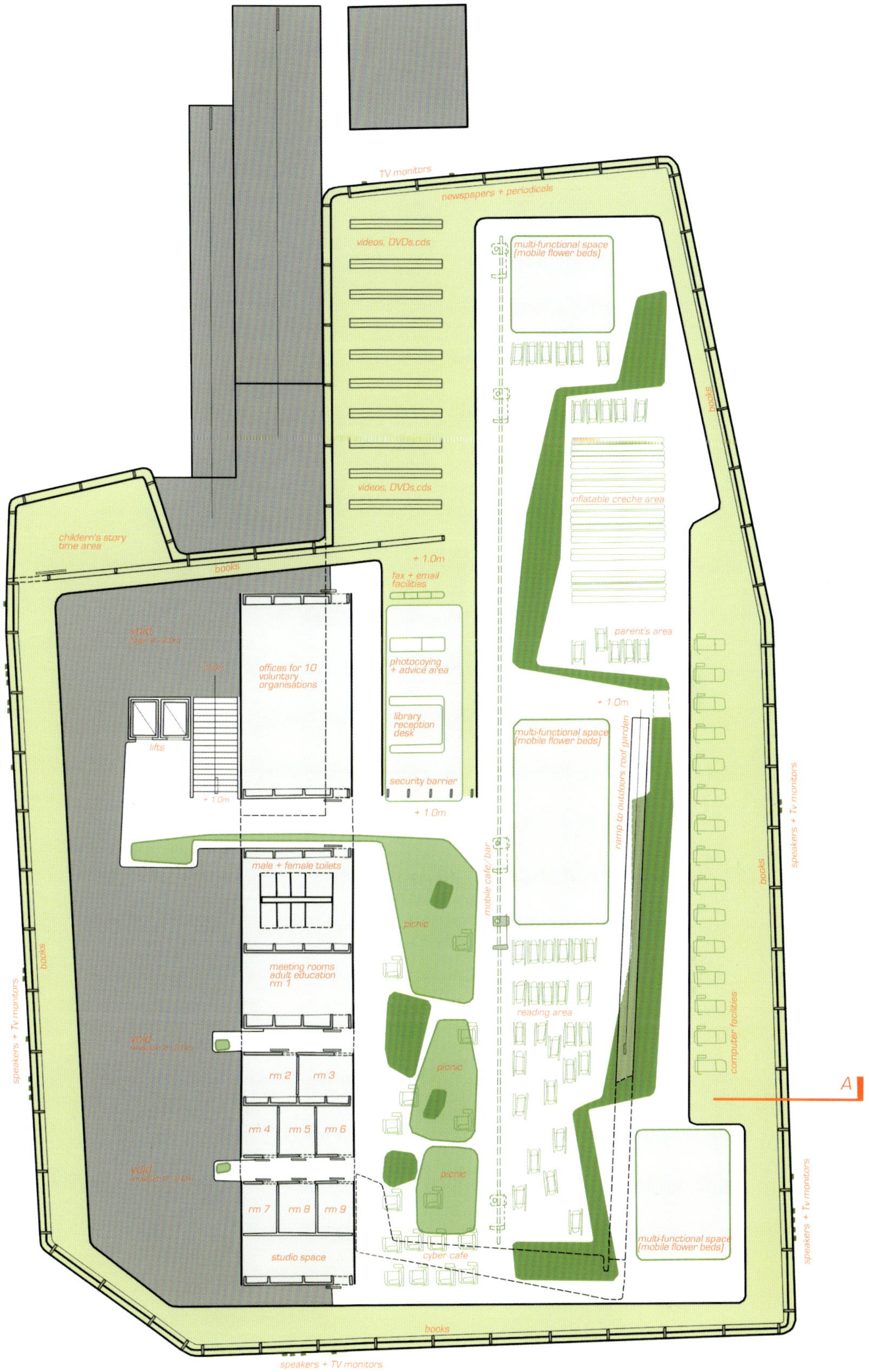
TV monitors
newspapers + periodicals
videos, DVDs,cds
multi-functional space (mobile flower beds)
books
inflatable creche area
childern's story time area
+ 1.0m
fax + email facilities
parent's area
offices for 10 voluntary organisations
photocopying + advice area
library reception desk
lifts
security barrier
ramp to outdoors roof garden
male + female toilets
mobile cafe/ bar
picnic
meeting rooms adult education rm 1
reading area
void
computer facilities
rm 2
rm 3
rm 4
rm 5
rm 6
rm 7
rm 8
rm 9
studio space
cyber cafe
A
speakers + Tv monitors
speakers + TV monitors

12

13

14

15

16

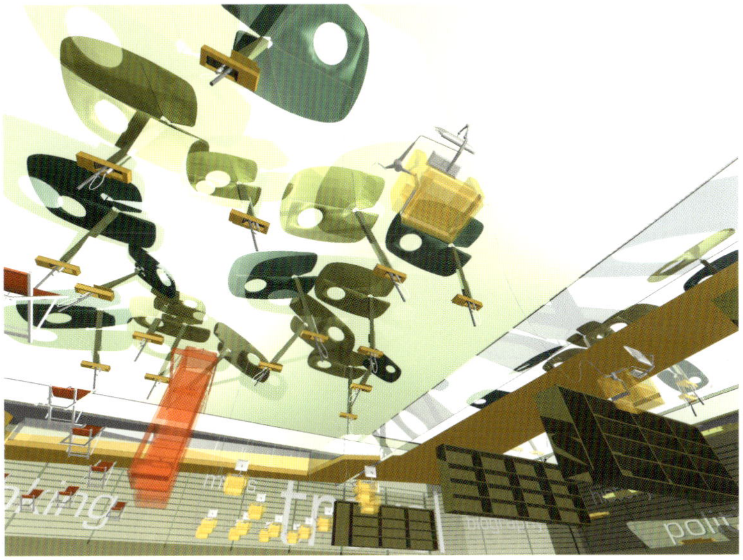

17

18

19

13 *View of courtyard from internet area* **14** *Inflatable sofas with internet facilities* **15** *Worm's-eye view of deck chairs and paper butterflies* **16&17** *Worm's-eye view of courtyard* **18** *View of courtyard with mobile café and oversized flower shades* **19** *Deck chairs for newspaper reading area*

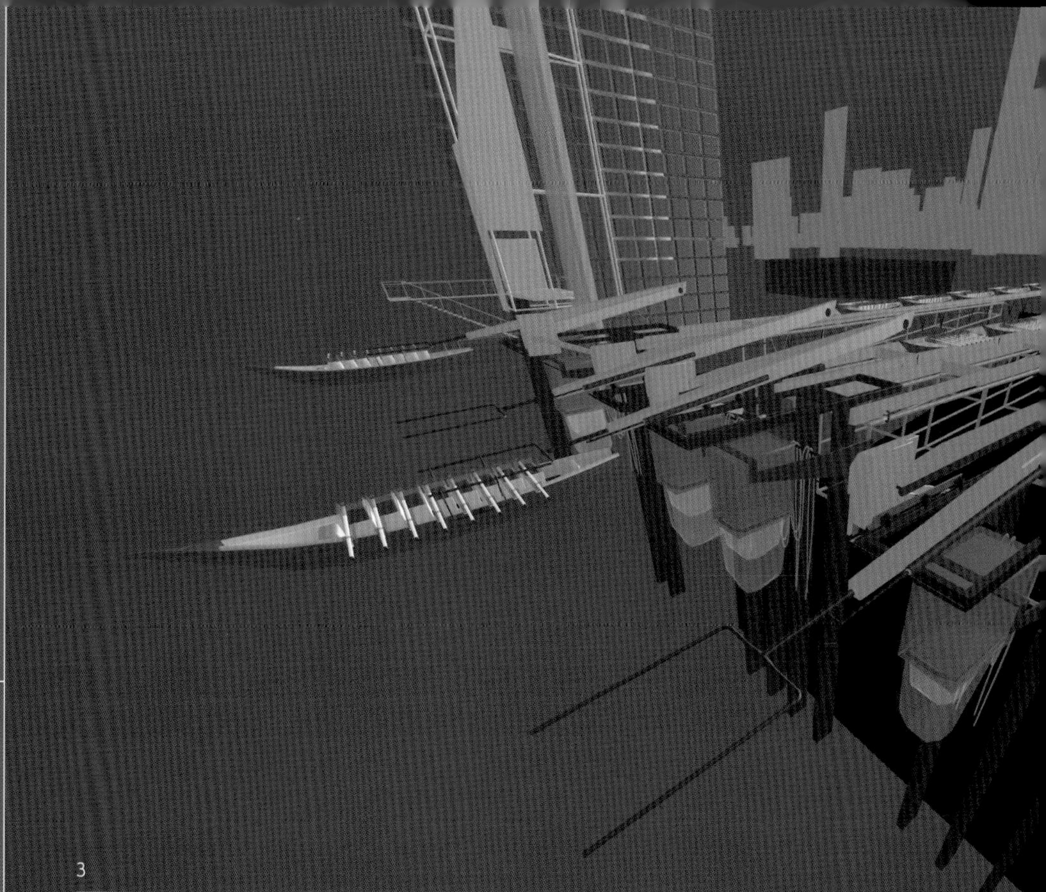

2

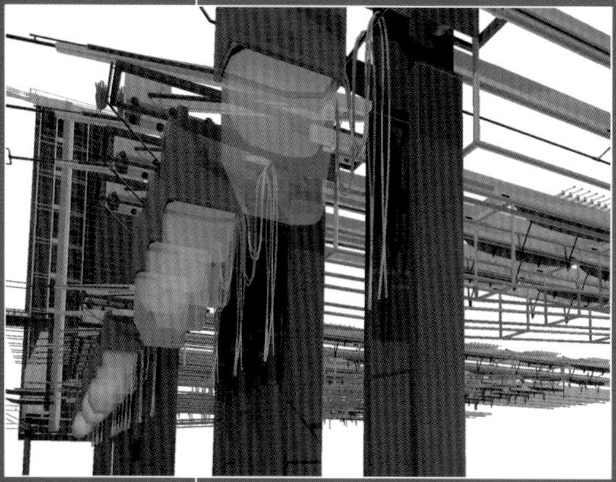

1

3

4

1 *Water bags acting as counterbalance to lift structures* **2** *Park in context* **3&4** *Worm's-eye view of park from existing meadow* **5** *Structure of park in horizontal position with floating boat-garden*

The boats of this floating garden symbolically celebrate the arrival of Haitian/French explorer, Jean Baptiste Point DuSable, the first settler in Chicago, and other subsequent immigration from various ethnic groups.

The **boats** of this **floating garden** symbolically **celebrate** the **arrival** of Haitian/French explorer, Jean Baptiste Point **DuSable**, the **first** settler in **Chicago**, and other **subsequent** immigration from **various** ethnic **groups**.

››› This piece of community landscape hovers delicately over an overgrown meadow, avoiding any physical contact to the green and the existing toxic ground conditions. The park is made up of an armada of floating boat-gardens, a skyscraper-plant-nursery and a drawbridge linking into Grant Park. The boats of this floating garden symbolically celebrate the arrival of Haitian/French explorer, Jean Baptiste Point DuSable, the first settler in Chicago, and other subsequent immigration from various ethnic groups.

Each floating boat-garden can be leased to individual members of the local community, members of which have predominantly ethnic origins. The boats act as planting trays, equipped with frost-protection clear covers and light-tubes. This park will display a tapestry of non-indigenous worldwide vegetation with a multitude of colour changes, a condition alien to the seasonal and severe climatic conditions of Chicago. The scheme also develops an ecological cycle of migrated plants, where a new ecosystem begins to foster.

The individual boat-gardens are gently placed on a series of lightweight pier structures pinned into the water's edge, while the meadow remains untouched. By day, all the floating gardens are deployed onto the lake by remote-controlled cranes. In doing so, the pier structures lift into their vertical configuration, revealing the overgrown meadow again. This performance mirrors that of the drawbridges around the city. On a diurnal cycle, the structures return to their horizontal positions, collecting the floating gardens and shifting them back in place for the night. Movements of boats are either remote-controlled or sailed into the lake. The choreography and arrangement of the park on the lake will be endless.

The skyscraper-plant-nursery is an inhabitable, south-facing glass structure, echoing the dominance of glass façades in Chicago. This structure cultivates non-indigenous flowers, vegetables and rare seedlings and it supplies plants to the floating boat-gardens and possibly to the rest of Chicago. Each individual glass seedling box is accessed via a vertical framing device similar to that of a window-cleaning system on neighbouring skyscrapers. The plant-nursery is capped by a sky garden with hydroponic trees. The trees symbolise freedom, democracy and liberation. Exalted views of Lake Michigan and the city allow the community to experience spatial conditions normally accessible only to the exclusive few.

As well as being the entrance to the floating gardens and DuSable Park, it also defines the end of Grant Park. At the bottom of this vertical structure are the public wash facilities, gardening tool/material storage cupboards, a retractable open-deck market and a small kitchen. On Sundays at the end of each month, fresh produce from the floating gardens can be sold on the open market. For a small fee, the kitchen can prepare picnic baskets using local produce. On a clear midsummer's evening with Chicago city as the backdrop, the community can dine in boats, amongst the floating gardens on Lake Michigan.

DUSABLE PARK, CHICAGO, USA

PARK OF SAND

research project

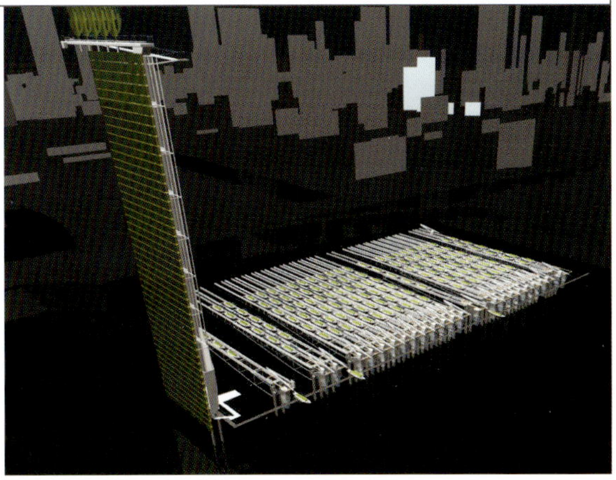

6

7

8

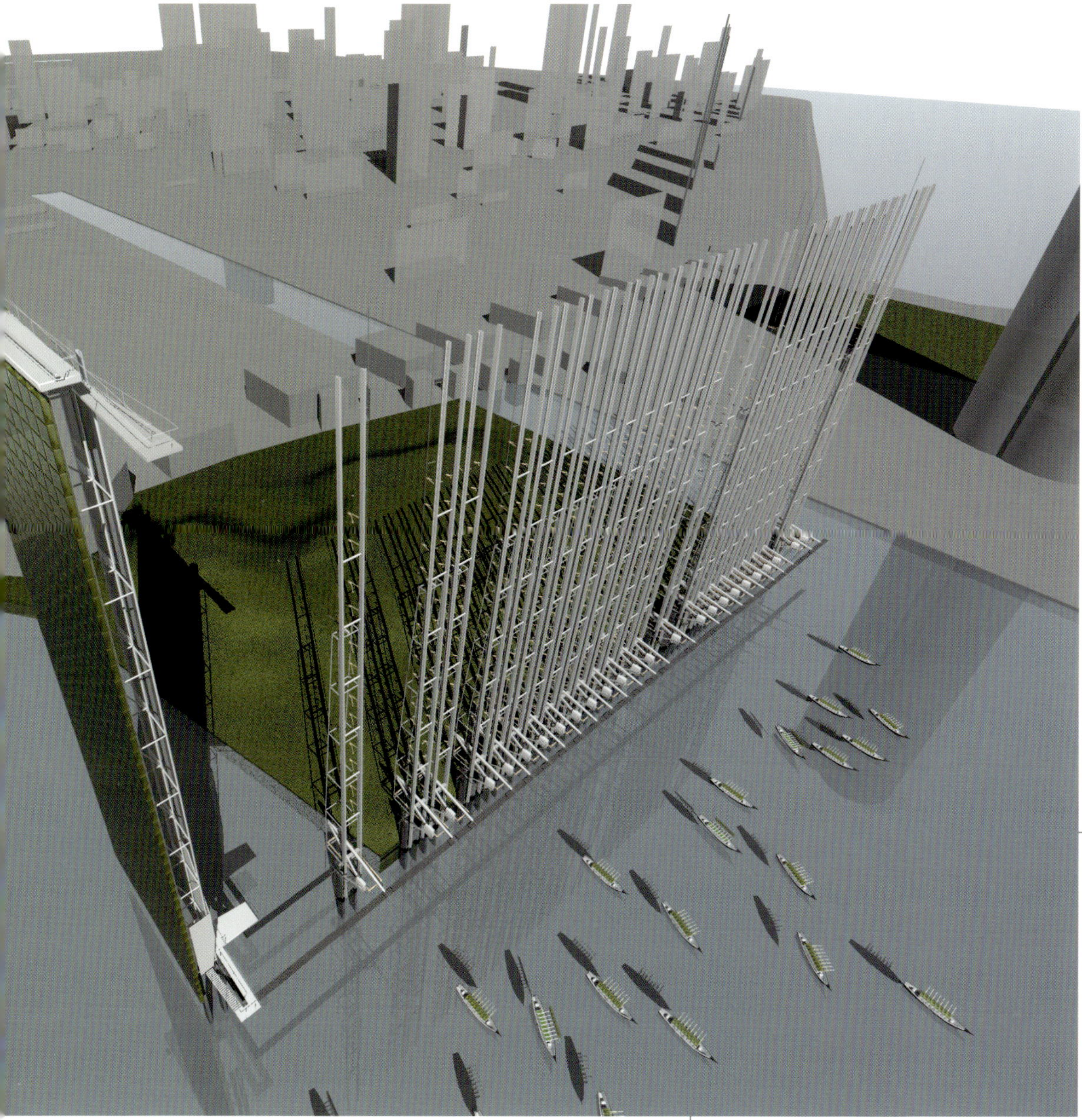

6 *New park with boat-gardens hovers over toxic meadow* **7** *Boat-gardens are launched into Lake Michigan during the day* **8** *Bird's-eye view of new park* **9** *Close-up views of structure of park* **10** *Floating boat-gardens*

9

10

11

12

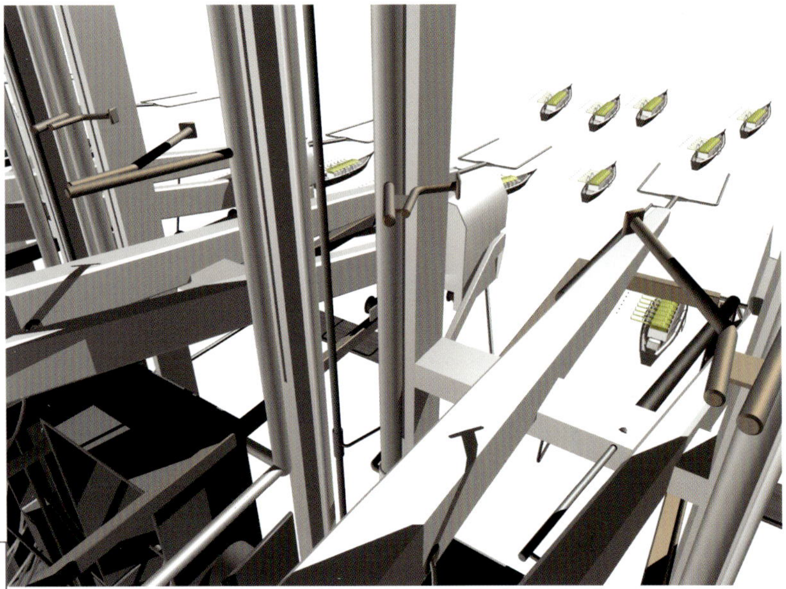

13

14

15

16

17

18

11 *Structure in daytime mode* **12** *Floating boat-gardens* **13,14,16–18** *Close-up views of structure of park* **15** *Worm's-eye view of floating boat-gardens*

19

19&21 *Close-up views of structure of park*
20 *Worm's-eye view of park from existing meadow*
22 *New park hovers over toxic meadow*

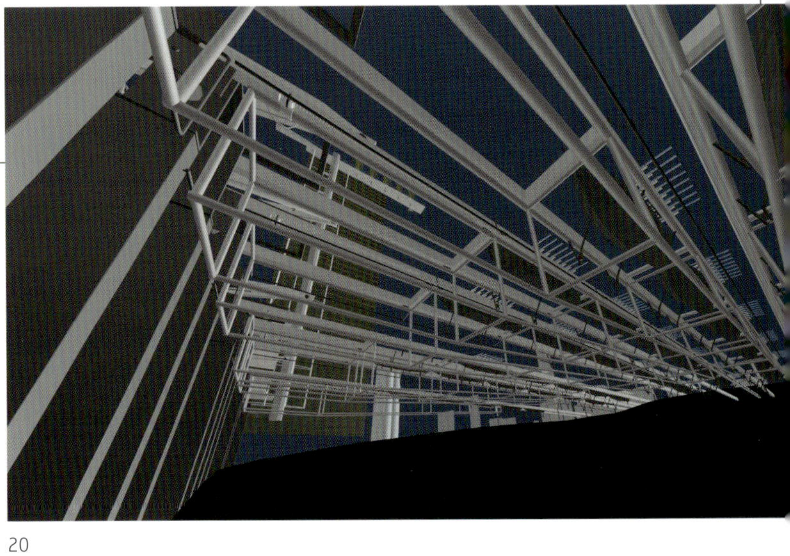

20

21

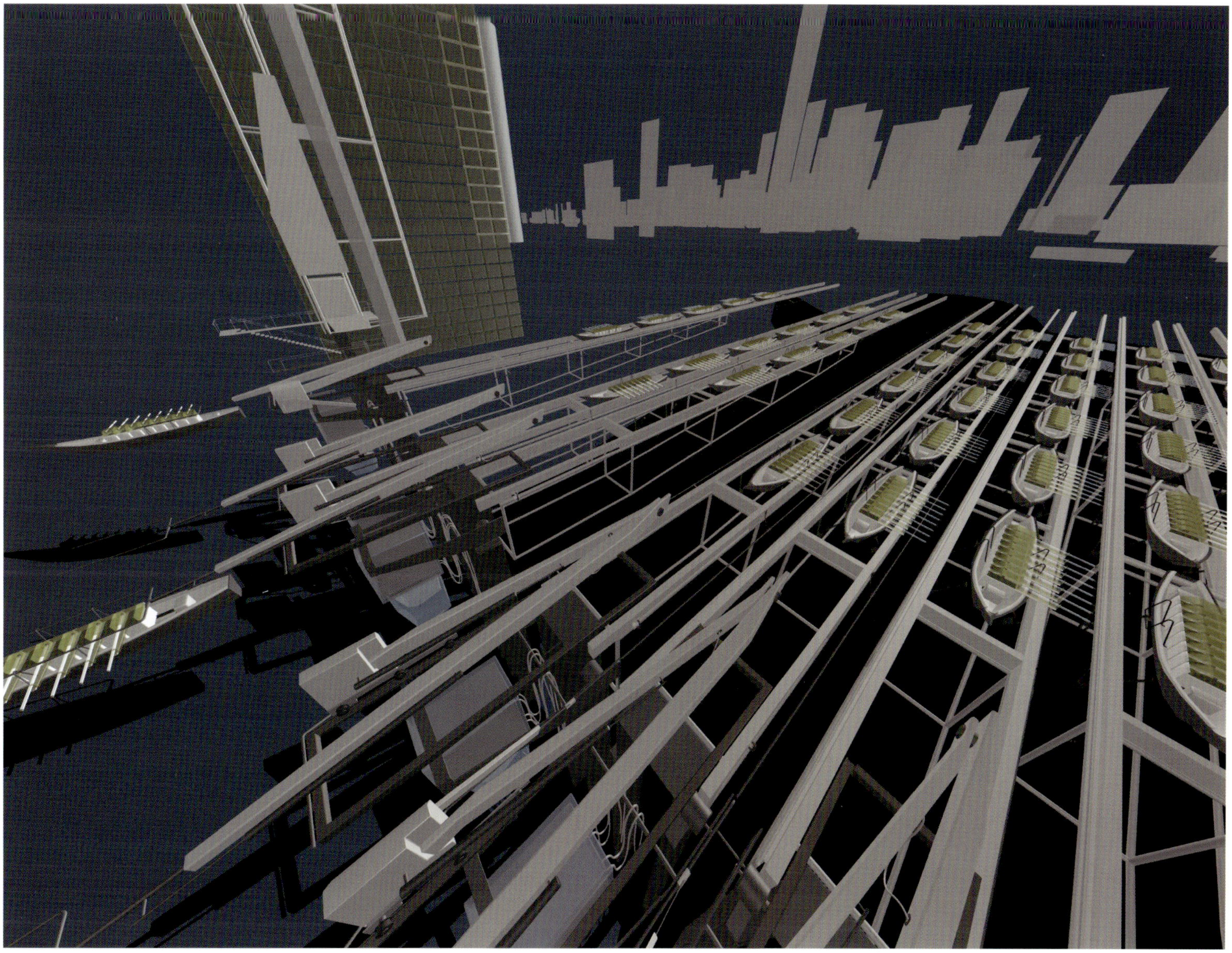

22

1

2

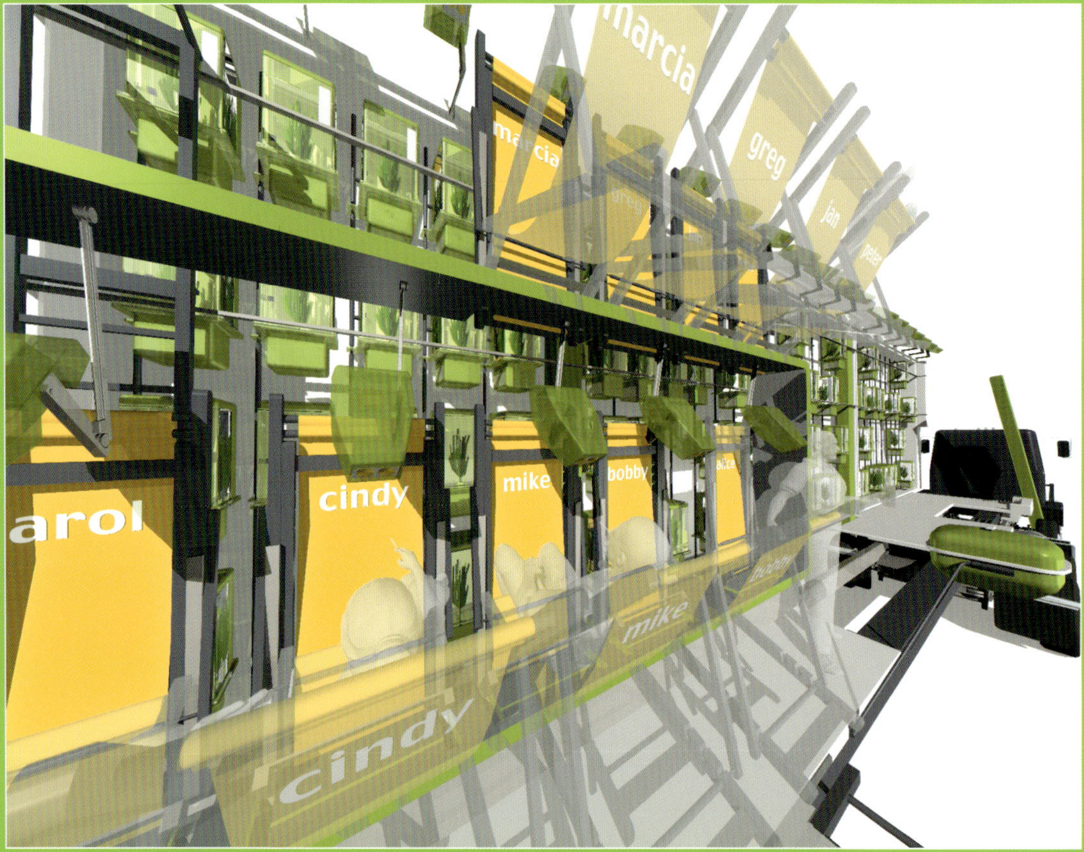

3

››› Christmas, Thanksgiving, Hanukkah, Eid, Ching Ming, Divali — ostensibly times for transcendental celebration, inevitably times of familial woe. The very idea of overcooked turkey and laugh-a-minute in-laws are guaranteed to strike dismay and consternation in the hearts of millions the world over. What we need is a neutral venue away from the pressure-cooker environment called home. What we need is a space to chill, a space where bickering, sniping and tedium dissipate in a haze of dreamy white cloud.

The dwelling place, in its most literal terms, is a shelter and gathering space. The words house, home and dwelling are mired in foretold relationships and prescribed associations — the kitchen is for cooking, the dining room for dining, the bedroom for bedding, the bathroom for bathing, the living room for … living?

For economical reasons, the majority of urban homes today are modest sized apartments. While the typical family members increase over several generations, the Victorian idealism of the domestic spatial arrangements becomes impossible to achieve.

But what is this beast parked over the street? Is it a house? A truck? A garden? A machine for living on? The answer is simultaneously an advertisement and actualisation of a transitory moment, a picture-postcard of happier times and sunnier climes. An extended family of nine perch showcased in an oasis of green, chatting amicably or snoozing in the sun with the barbecue wafting scents of wellbeing to all and sundry. But like any advertisement or postcard, the veil of substance is paper-thin and easily sundered.

The heart of the home where the family may gather and interact socially has gone through many incarnations, from the heart(h) to the dining table to the television set. Continuing this trend, the hanging gardens of wanton harmony lack such a focal point altogether. Privacy, security and comfort, those cornerstones of the home are all absent, save only in the most superficial, empty terms. There is no roof. There are no curtains. The barbecue is a sham and familial accord comes only from smoking the endless rows of hydroponically grown dope from the garden. This is *home* for the holidays!

1&2 *The garden is open to the elements, flooded only in light from bi-directional luminaires that light the plants while bathing the family in UV radiation for that mid-winter tan* **3** *Deckchair on mobile frame that traverses the length of the garden* **4** *The nine deckchairs make reference to the quintessential all-American happy family from the 70's TV series* The Brady Bunch **5** *Billboard advocating the lifestyle of the happy family while concealing the illicit substances that make such harmony appear possible*

4

LONDON, UK

THE HANGING GARDENS OF WANTON HARMONY

research project

5

6

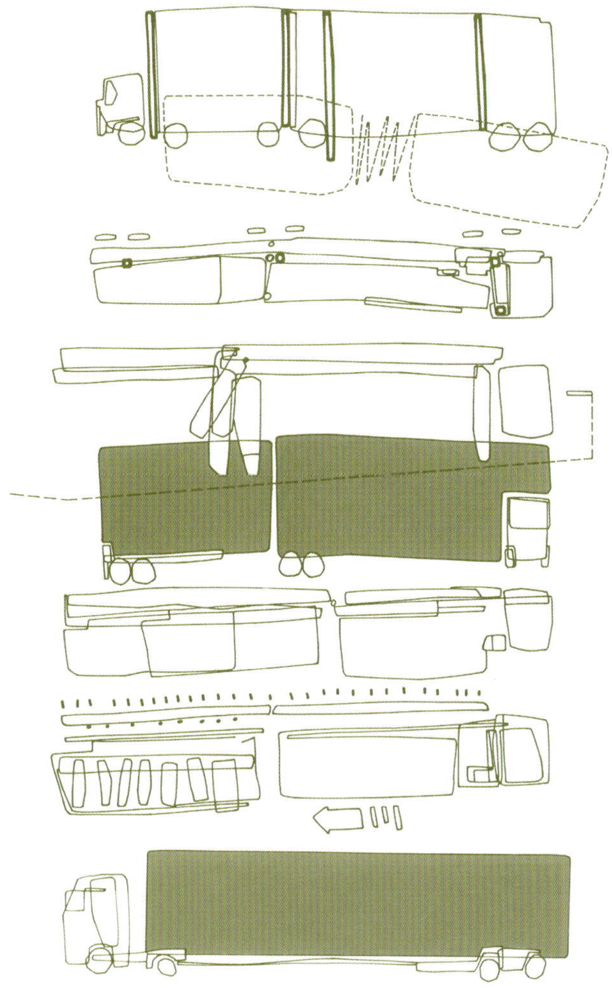

6 *Studies of the hanging garden* **7** *Sketches of the billboard* **8** *Elevation of hanging garden* **9** *Hydroponic growing unit with integrated pipes providing nutrient flow and carbon dioxide to promote growth of the marijuana plants*

7

8

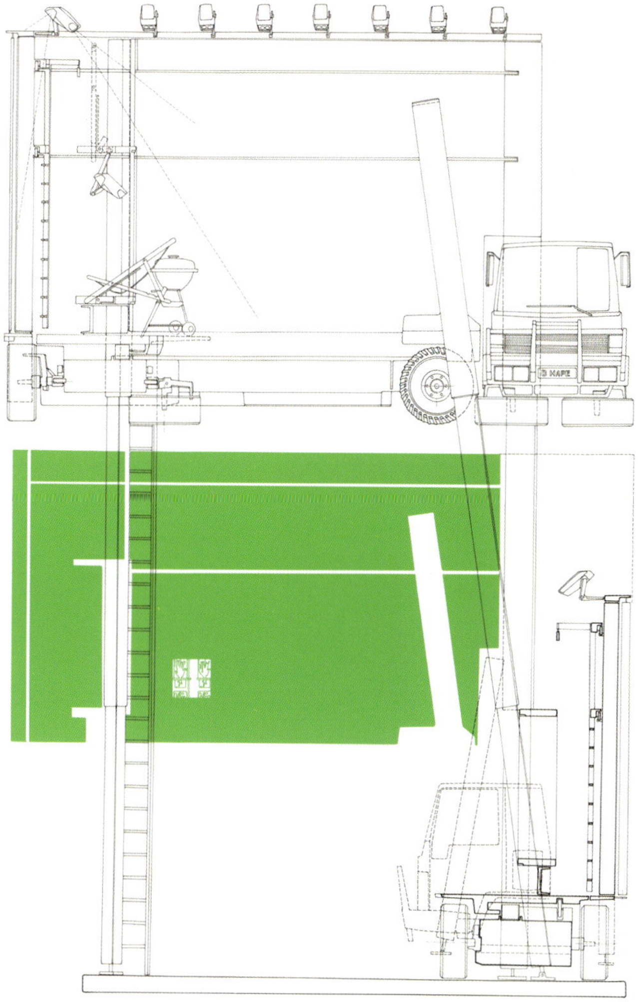

9

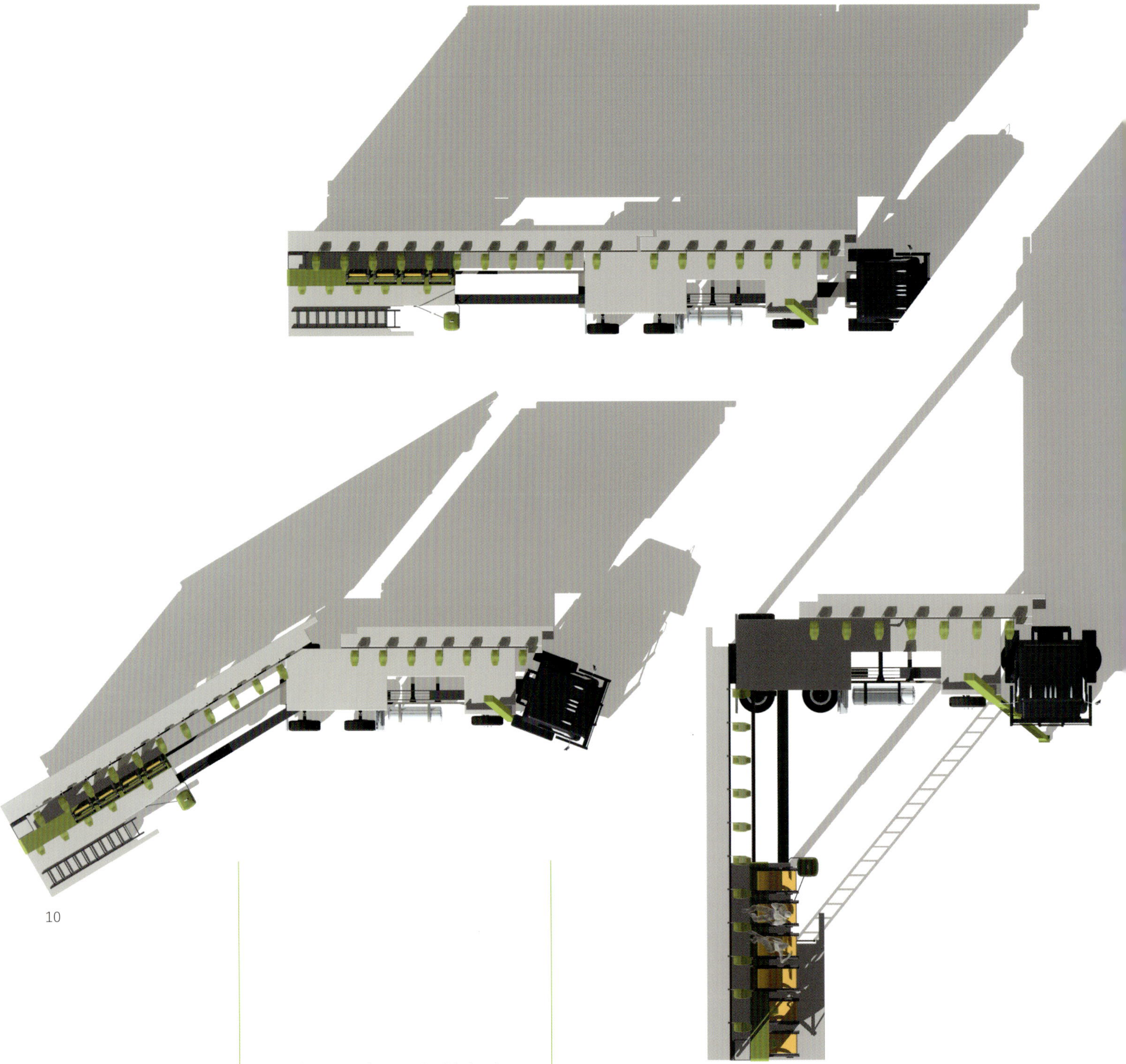

10

10 *Plan options: choreography of the hanging garden* **11** *The hanging garden is a modified HGV with a wall of hemp plants that parks across the road and elevates itself on tripodal hydraulic legs, away from the hustle and bustle of the street* **12** *Front view* **13** *View from above*

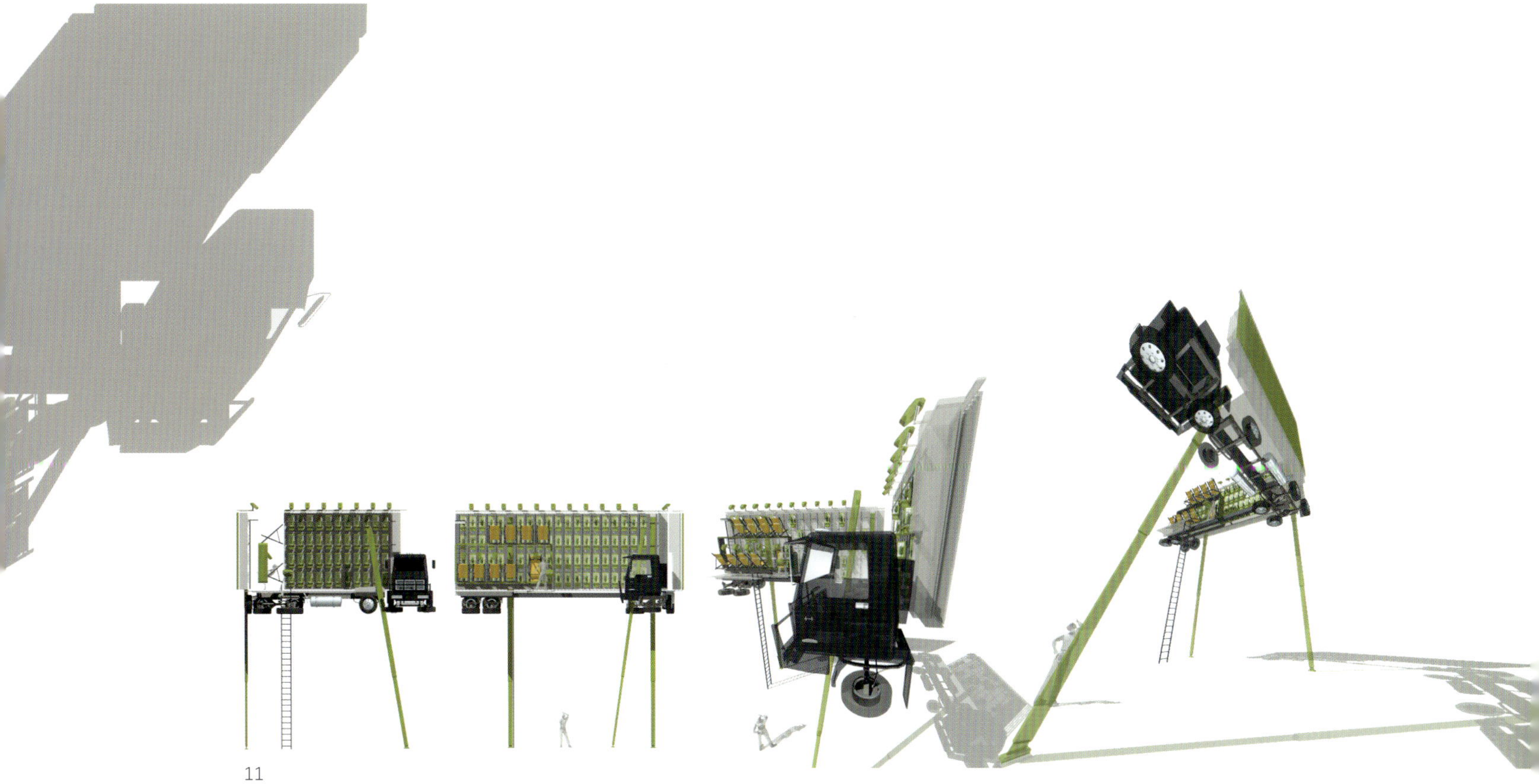

11

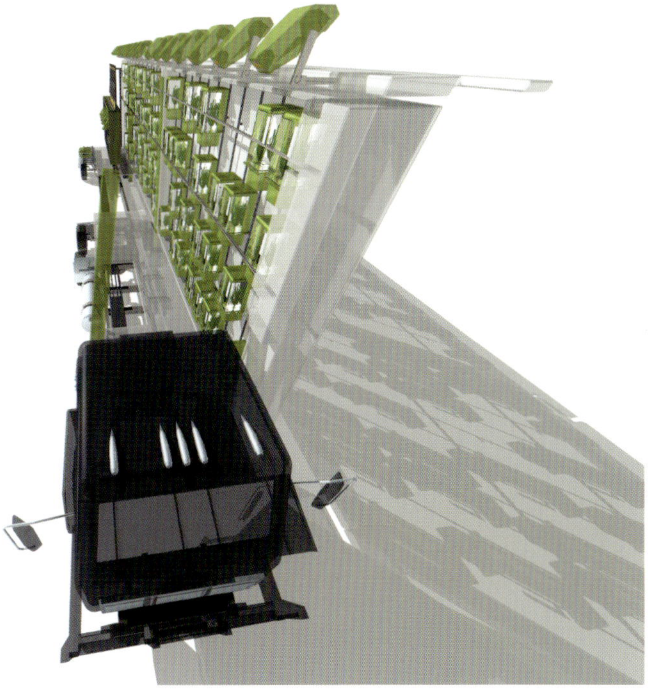

12

13

1

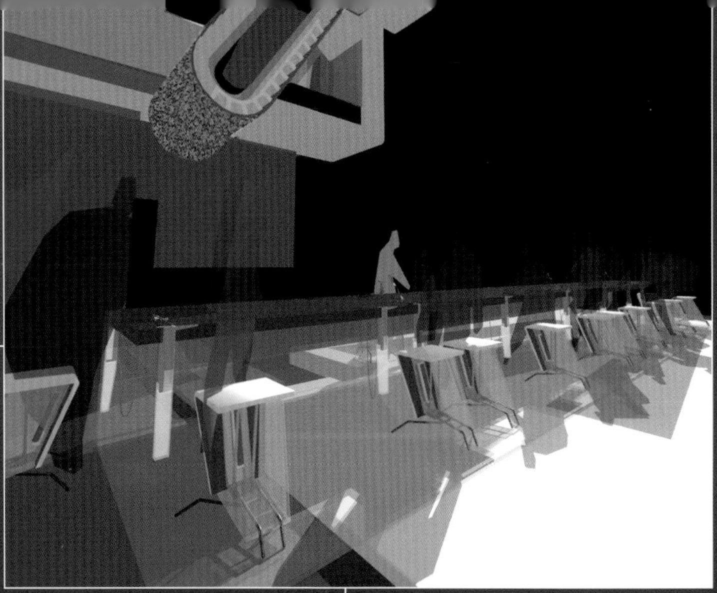

2

3

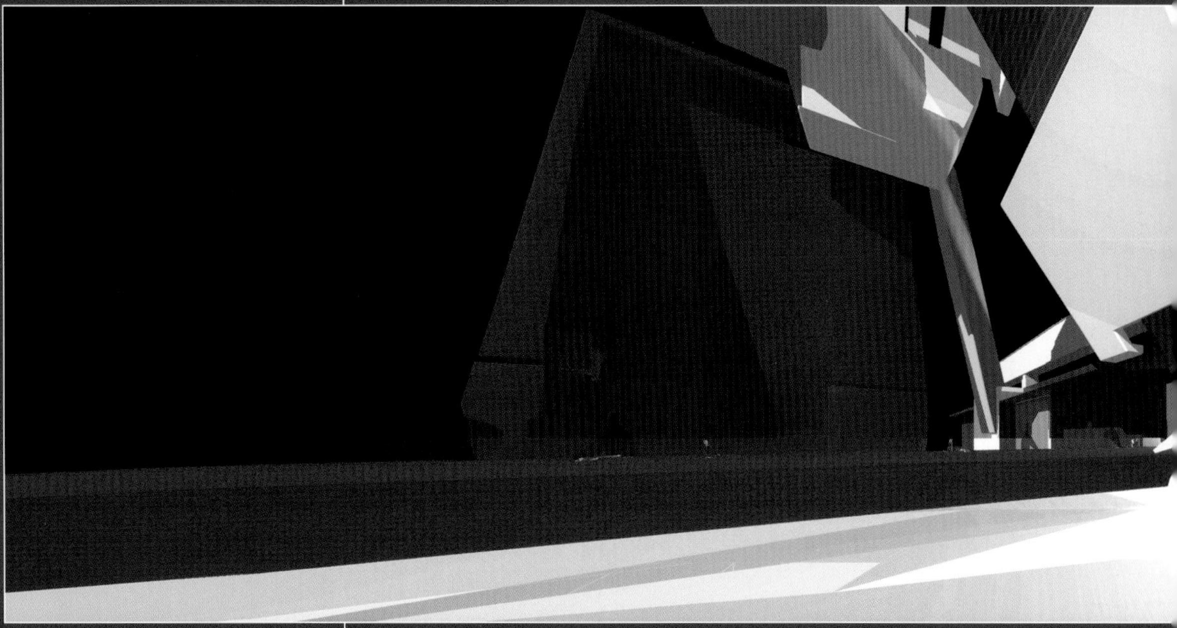

4

1 *Cow* **2–4** *Dining area*
5 *Sketch of the penthouse*

When owners of a cow arrive at the visitor centre, the gates concertina together to create a narrow pathway through which the visitors can access their respective cows.

When owners of a cow arrive at the visitor centre, the gates concertina together to create a narrow pathway through which the visitors can access their respective cows.

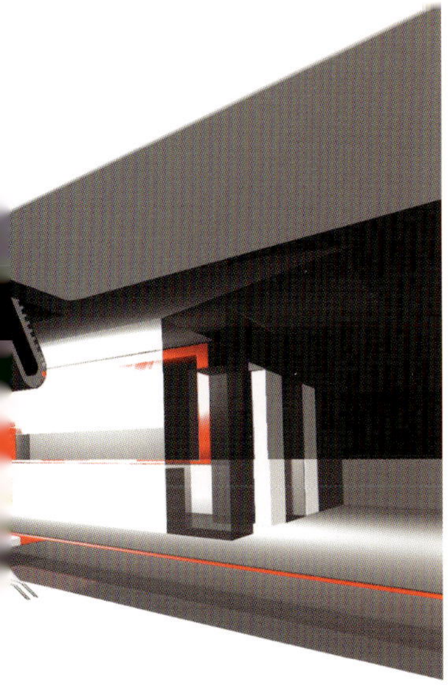

The basic premise of the 'World of Cow' is the suspension of a Wagyu calf and its living space over a restaurant in which it is later served up on a plate. Within this linear living strip, the cow inhabits a bedroom (with sun shades), massage parlour (replete with alcohol and unguents), living room (for receiving visitors) and a garden (a finely manicured lawn).

From the moment of her arrival from Kobe, the calf is sedentary. She is carried from place to place in her own carriage to feed, sleep and bathe. She has her own personal physician to ensure a clean bill of health, and a masseur to prevent her muscles from atrophying. She has no need to move. Slip-joints in the carriage foot supports allow space for growth and small shifts in movement.

The strip on which the individual farms are located is separated from the riverbank by a 2-metre-wide chasm, creating an artificial island. The only point of passage is via a series of gatehouses, within each of which is a guard. Or what appears to be a guard. Of the thirteen gatehouses, only one is manned by security personnel; dummies, their features hidden behind a monitor screen, occupy the other twelve. When owners of a cow arrive at the visitor centre, the gates concertina together to create a narrow pathway through which the visitors can access their respective cows. Hanging from a pole within the units are Barbour jackets and Wellington boots. A tray providing disposable jacket-linings and polythene socks allow manicured urbanites to assume the guise of seasoned crofters without sullying their clothes.

Behind the watchman is a small cupboard into which the dummy is stuffed. When the guard needs to relieve himself, he slides open the door of the cupboard in which a dummy is housed. The sliding mechanism contains a counterbalance that conveys the dummy smoothly out of the opening and into the vacant seat of the departed watchman.

At any time, the calf is in one of five positions:

1 Dining room: 7 metres above ground level, the cow's carriage cantilevers over the river. A conveyor belt surfaced in wild fescue provides continuous food for the cow. A slow rotation system ensures even consumption of the grass and prevents patches becoming worn. Fluorescent tubes beneath the belt give out uninterrupted light to help replenish what has been consumed during the day. The owners may also watch the cow eat in this location from the adjacent sofa.

2 Checkup room: the carriage occupies the space normally housing the sofa that rotates out to accommodate the unit. Here the

LONDON, UK

URBAN COWFARM

research project

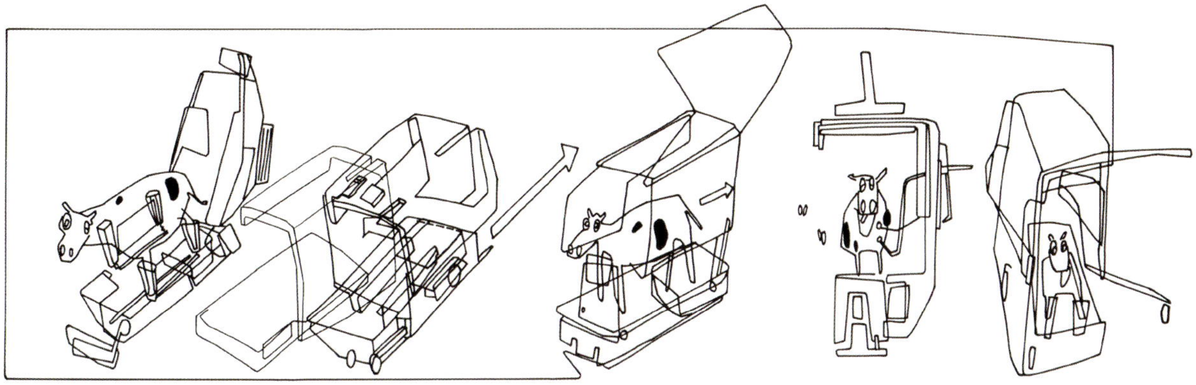

6

7

8

6&7 External view 8 Side elevation 9 Sketches

yer cow is so hap-py ne-ver sad

9

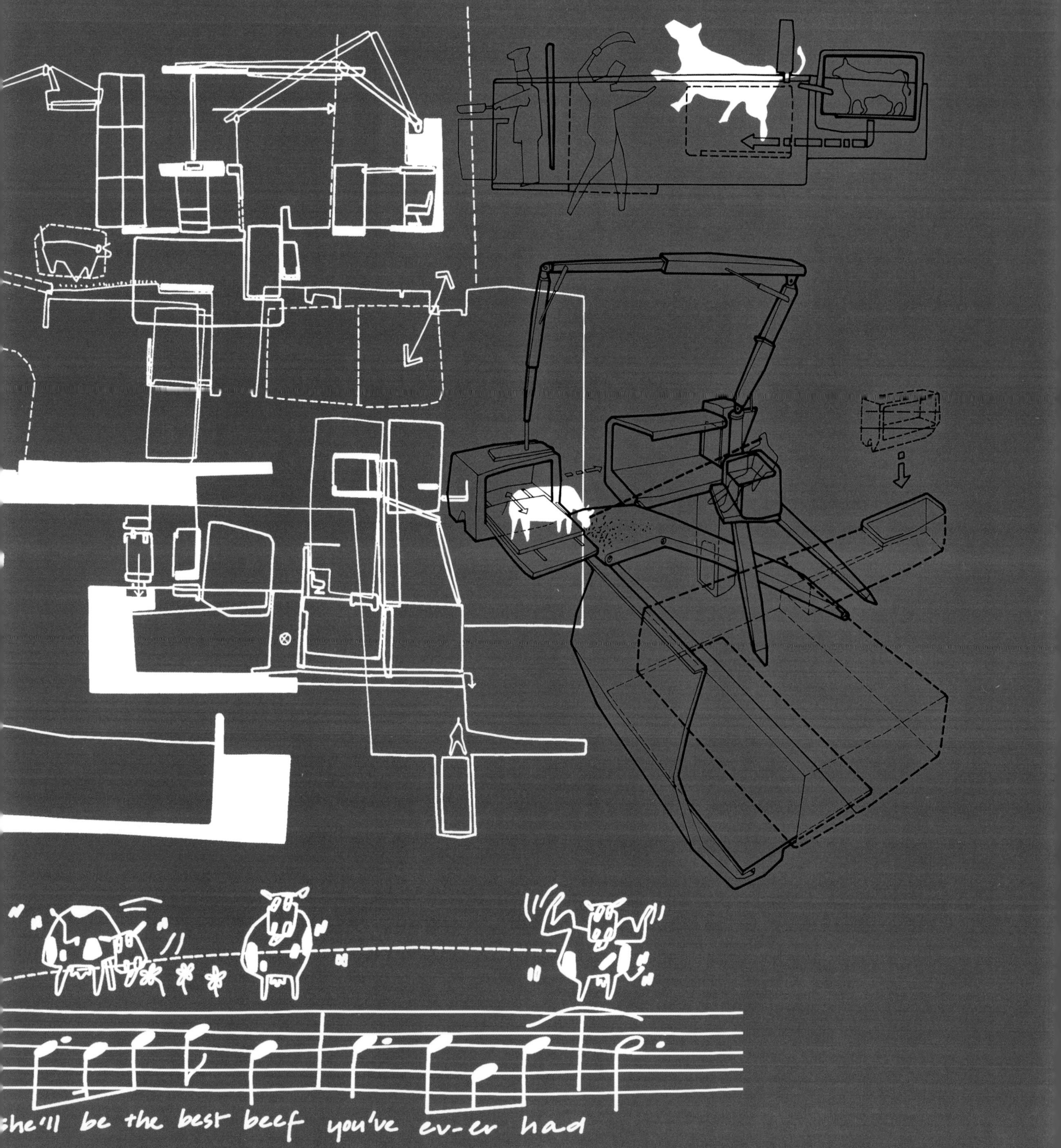
she'll be the best beef you've ev-er had

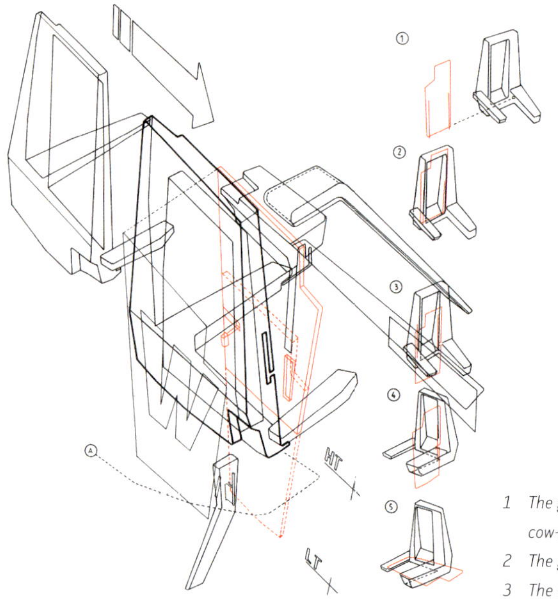

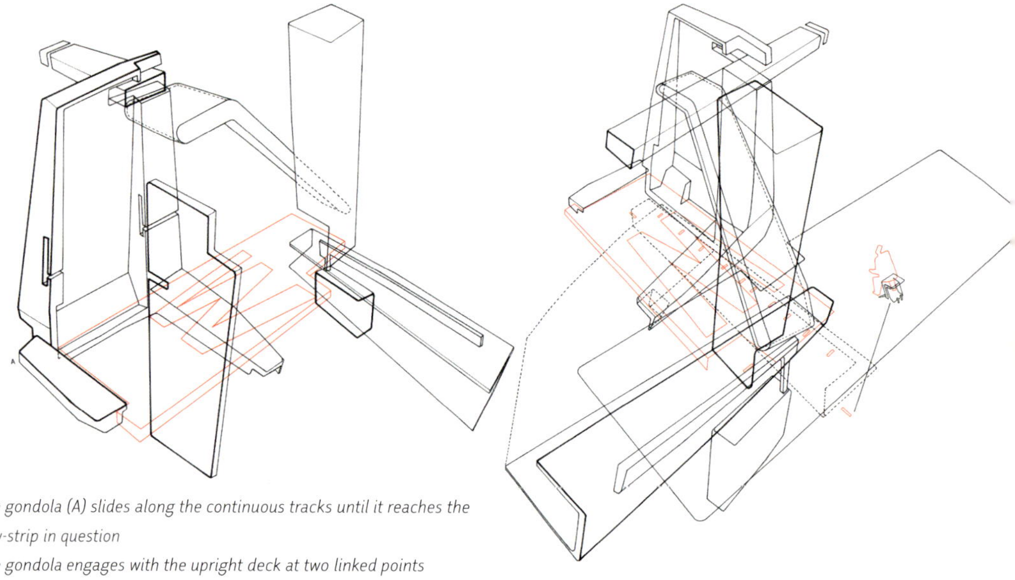

10

1 The gondola (A) slides along the continuous tracks until it reaches the cow-strip in question
2 The gondola engages with the upright deck at two linked points
3 The deck drops vertically with the tide, still connected to the point-tracks, until it engages and locks at the pivot points
4 The gondola detaches from the deck and rotates 90° clockwise at the pivot points
5 Once the gondola locks into place the deck detaches from the track and is lowered until horizontal. The dining table is then manually swung into place, ready for the banquet later that evening

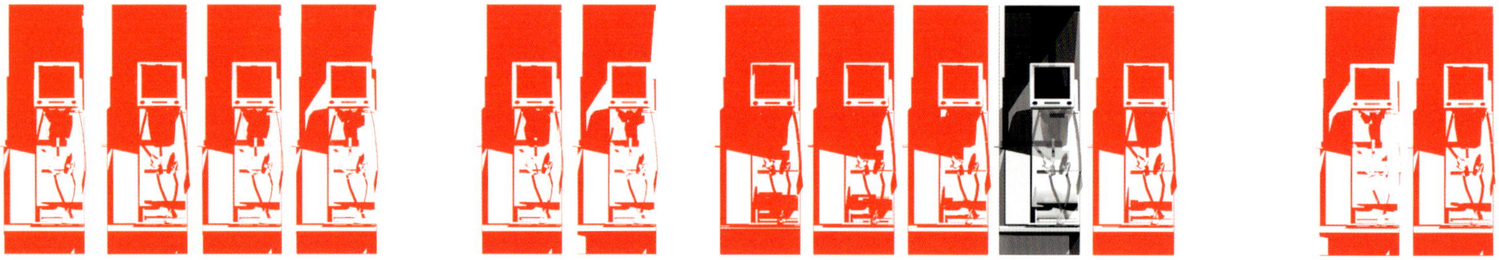

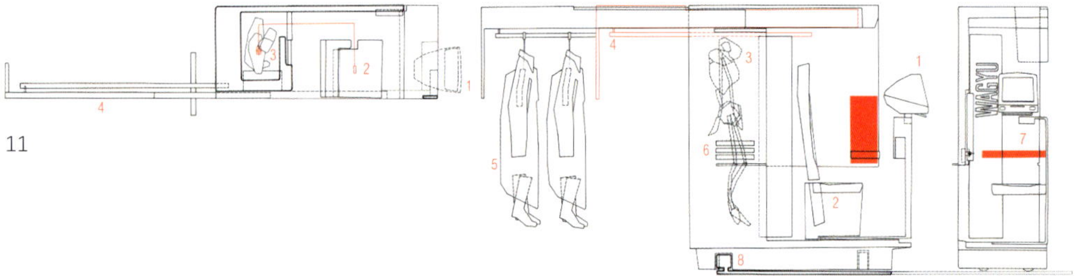

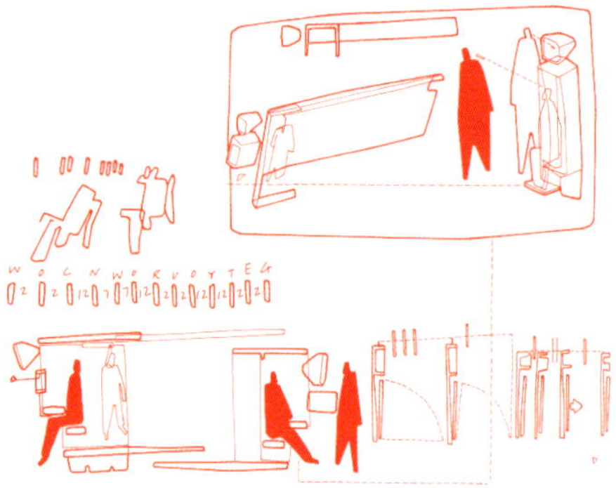

11

1 Visual display unit
2 Chair
3 Dummy
4 Extendable rail
5 Barbour and wellies
6 Jacket linings
7 Keyboard
8 Sliding track

cow is wired up to a computer that examines its vital statistics, fat content and marbling grade. She may also be inspected by her personal physician in this position.

3 Bedroom: the carriage is lowered three-quarters of the way into the ground, leaving sufficient space for fresh air to enter. The subterranean condition also prevents vandals who have circumvented security personnel from baiting or tipping the cow. A feeder bottle containing beer hangs down at head-height in the event of night-thirst.

4 Massage parlour: the carriage is lowered completely underground. The side panel folds down, allowing the masseur access to the cow. She is then rubbed down with plum wine, giving her coat a healthy sheen.

5 Kitchen: the carriage slides horizontally underground to a tiled area where the calf is chopped, hung and cooked.

The floor of the dining hall alternates between vertical urban signage and a horizontal dining pontoon. Discreet markings on its surface indicate the positions of the dining table and seat positions. The table is set for thirteen: twelve around one side, and a solitary seat opposite, illuminated by a shaft of light. The ceiling of the hall, in line with the dining table, is a 1-metre-wide grass strip, shifting infinitesimally slowly on a conveyor belt. Beyond the table is the curved screen of the gondola, folding beneath the platform. Water from the river washes into the space in rhythmic waves, creating a faint aural backdrop to conversation.

12

13

14

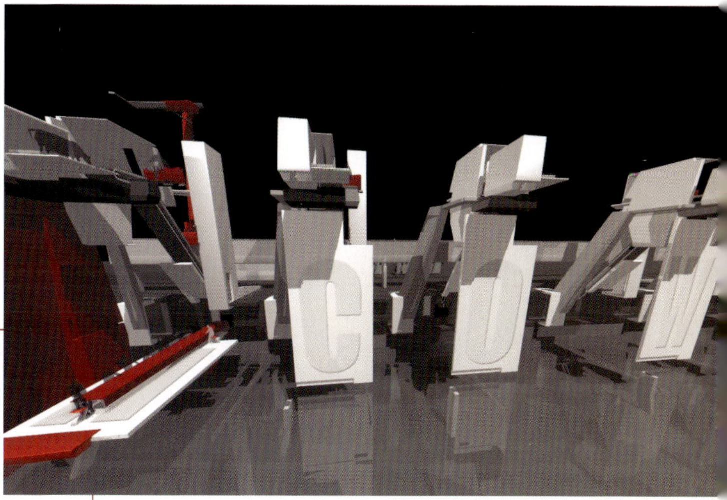

15

10 *Configuration of the building* **11** *Security pods* **12-15** *External view*

16

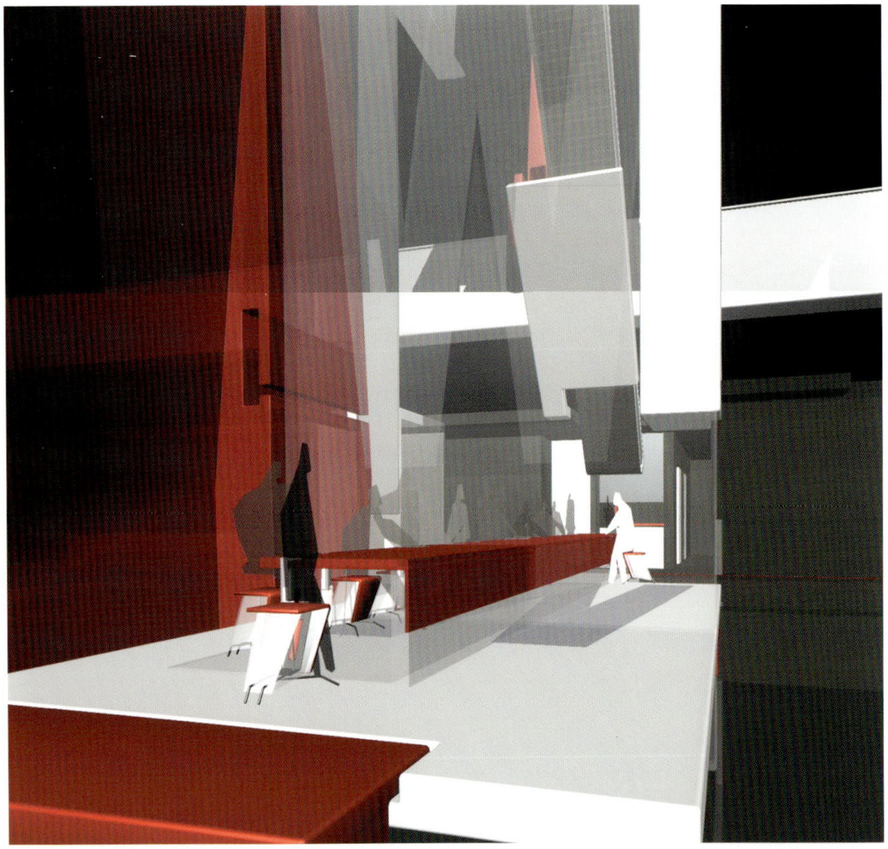

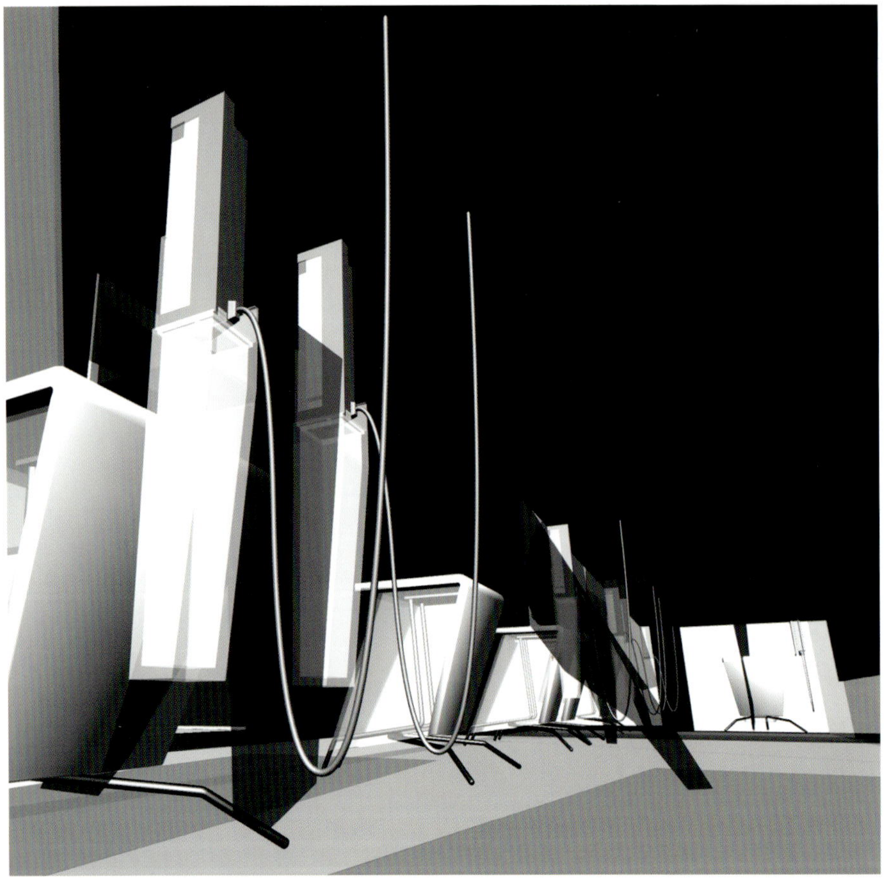

17

18

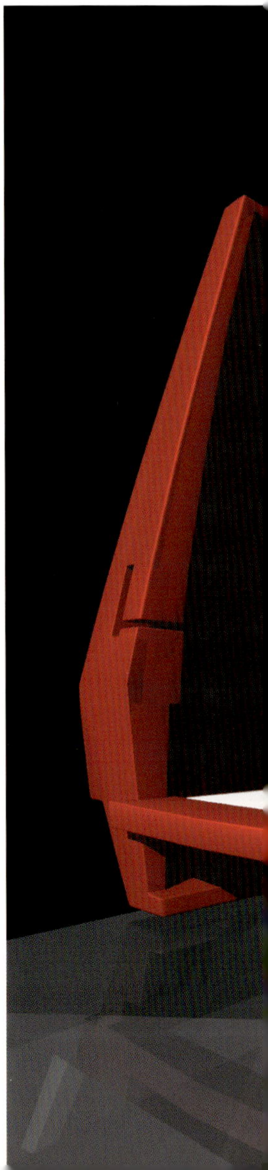

16&17 *Dining area and interactive stools* **18** *External view into dining area below and penthouse above* **19&20** *External view* **following pages** *Owner conversing with the sacred animal*

19

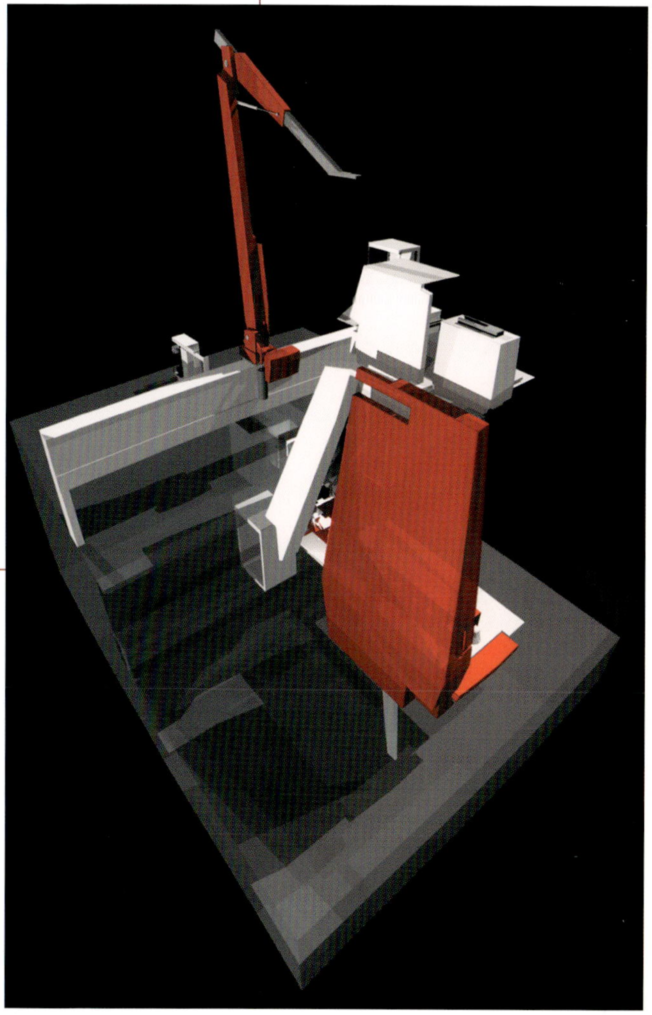

20

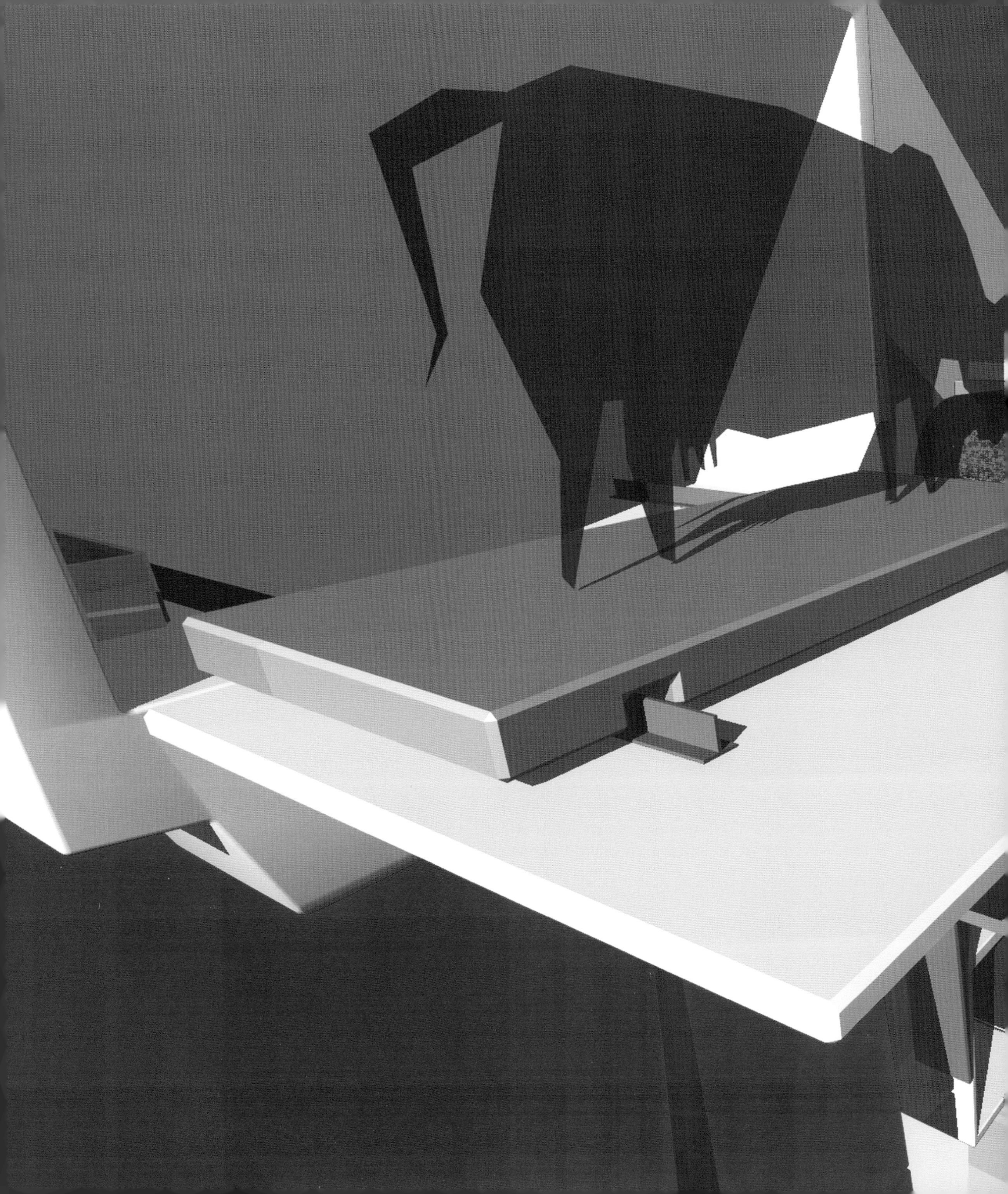

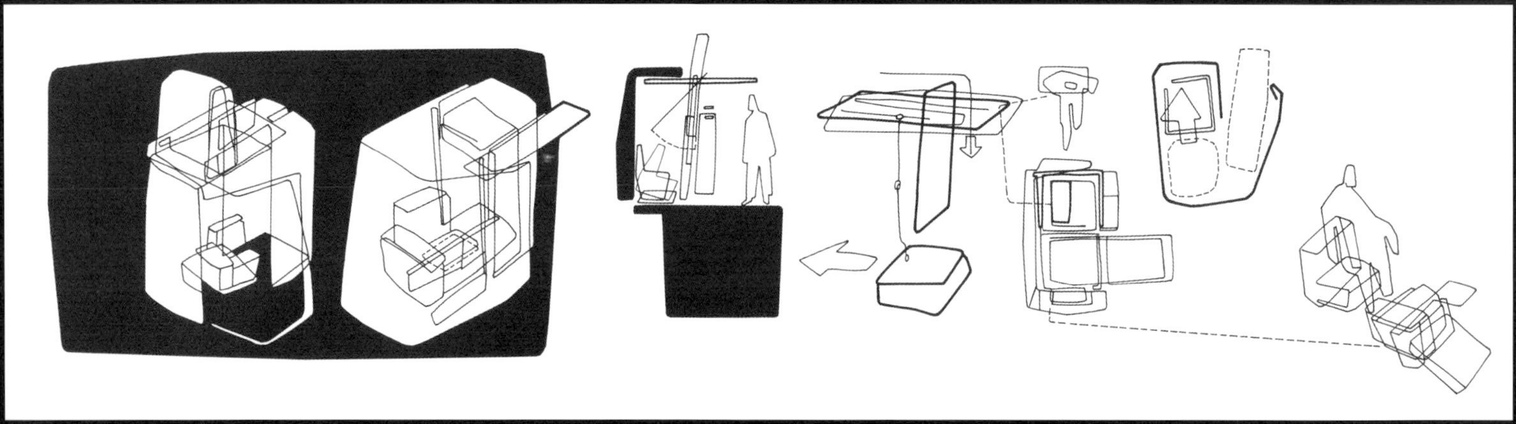

1

customised removal
tool for replacement
and maintenance
ground plane
recessed cover plate
tool socket
loudspeaker
aerial
drainage reservoir
ground socket

2

The public telephone has seen the many vicissitudes of life in the late 20th century. Its unrivalled distribution in almost every city of the world makes it the ideal forum for disseminating services and information. Changes in the way we communicate, however — WAP technology, conference calling, webcams and other computer-related outgrowths — have led to the decline of the traditional booth as a means of conveying information. The need for new functions and programmes for the booth has become ever more pressing with increasing space demands and changing patterns of life. The following list compiles important dates in the history of telephony:

1700: Defined as any device conveying sound over a distance, the first telephone consists of two vessels in separate rooms connected by a piece of string, much like the toy children construct in the late 20th century.

1729: English chemist, Stephen Gray transmits electricity over almost 300 feet of brass wire and moistened thread.

1837: Samuel Morse invents the first workable telegraph. Telegraphy replaces the Pony Express, clipper ships and other slow-paced means of communicating.

1861: Johann Reis completes the first non-working telephone. Made of a sausage skin, a knitting needle, cork and a piece of platinum, it was able to transmit music, but not intelligible speech.

1876: Elisha Gray and Alexander Graham Bell invent the first working telephone, patent no. 174 465. American President Rutherford Hayes is quoted as saying: 'This telephone is an amazing invention, but who would ever want to use one of them?'

1885: The American Telephone and Telegraph Company (AT&T) is born, the most influential and one-time richest company in American corporate history. The telephone is credited as having made the skyscraper possible, creating a new type

3

LONDON, UK | JERRY SPRINGER MUSEUM

research project

1 *Confession booth studies* **2** *Listening Plain* **3** *Existing telephone booth* **4** *Confession booth elevations*

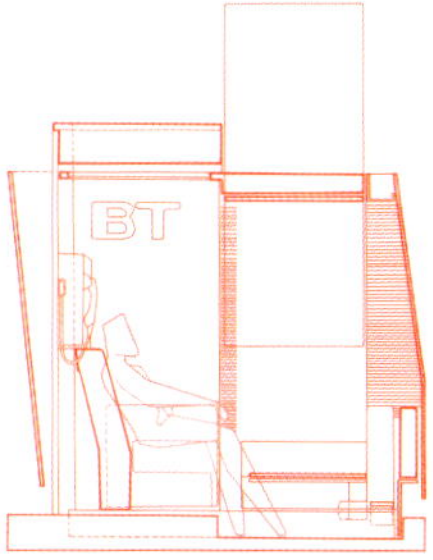

4

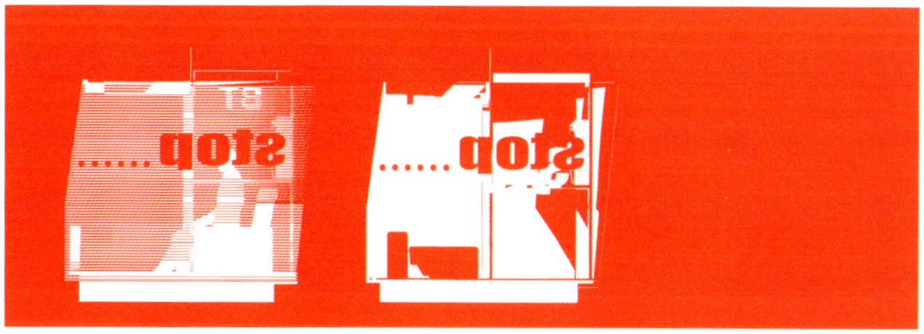

of city redolent of the fairy-tale constructs of mythical nations.

1889: The first public coin telephone appears in Hartford, Connecticut. Payment was given to a nearby attendant.

1950: AT&T establishes a telephone network allowing manual exchanges to be placed through a discrete operator.

1965: An electronic switching system becomes the industry standard. London's red booths become a cultural icon.

1990: London: telephone booths are claimed by the sex industry. Advertisements offering the full range of sexual services plaster the kiosk interiors. In other countries, less prurient notices adorn the cubicle walls.

2004: Telephone booths: the GlassStop™ assume additional functions. A temporary living room is created within the city by wrapping a vari-focus glazed screen around the existing units. Fitted with an armchair and a television, it provides a place for people to rest between shopping, or before an evening rendezvous, without having to purchase a coffee or beer. Making use of the phone power points, notably in London, the public telephone has been converted into a modern-day confession booth where people may divulge their personal failings to an audience several miles distant.

The defunct telephone kiosk has found a new lease of life in the form of the CONFESSION BOOTH. Paradoxically, the dissolution of faith in our secular metropolis has not seen a corresponding disappearance in the need to confess. Guilt and absolution, it appears, are not the sole preserve of Catholics. The success of the phone booth as a ground for confession rather than straightforward conversation can be put down to the physicalisation of the site. In an age of mobile communications and worldwide access, penitence is more than ever equated with physical hardship – the ritual of pilgrimage remains an integral part of redemption. The confession is broadcast live to the Listening Plain, a custom-built park where the intended confidante of the message, or general public, may tune in. At the end of the session, a disc of the confession is provided, giving the penitent a physical record of his or her transgressions. The recording may then be sent to a specific party, or kept in a personal collection as a permanent reminder of errancy.

The Listening Plain proposes a radical reconditioning of public horizontal spaces with minimum visible intervention. Tiny infrared receivers and loudspeakers are inserted into the existing floorplate to create a matrix of listening stations, broadcasting an aural membrane of whispered conversations, confessions and revelations. The true architecture, however, is not the soundscape, but the spaces created by the listeners – individuals ranging from the young to the old, the rich to the poor, the stick-like to the obese. Visitors to the plain twist into strange positions – crouching, kneeling, squatting and reclining – in order to eavesdrop on occluded conversations transmitted from strategic locations within the city. In the process, they inadvertently form a living membrane that changes in texture according to the time of day and season. This layer of undulating material, ranging from bare skin to fur coats and scarves is clearly visible from afar and on high.

5

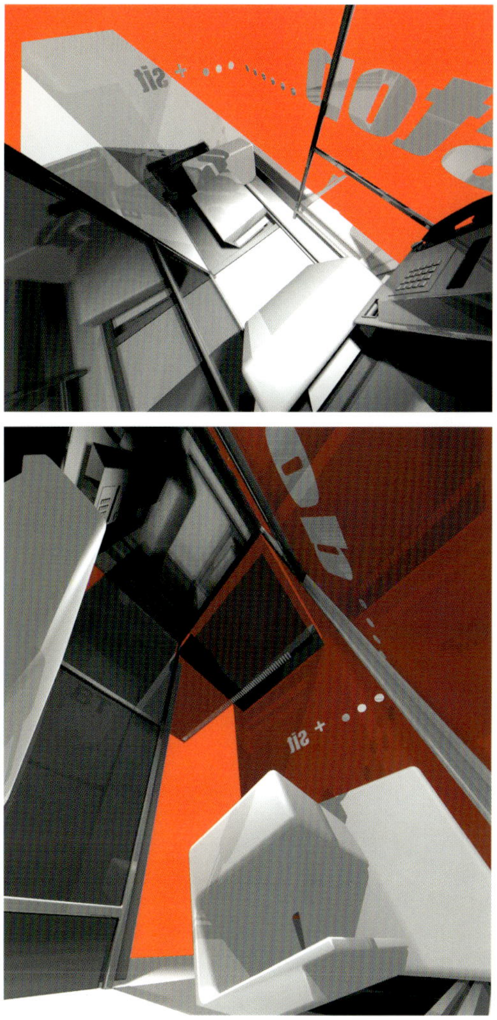

6

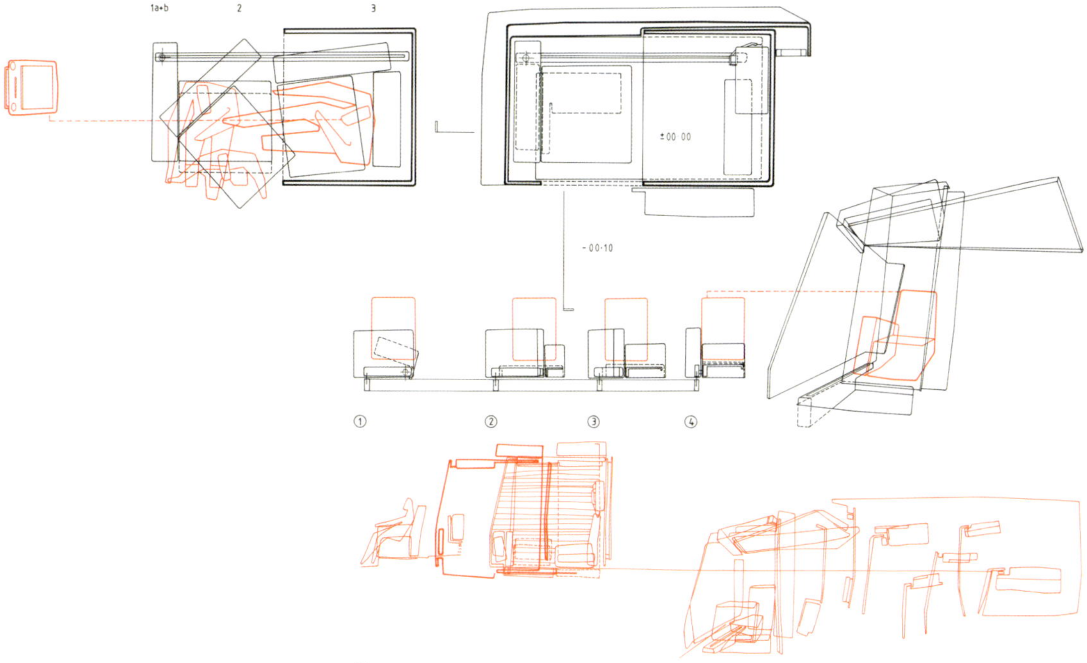

7

5 *Confession booth open and closed*
6 *Confession booth interior*
7 *Confession booth interior studies*

TELEPHONE

Opposite *Confession booth interior*

9 *Confession booth mechanism studies*

10 *Confession booth open and closed*

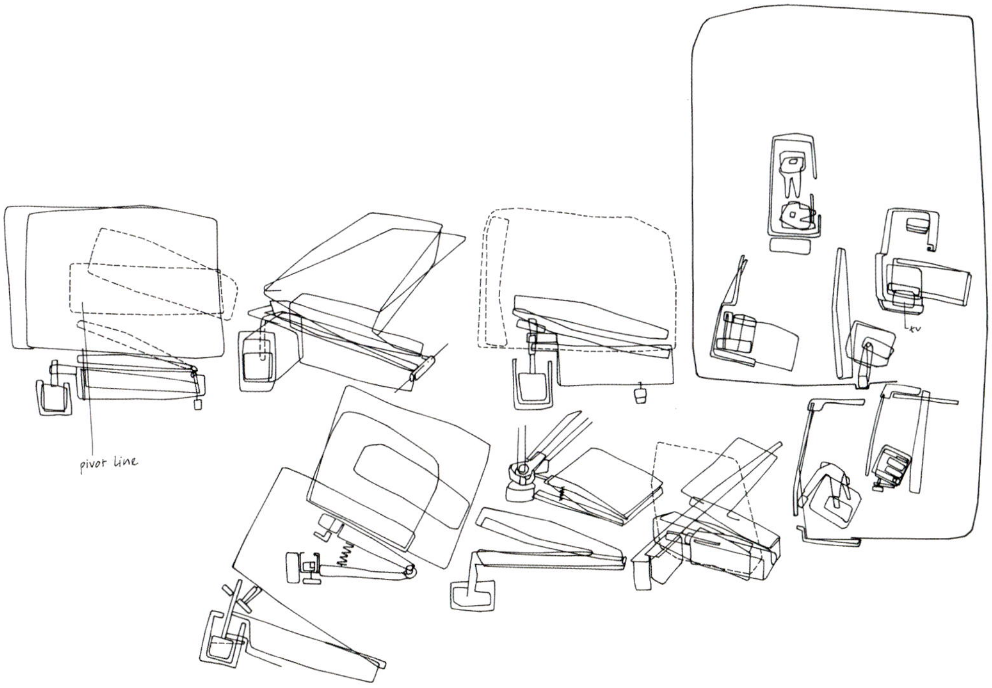

9

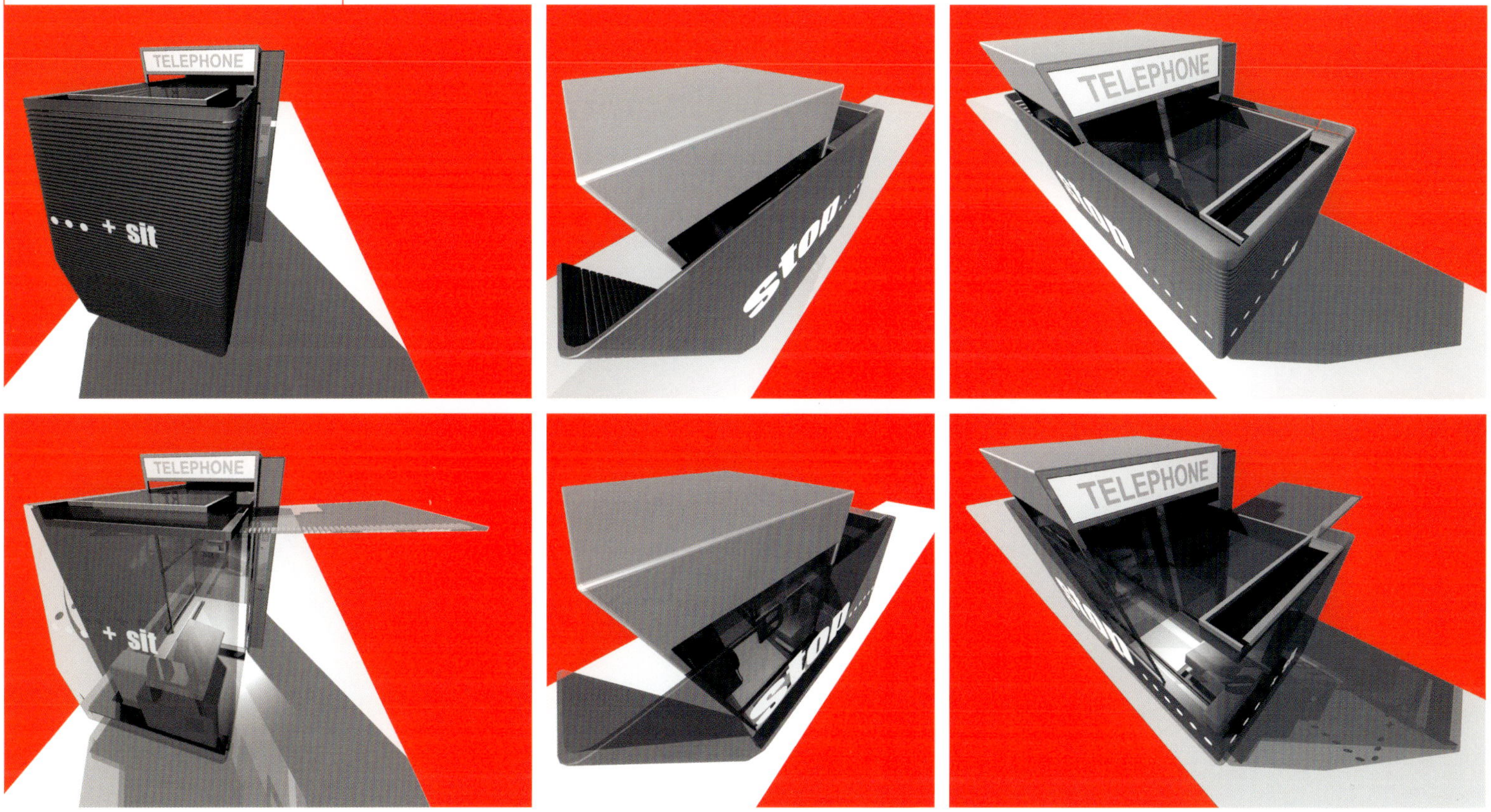

10

Something strange has been happening to Trafalgar Square over the past few years. A series of seemingly innocuous structures have gradually insinuated themselves into the square and its environs. Seen in retrospect, they conflate to form some kind of demented masterplan founded on violence and lunacy — a Friday evening in the centre of London could well be mistaken for a convention of escaped mental patients with screams, brawls, rants and pigeons flying through the air. The area, by accident or design, is zoned into strips, each providing their own idiosyncratic take on public space.

Zone 1

National Portrait Gallery. The first insertion into the area is a subtle one, consisting of a single painting mounted on the entrance stairway. It shows a woman frozen in the act of letting loose a lung-bursting scream. Sitting soberly next to her is a portrait of Her Majesty Queen Elizabeth II. The first portrait is in fact a digitised image, changing every few minutes. In a gallery full of portraits, an art form inextricably linked to the moment, it is the sole shifting element, displacing the compound viewer from the comfort of familiarity. It transpires that the image is that of one of the screamers from Zone 2, abstracted from its context and sound.

Zone 2

Screaming gallery/sound columns. Five airshafts pierce the body of the National Gallery. Reflective sound tubes, several metres in diameter, and approximately 20 metres in height are suspended from the tops of these, into which the public may enter to bellow and shriek to their heart's content. A small percentage of the sound is reflected back into the tube, amplifying the scream in the ears of its source. The remainder is channelled via angled convex surfaces down to sound hotspots on the west side of Charing Cross Road, simultaneously shocking conservative gallery-goers and delighting their protesting offspring in tow.

Zone 3

Sofa therapy/confessional. On a sunny summer's day, banks of coffee tables sit on the green manicured lawn outside the National Gallery. Two people are seated on each adjacent sofa, engaged in earnest conversation. One of the pair is invariably a psychiatrist, the other a member of the general public. A fine porcelain tea service rests, untouched, on the coffee table. In an age where the term patient is deemed politically incorrect, the therapist is distinguished only by his attire of flannel shirts, corduroy trousers and brogues. For the price of a coffee, punters may take advantage of a free counselling service in the heart of London.

Zone 4

Bus stop messaging. The Trafalgar Square Bus Station is the nucleus

2

1 *Zone 02: Screaming gallery* **2** *Zone 01: National Portrait Gallery with live portrait* **3** *Zone 03: Sofa therapy* **4&5** *Zone 02: Screaming gallery's sound column*

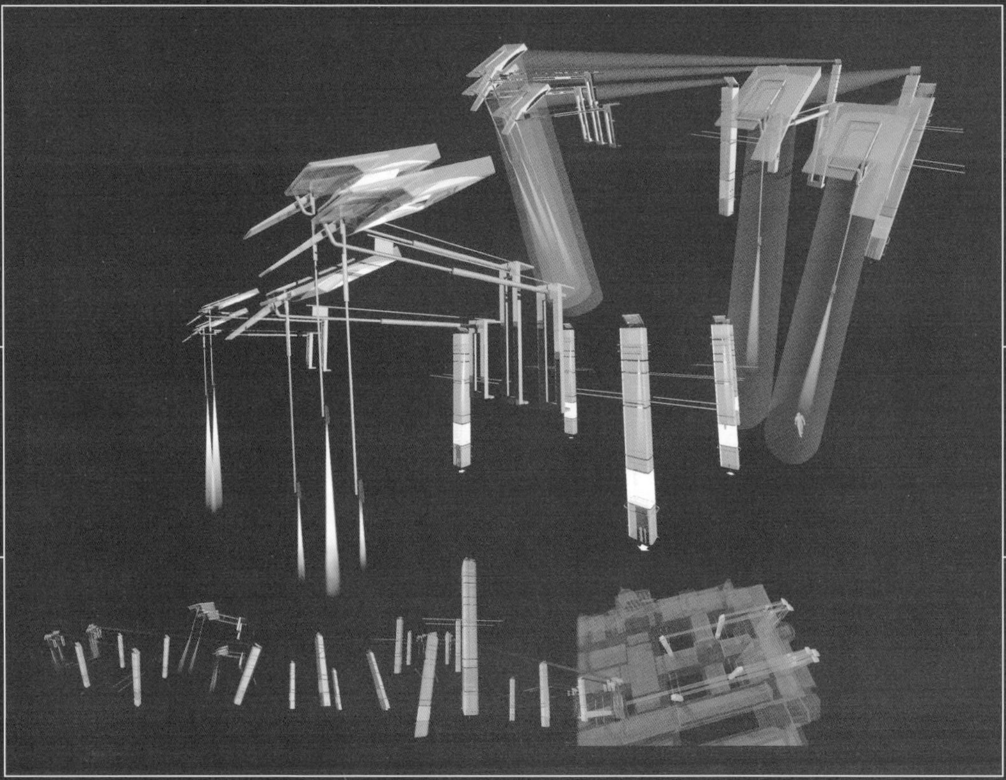

1

A Friday evening in the centre of London could well be mistaken for a convention of escaped mental patients with screams, brawls, rants and pigeons flying through the air.

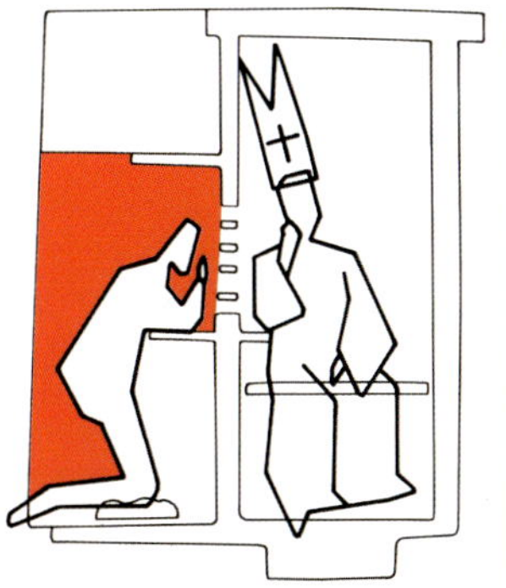

4

3

5

LONDON, UK

TRAFALGAR SQUARE

research project

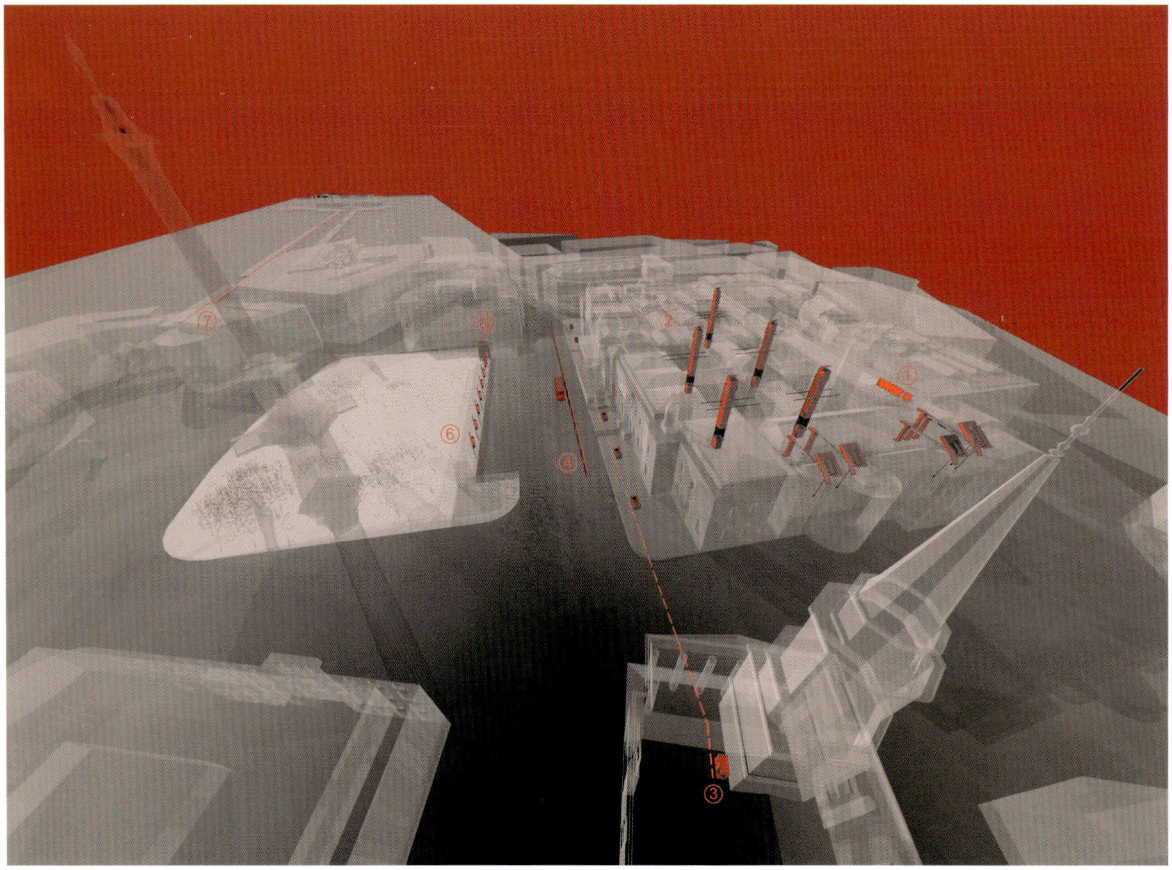

6

7

8

9

of the bus text-messaging service. Reminiscent of Jenny Holzer's digital displays in art galleries around the world, over-sized letters on full-height LED screens scroll fragments of text over a 50-metre expanse. The message, part of the Naming and Shaming programme, is broadcast to all London bus stops bearing electronic displays.

Zone 5

The Fourth Plinth. The last of the four statue-bearing plinths has been vacant since its inception for want of a suitable hero. After much deliberation, Westminster Council has finally approved the use of the plinth as an autonomous soapbox where the public may voice their opinions on whatever topic takes their fancy. Each cause and their anarchic champions come complete with their bands of ardent, similarly deranged adherents willing to die, or at least fight, for their respective beliefs. Fortunately, the council has had the presence of mind to install floor-recessed water jets that flood the square when crowds become too unruly.

Zone 6

Shooting gallery/sensory paving. The parapet overlooking the square is lined with miniature versions of the fourth plinth. Standing astride the platforms are not self-styled orators, however, but young hotheads engaged in the ever-popular pursuit of shooting animals. Striking ridiculous poses while sporting ear pieces and shades, competitors fire at the pigeons that inhabit the space, or more precisely, the paving beneath the pigeons which houses vibration circuits, causing the birds to flap and squawk into the air. Simulations of recoil from the guns, accompanied by a report through the earpieces further the illusion in the eyes of the shooters, while escalating the absurdity of the performance in the eyes of surrounding spectators.

6 *Overall bird's-eye view of square with interventions* **7** *Zone 05: The Fourth Plinth* **8-10** *Zone 06: Shooting gallery*

10

11

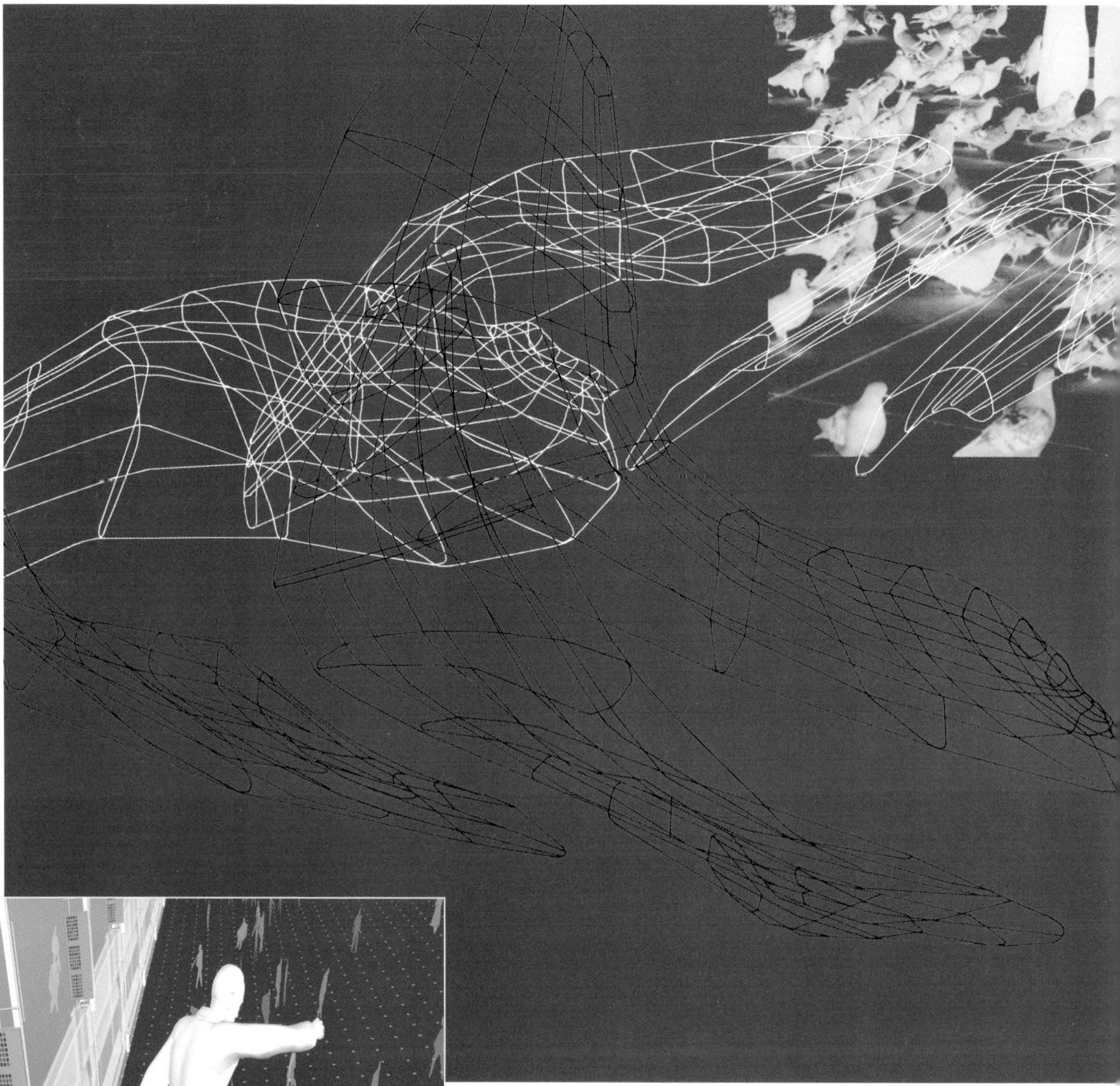

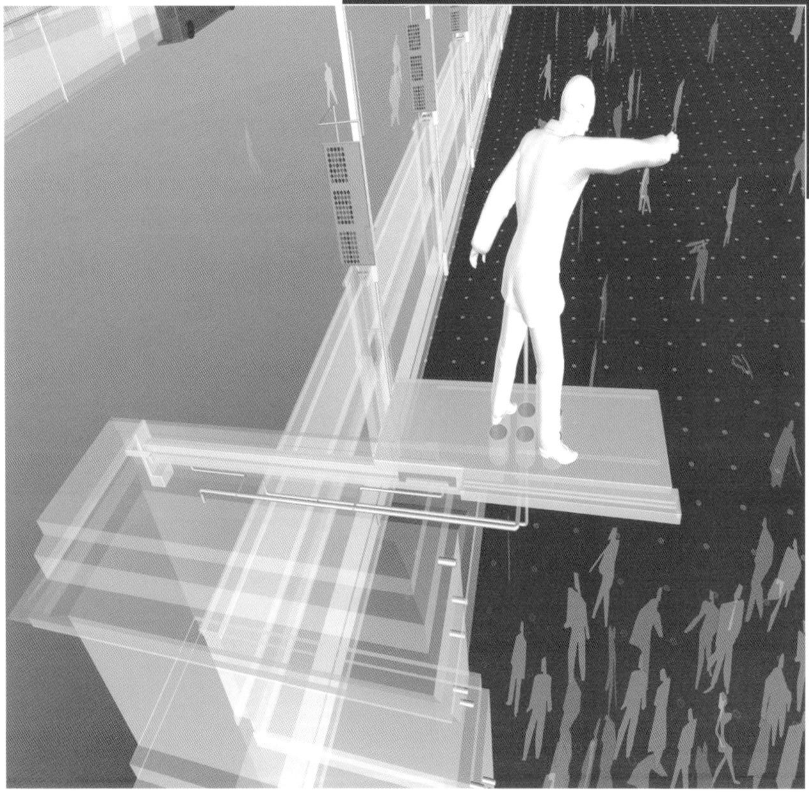

12

13

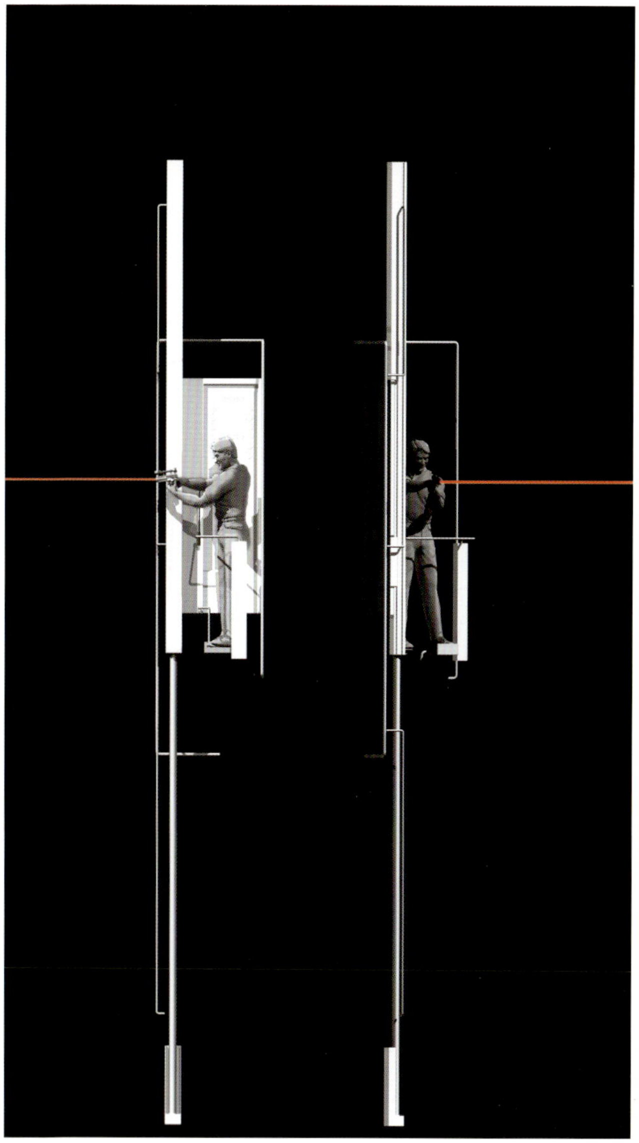

14

11&14 *Zone 06: Shooting gallery*
12&13 *Zone 05: The Fourth Plinth*

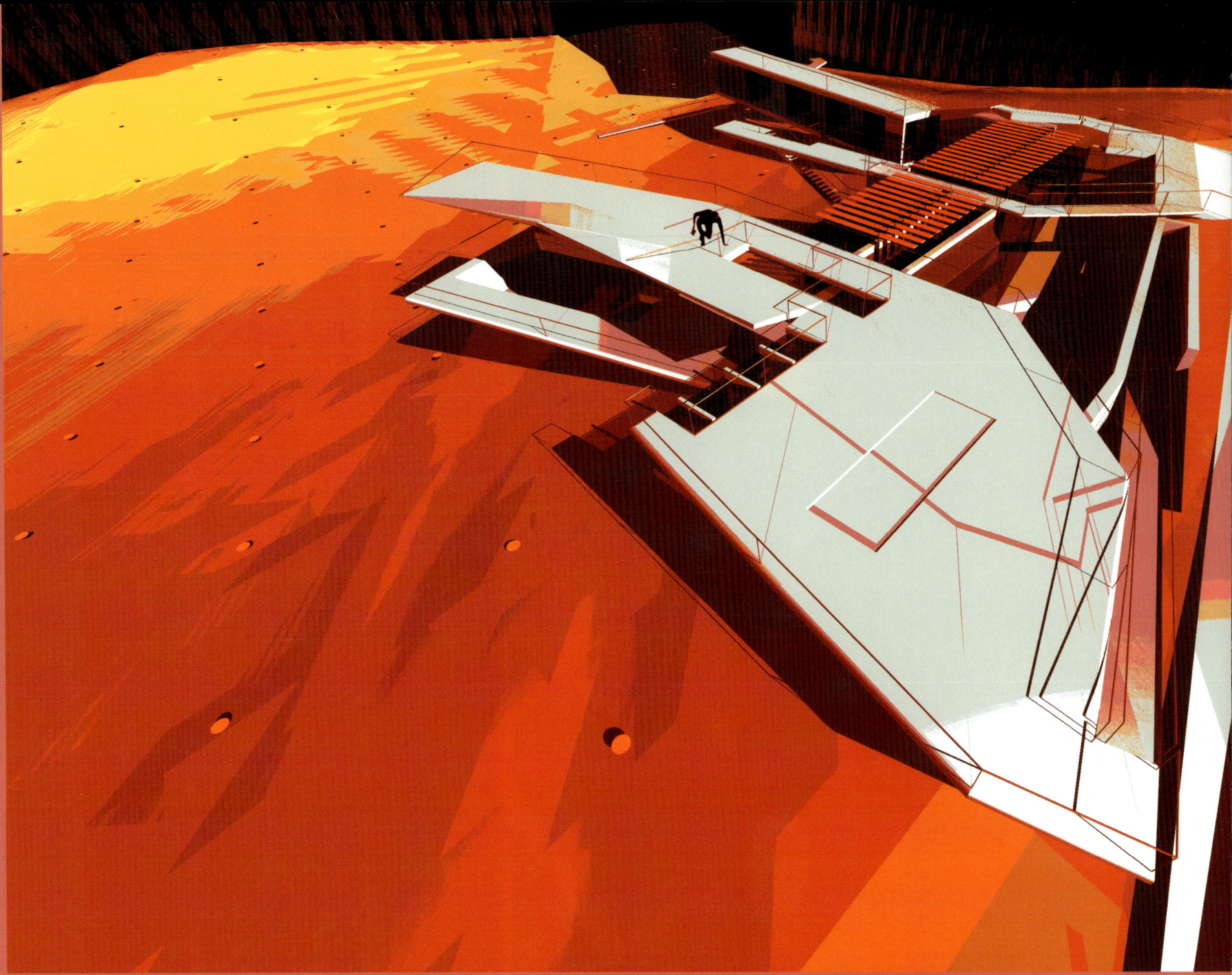

1

2

››› The country house is devised as a modulating garden wall by which occupants can refer to and redefine the landscape. The datum is established from the site's summit across the undulating plane – tips of the hedged horizon emphasise the slope of the land. Stretching out below, a grid of recessed lights describes the contours of the landscape at night.

A series of inhabitable horizontal concrete platforms forming the main house extend from the garden wall, replicating the stepped landscape. The garden wall starts with the office unit, away from the main house thus allowing privacy and providing security, while doubling as the gatehouse. From here, the stone drive leads to the entrance viewing deck overlooking the sunken courtyard garden below.

On the bridge across the courtyard, one arrives amongst a carpet of mechanical flowers with heat and smells of domesticity vented from the spaces below. The flowers present a fluctuating landscape to the building's upper surface, responding to the activities below – closing, opening, tilting as desired. The path continues out onto a cantilevered deck that flexes slightly with human movement leaving the impression of hovering in mid-air. A staircase leads down to the main communal spaces.

The internal courtyard is bordered by a living room, principal bedroom, kitchen and pool. The principal bedroom, distinct from the main body of the building, occupies a pivotal sight line – a view from the courtyard through the bedroom to the driveway entrance is maintained and vice versa. The pool area combines an outdoor eating and entertaining space with water recreation, wrapped in a 'heated envelope'.

The secondary bedrooms reach out into the landscape with a connection to the lake. This glass wing is subdivided by a series of aluminium service units, each containing an ensuite bathroom and storage cupboard. These units move effortlessly using existing air-lift technology, allowing the building to adjust to the needs of the occupants – single, double, children's and guest rooms can be established as best suited. This recreation or secondary living room has the added benefit of being either a secluded sitting room or children's den.

LANCASHIRE, UK COUNTRY HOUSE

competition entry

1 *View of main house from office* **2** *Cross section* **3&4** *Various conditions of the mechanical flower shading system* **following pages** *Overall bird's-eye view of house from garden*

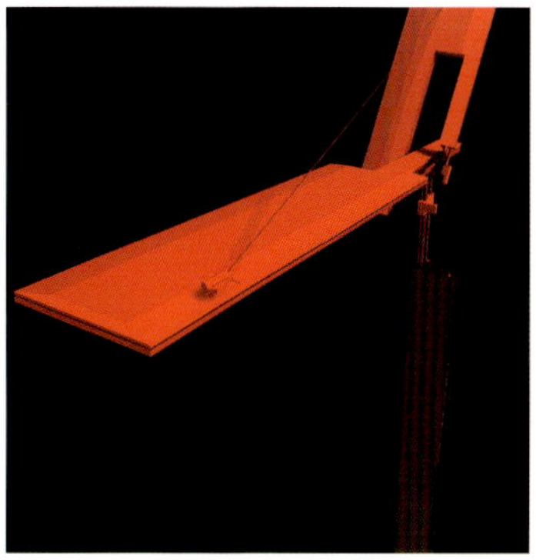

3

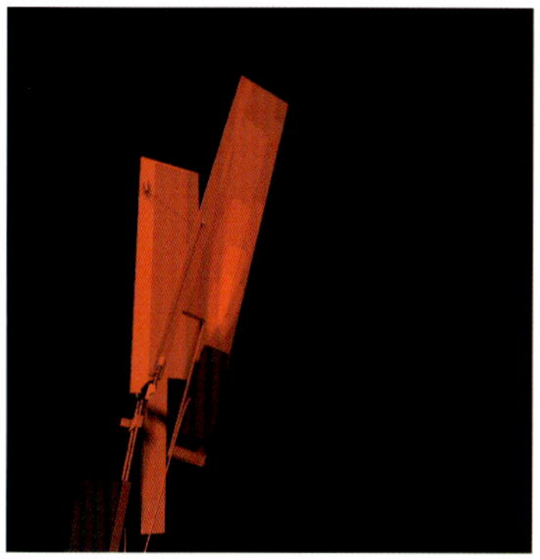

4

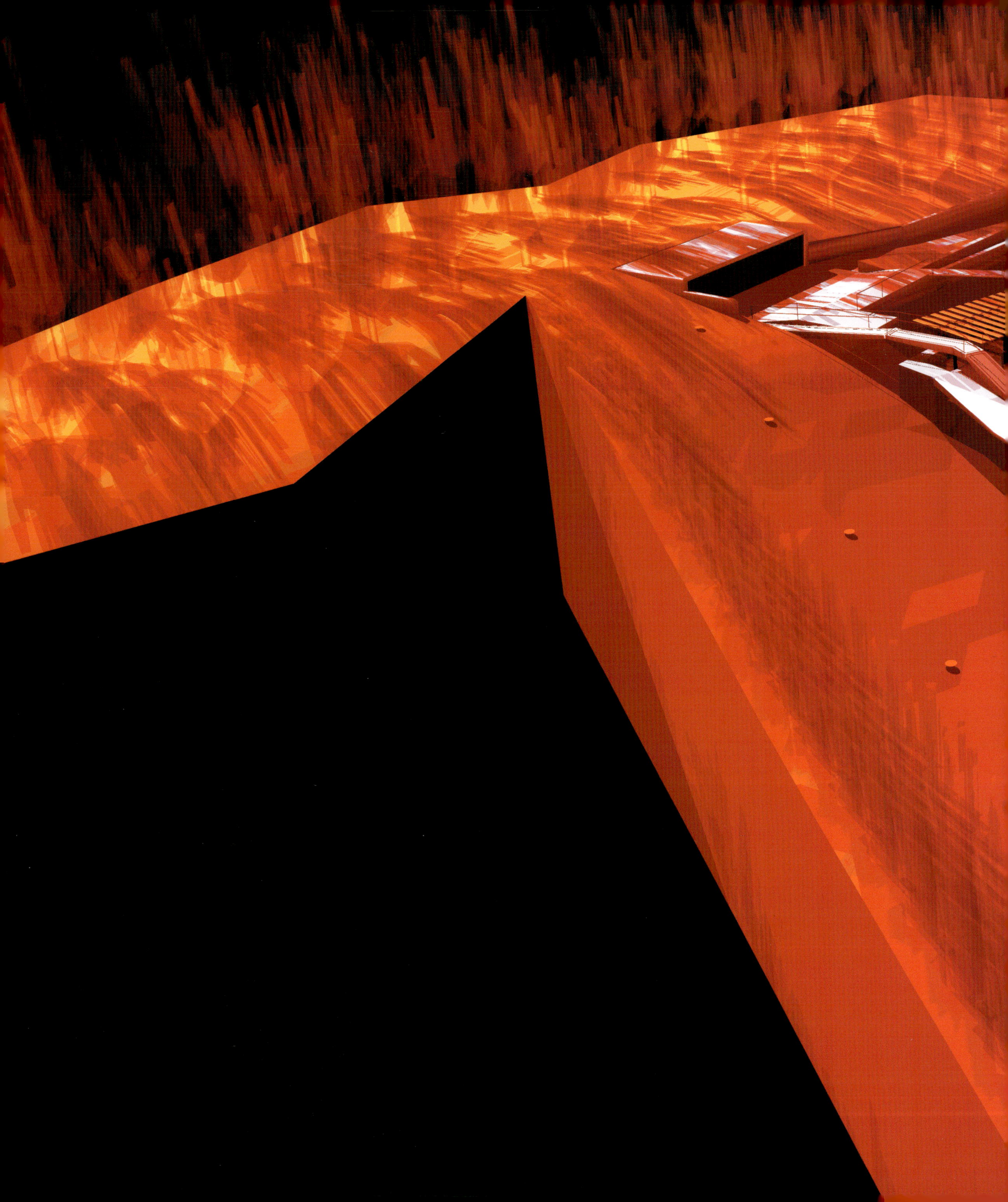

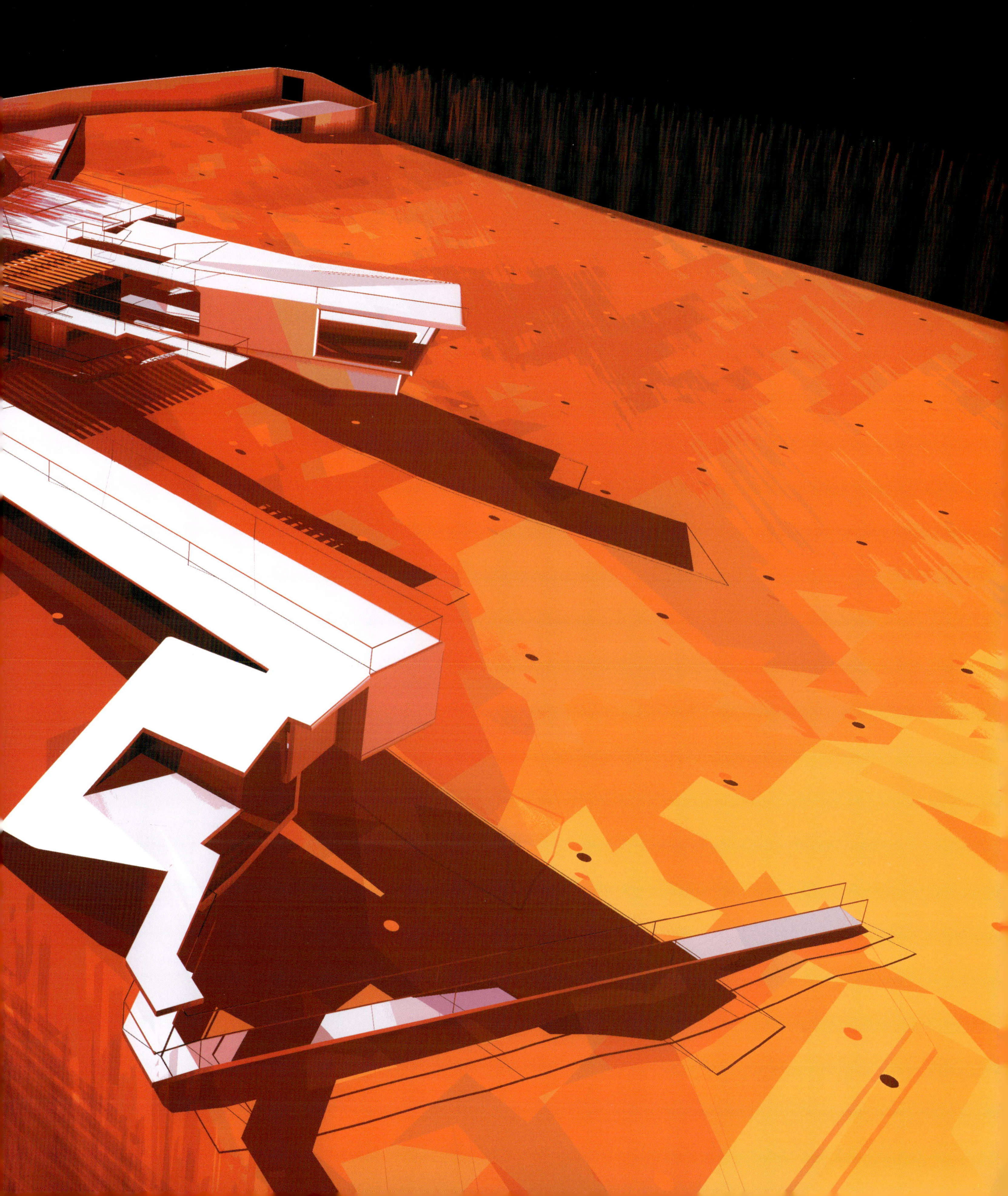

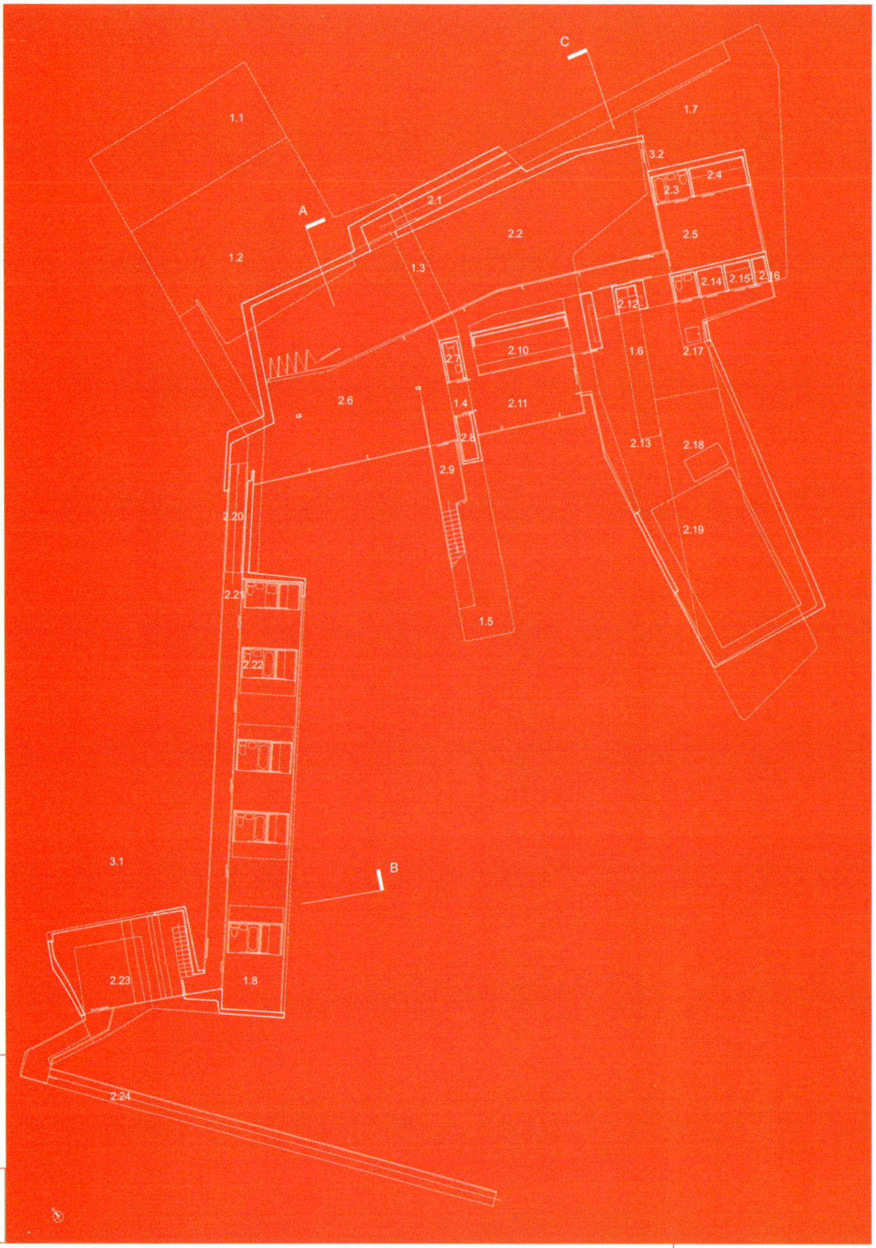

6

7

6 *Overall plan* **7** *View from lawn garden showing balcony* **8** *View from hillside* **9** *View over main entry walkway with shading up* **10** *View over main entry walkway with shading down*

KEY

UPPER LEVEL

- 1.1 Garage: 4 parking spaces and maintenance area
- 1.2 Garage apron: car standing and vantage point
- 1.3 Entrance walkway
- 1.4 Grille: kitchen vent, central heating boiler vent
- 1.5 Entrance observation deck: cantilevered timber deck providing 360-degree viewing of house and gardens
- 1.6 Barbeque vent, opening allowing light through to outdoor dining area
- 1.7 Upper pool platform: entertaining space, underside above pool containing radiating heating elements
- 1.8 Accommodation wing platform: sundeck

MAIN LEVEL

- 2.1 Pool platform with access ramp
- 2.2 Internal courtyard: Japanese Zen garden
- 2.3 Ensuite bathroom
- 2.4 Walk-in wardrobe
- 2.5 Principal bedroom: opposing glass walls allowing views into courtyard and back to drive entrance and office
- 2.6 Living room: retractable screen allowing direct access to internal courtyard and views through the length of the site
- 2.7 Toilet/boiler
- 2.8 Cloakroom
- 2.9 Entrance terrace
- 2.10 Kitchen: glazed roof
- 2.11 Dining area with access to pool
- 2.12 Barbecue area: stove, preparation table, fuel store
- 2.13 External pool area with heating elements mounted in underside of upper pool platform
- 2.14 Steam room
- 2.15 Sauna
- 2.16 Pool machine room
- 2.17 Shower
- 2.18 Outdoor heated spa
- 2.19 Heated outdoor swimming pool: 10 x 6 metres, depth 1 – 2.2 metres
- 2.20 Ramp to accommodation wing
- 2.21 Accommodation wing
- 2.22 Bedroom service units: flexible, self-contained units comprising ensuite bathroom and storage space. Unit positions may be quickly and easily changed, creating bedroom spaces of varying volumes. Water, electricity and waste are connected via self-sealing pipes arranged in staggered docking terminals.
- 2.23 Recreation room: stepped room provides accessible under-floor storage and optimum viewing arrangement for family entertainment
- 2.24 Garden access ramp

EXTERNAL

- 3.1 Private garden: 'secret garden' terraced and planted
- 3.2 Side gate: domestic waste and refuse area

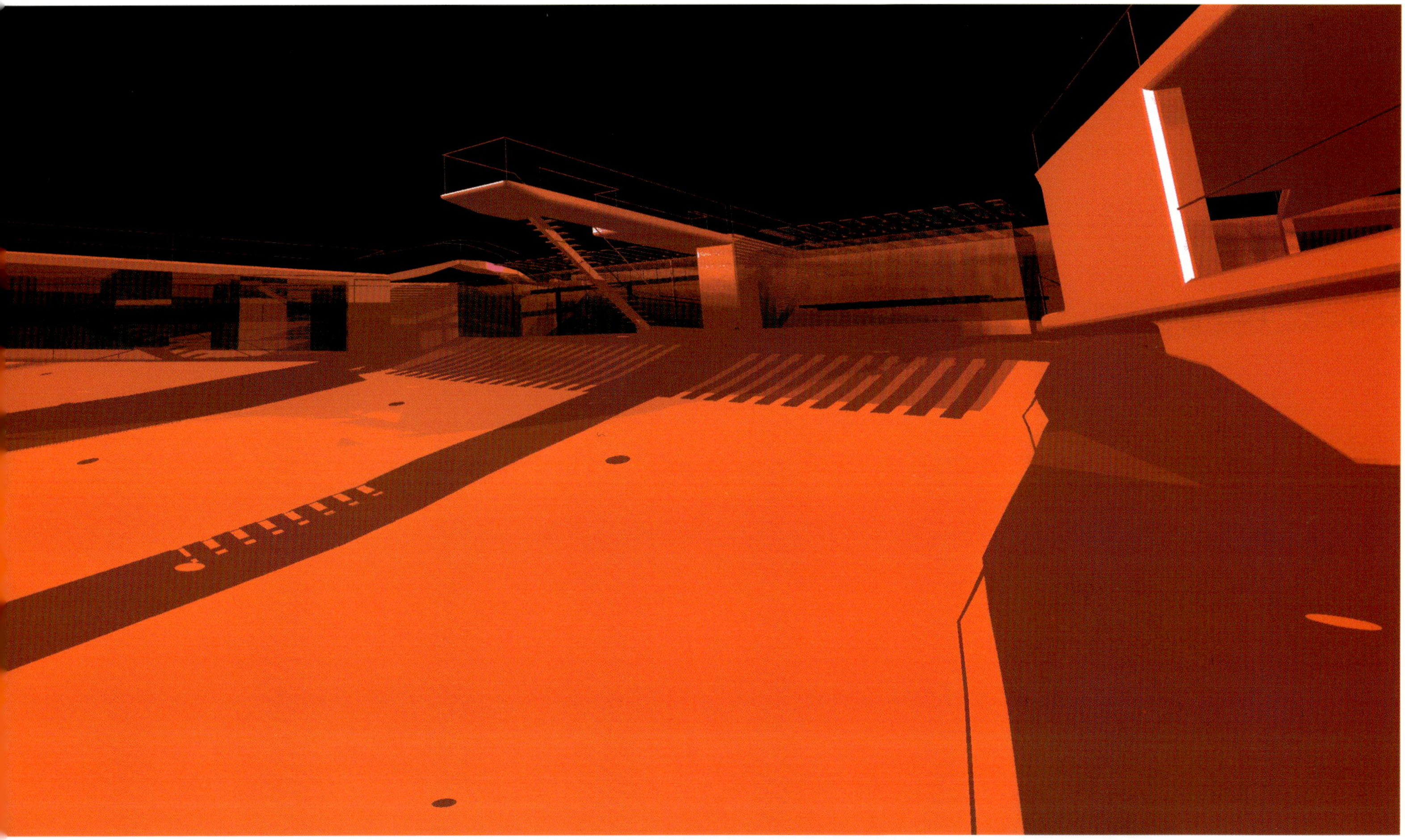

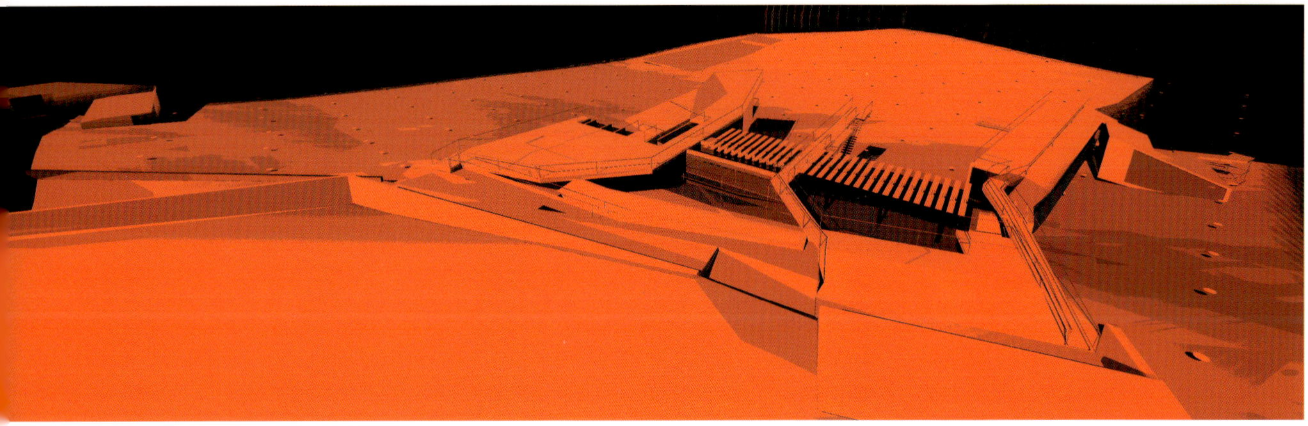

8

9

10

This proposal for Chummy's Seafood Pavilion sets out to reconcile the functional simplicity of a food vending outlet and the romantic lyricism of a coastal location. It comprises two components: the kitchen/stall core and the modulating 'shell-wrap'.

The working area of the stall is an exercise in stripped-down simplicity. Continuous work surfaces made of stainless steel contain the refrigerated displays, sinks and servery, with storage and cooking facilities fully integrated within the structural housing. The internal spaces are arranged for maximum efficiency, zoned into cold and hot food areas in one plane, and public and private areas in the other.

In stark contrast is the ultramarine-clad shell that extends out into a sinuous tail overhanging the land and water. Clearly visible from all directions, notably from the ferry terminal, the hotel and from Gi-Gi's Café, the tailpiece is a visual landmark that forms the centrepiece of a triangulated vista.

The shell wraps the functional core not only figuratively, but also dynamically, a development new to current architectural discourse. The cyclical nature of the tides and seasons is mirrored by the periodic unfurling of the protective skin of the stall, which initially assumes the shape of its host. As the day progresses, the shell reconfigures to assume the line of the retaining wall and surrounding landscape to accommodate changing occupancies.

The construction of the piece is identical to that of a fibreglass hull, affording it protection from the elements in the same way as the moored boats nearby. In this way, it acknowledges the traditions of the

›››

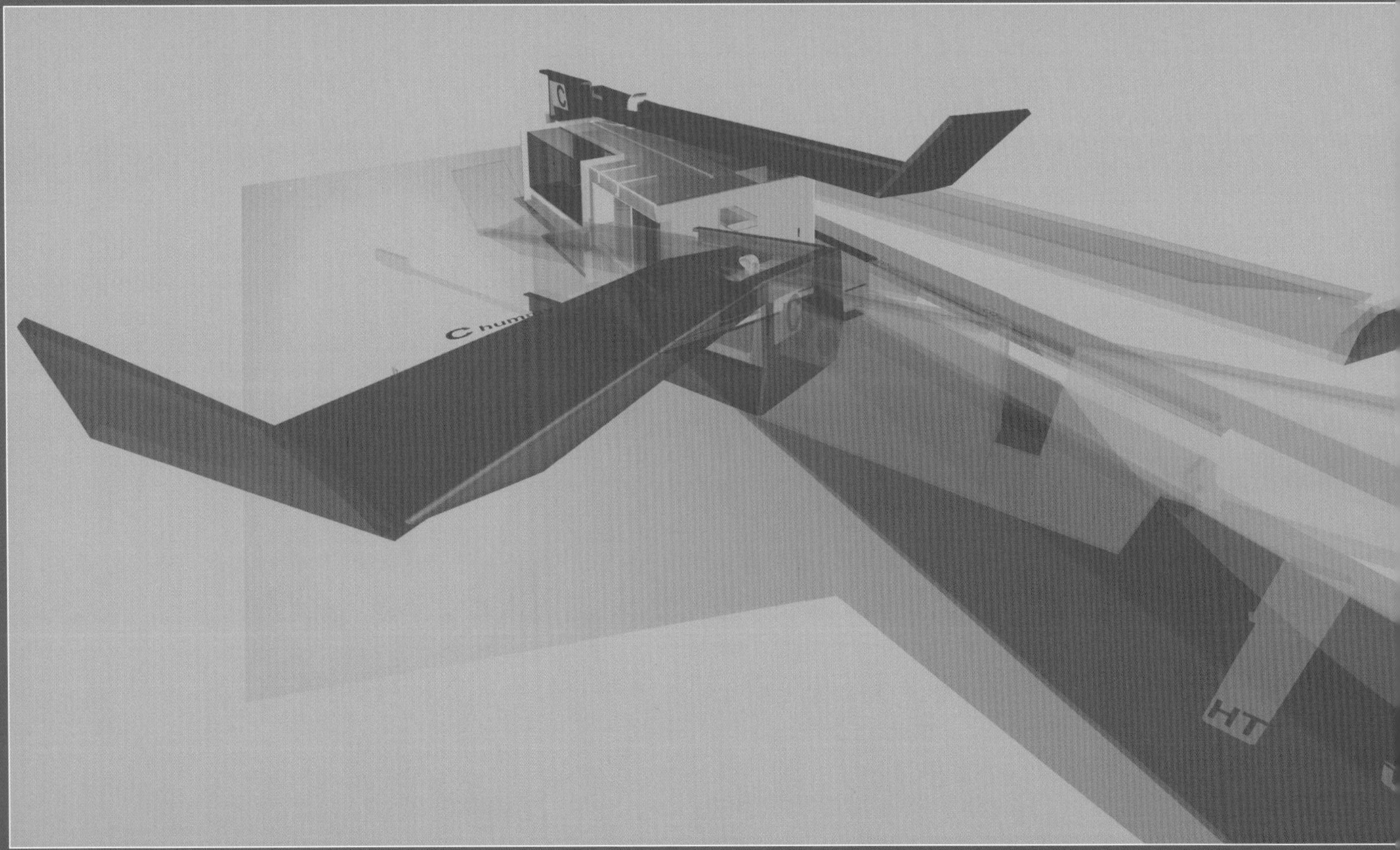

1

The construction of the piece is identical to that of a fibreglass hull, affording it protection from the elements in the same way as the moored boats nearby.

The construction of the piece is identical to that of a fibreglass hull, affording it protection from the elements in the same way as the moored boats nearby.

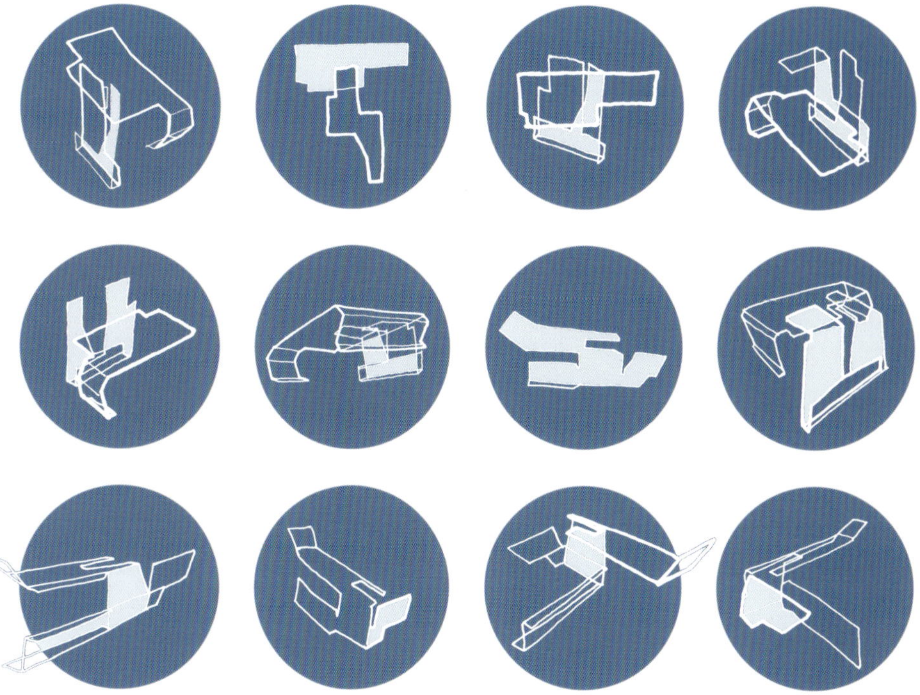

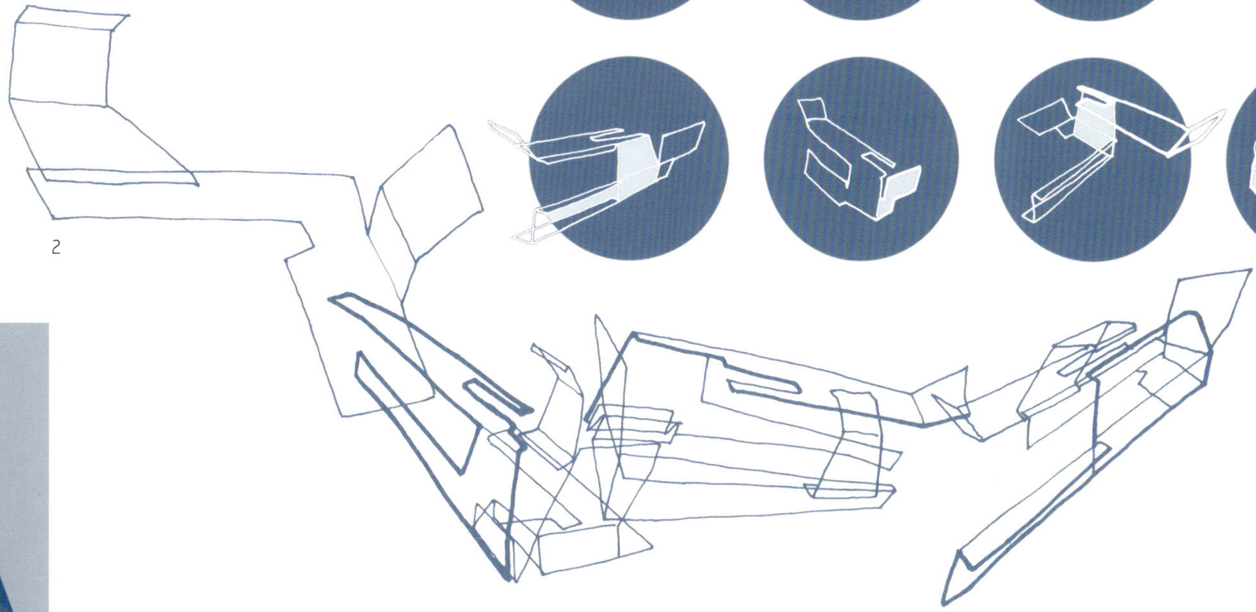

2

KENT, UK

FOLKESTONE SEAFOOD PAVILION

competition entry

1 *Multiple movement of pavilion*
2 *Choreography of pavilion*

area and the transience of marine culture while using materials and space in an innovative fashion; the mobile nature of the enclosure allows it to belie its status as object and begins to encompass its surroundings, both physically and visually.

The projecting endpiece is a flourish inspired by the tailfin of a fish as it propels itself through the water. Twisting in two planes, the tail cantilevers over the water when the stall is closed, the silvered underside catching the light reflecting off the water's surface in a caustic celebration, most evident from Harbour Approach Road. At opening time, the tail rotates and extends out in line with the stall to form a canopy and customer counter that slides along the back wall; an integrated platform provides a new vantage point and view out to the harbour for customers while eating, previously impeded by the height of the retaining wall.

3

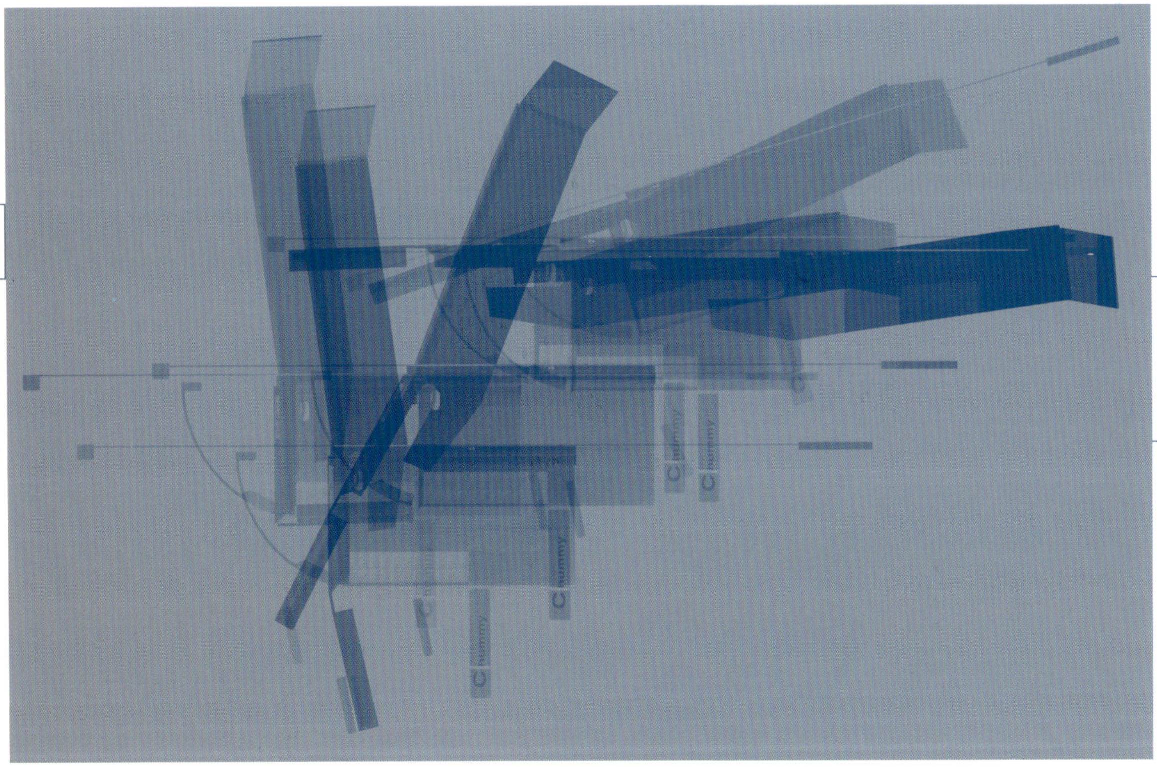

4

3&5 *Multiple movement of pavilion*

4 *Composite plan showing various spatial configurations*

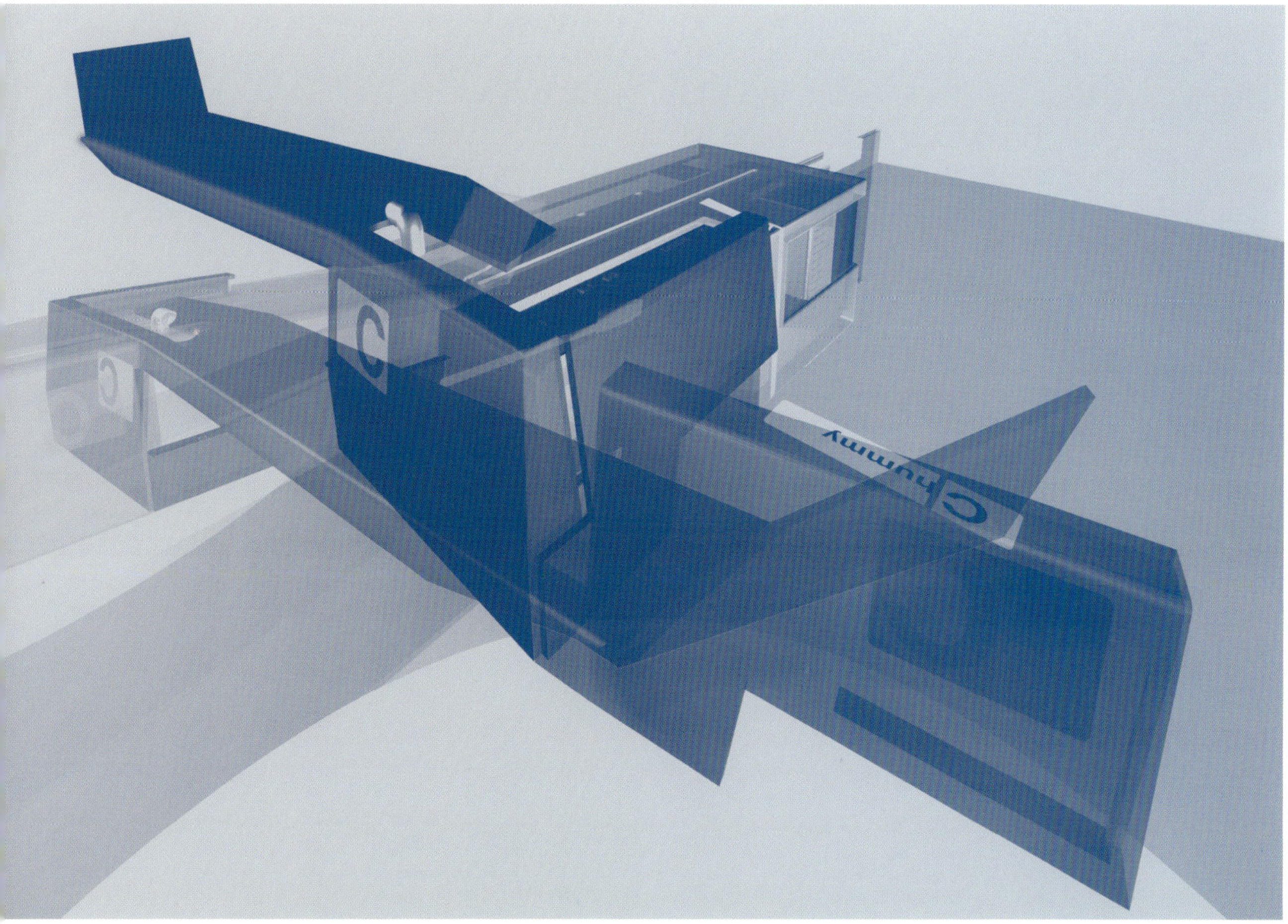

5

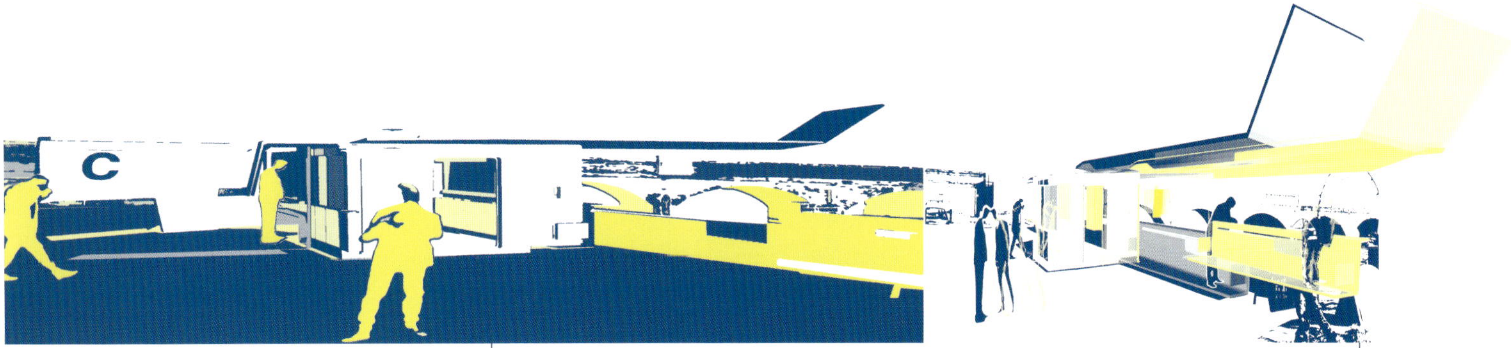

6

6&7 *Pavilion in context*

8 *Cross section*

7

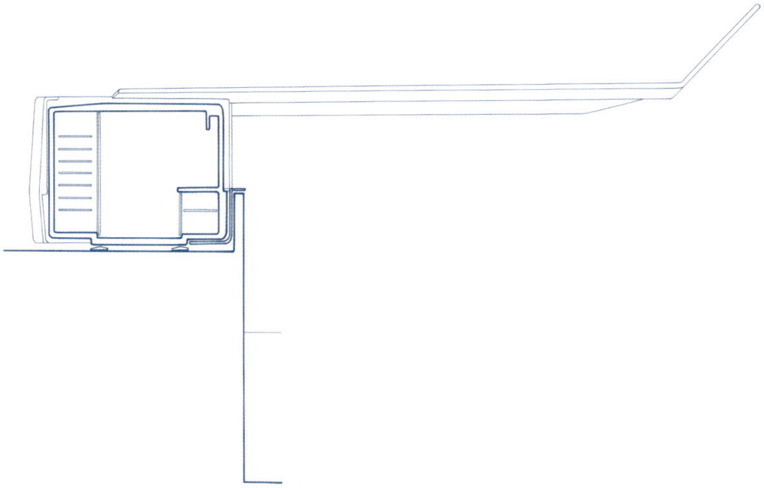

8

››› The Clone House is an enclosure that manifests the repetitive motifs of everyday life by projecting multiple histories within a single space.

A commentary on the patterned nature of routine existence, whether daily, weekly, yearly or generational, the Clone House simultaneously proposes a new system of house relationships and interactions.

The house is centred around four identical and interchangeable chambers. There is no hierarchy to these units, with identical views from each. The contents include a sleeping element, a computer workstation, and a glass overhead plane of uninterrupted sky. The four rooms may be hoisted up or stacked to reconfigure the space for different eventualities. The house can, as a result, accommodate up to five occupants, reflecting the changing spatial requirements as one progresses through life. The proposal is therefore represented as an eternal cycle, showing the seminal ages and relations in the protagonist's life and their associated spatial ramifications.

Communication between household members becomes both more intimate and more distant through devices that give rise to the occluded conversation, a non-verbal conversation consisting of glimpses, half-heard dialogue, echoes, unmade beds and vestigial odours. As the units are interchangeable, the lingering presence of the last occupant is always apparent. Last telephone calls and websites visited would remain on the workstation, potentially becoming a subject for verbal intercourse.

The house is the antithesis to the outward-looking modernist house. Having no direct view out other than the sky, activity is focused inward to form a domestic stage-set. From cloned modular beginnings, a paradoxical variegated mosaic of interrelated incidents and happenings emerges. The project should be read as a pre-emptive case study for intra-familial relations. Rather than using specific situations or lives that have not yet occurred, it manipulates physical and sensory boundaries to project scenarios, and to intensify their resulting eventualities.

1

2

1 View from living room up to bedrooms 2 The domestic stage: the internal courtyard in constant flux and animation performing to spatial demands 3 Exploded isometric showing all the 'interactive' elements for recordings and spatial reconfiguration

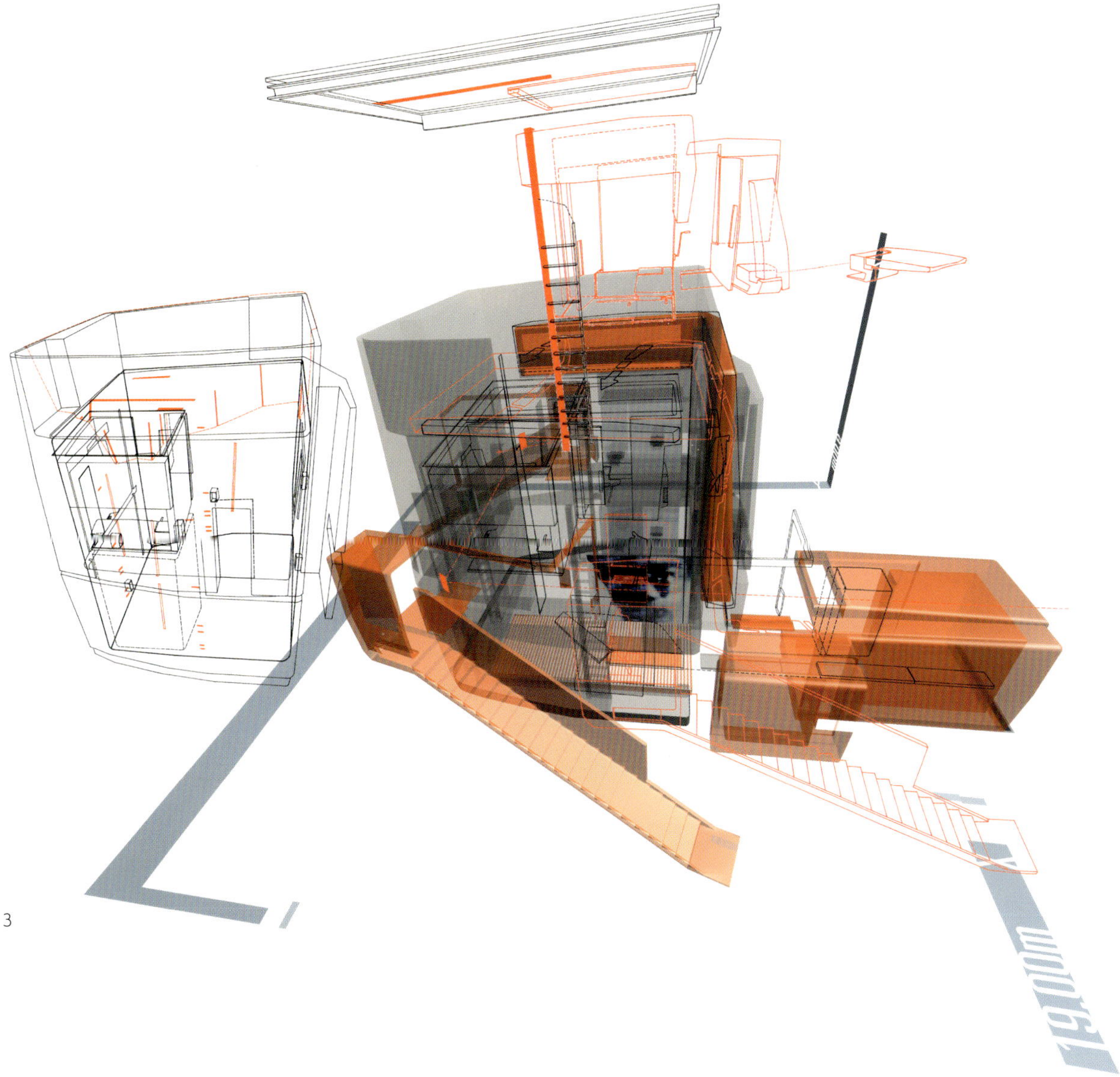

3

LONDON, UK

CLONE HOUSE

competition entry

4 *The house represented as an eternal cycle, showing the seminal ages and relations in the protagonist's life and their associated spatial ramifications* **5** *The lens moves in conjunction with the external stairs, reflecting the outside into the interior* **6** *Section highlights all mobile components (bedrooms and kitchen) in red* **7** *Sensory air column: the kitchen is linked to the roof via an air column and the extractor that allows upper-level residents olfactory, visual and auditory connection to the cooking/cleaning area via an 'interior window'* **8** *Entrance threshold: at the upper level entrance, a 300-mm void exists between the door opening and the floor of the room module. The human step completes the connection between exterior and interior, creating a threshold in absentia.*

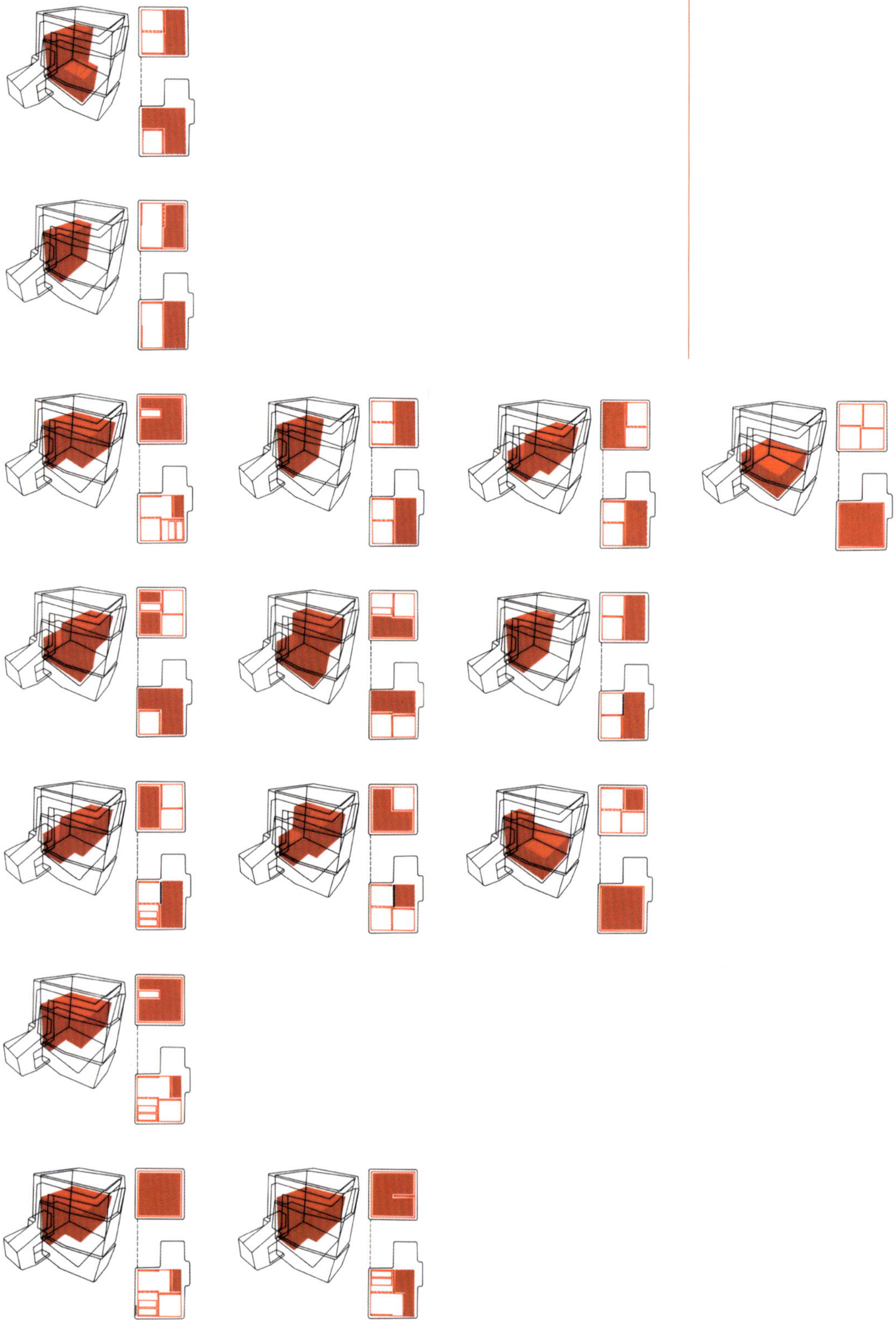

4

5

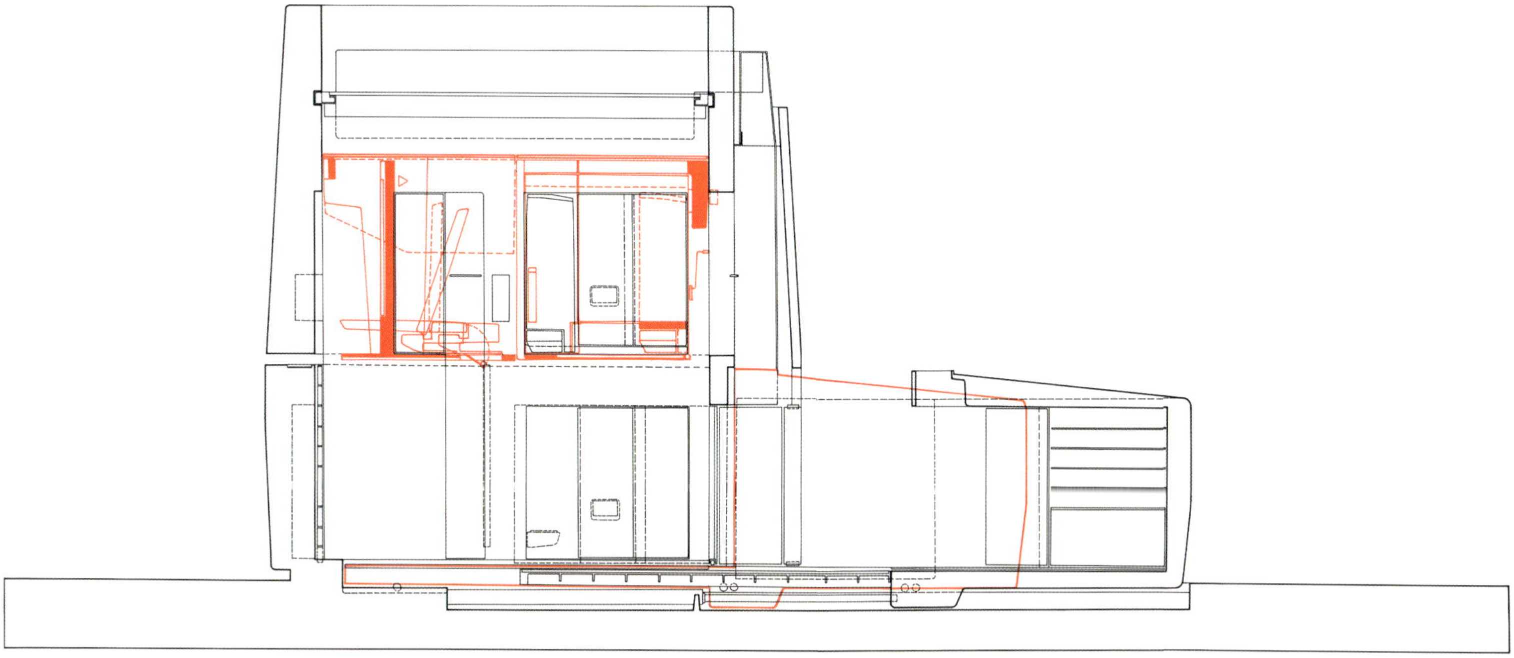

6

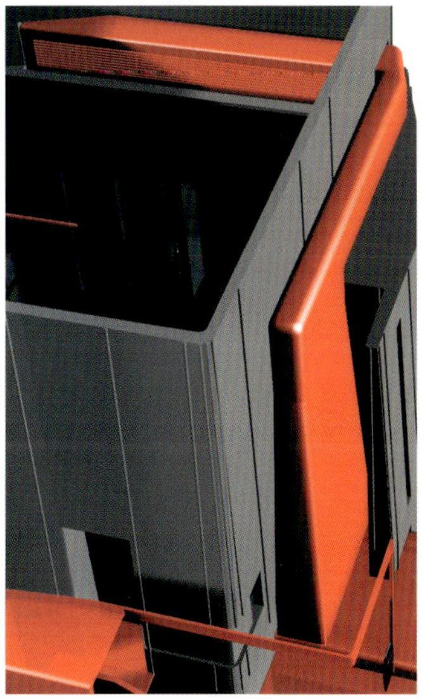

7

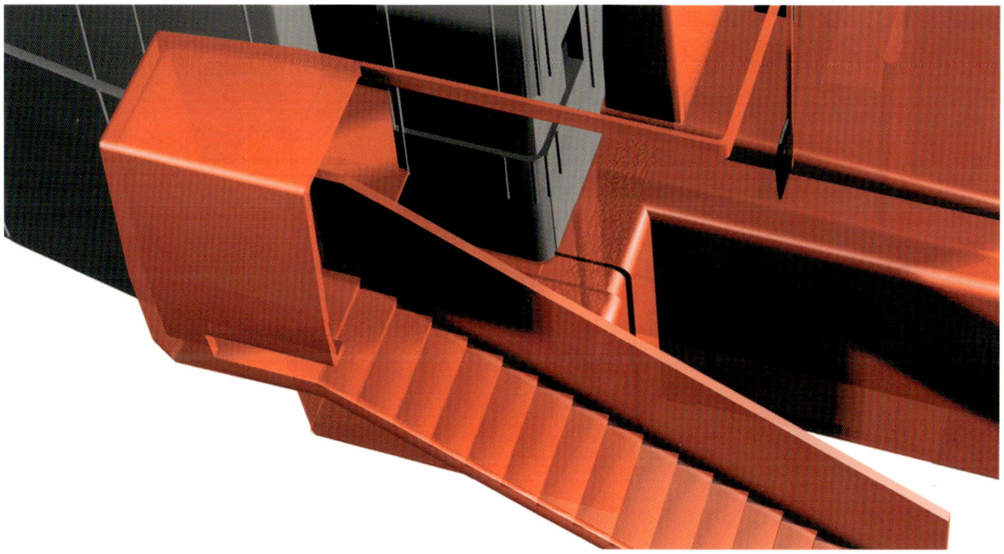

8

9 Ground floor plan highlights all mobile components (bedrooms, kitchen and stairs) in red **10** *Bed unit: these modular units attach to the floor of the rooms and house the workstation which connects to the full-height AV screen. The units fold to form a chair, converting the space into a study* **11** *The house is the antithesis to the outward-looking modernist house, focusing inward to form a domestic stage-set* **12** *External mobile stairs ensure complete autonomy to each of the bedroom studios*

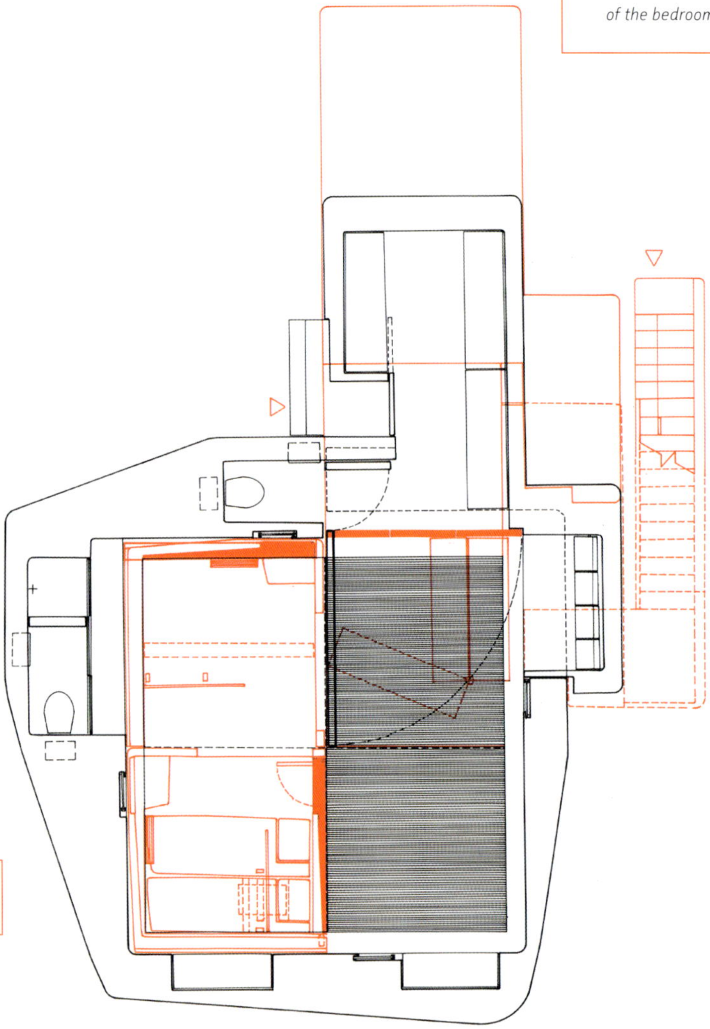

9

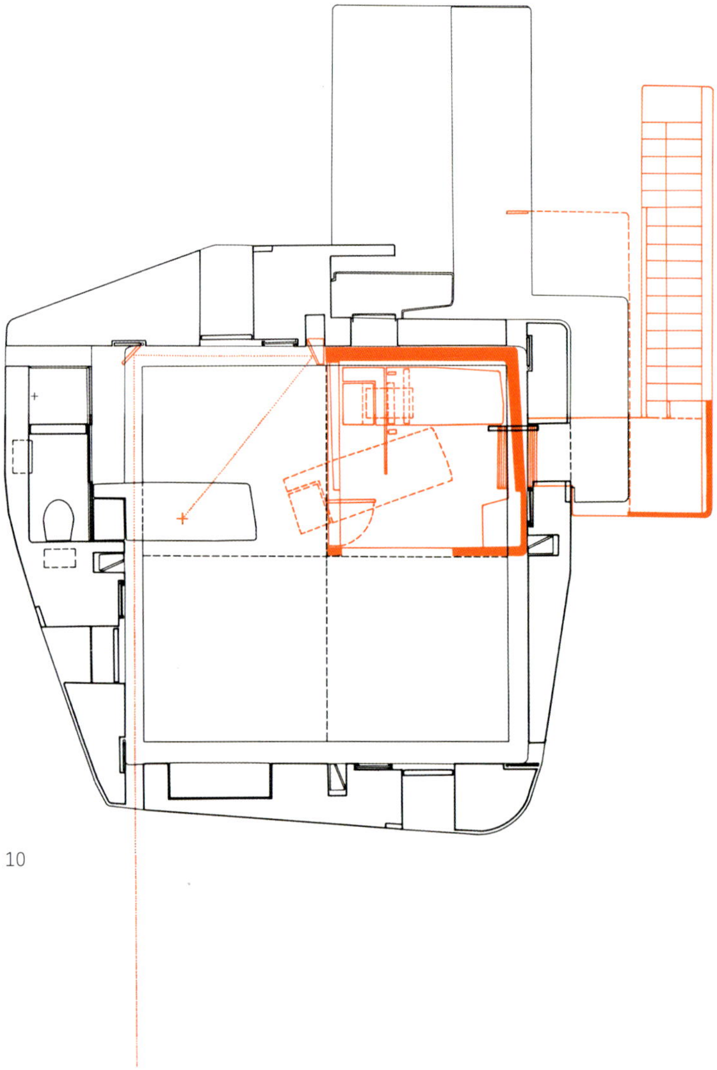

10

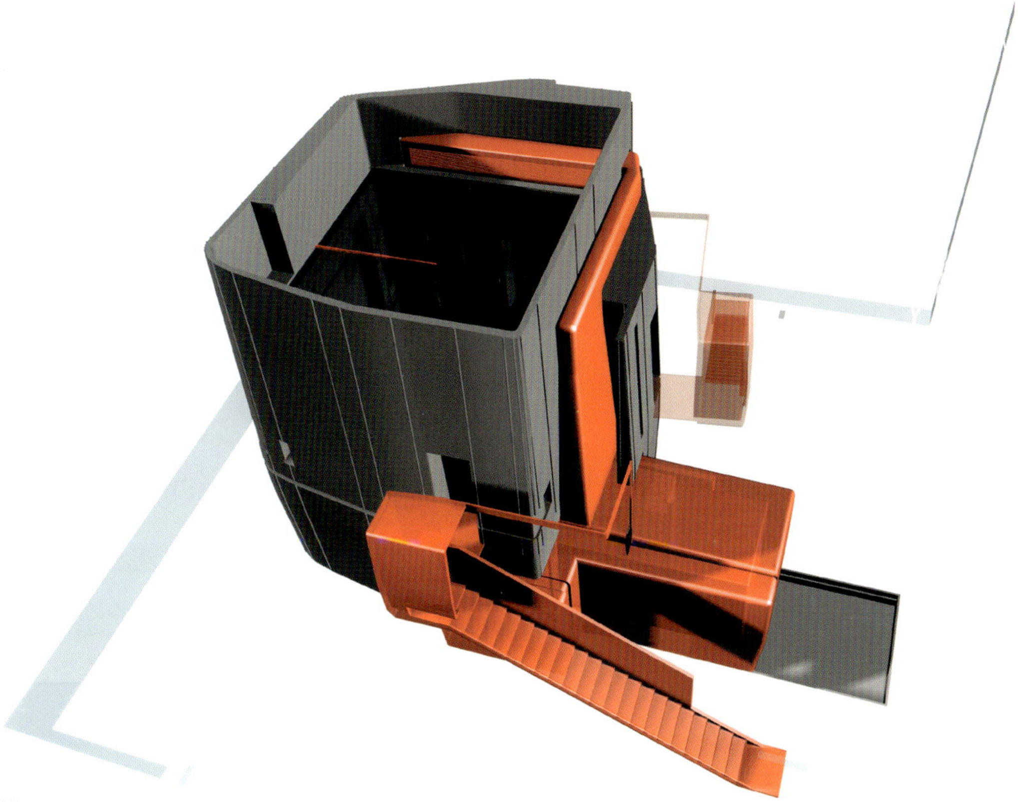

11

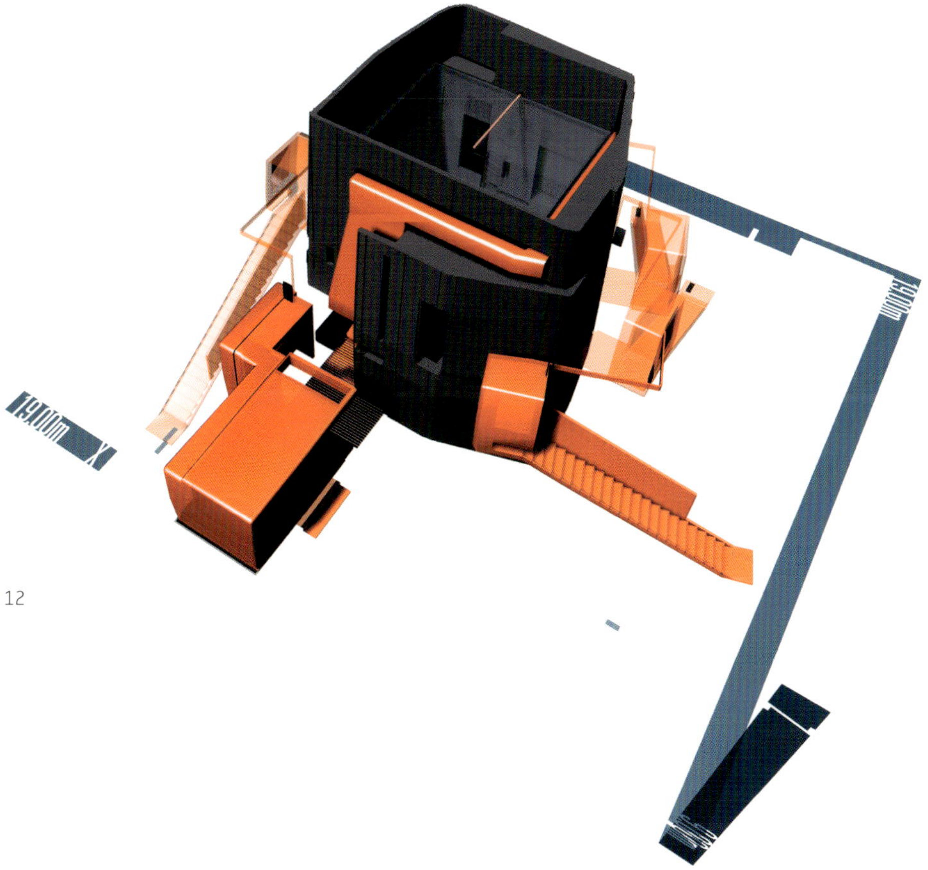

12

1

2

Space packs will generate a charged membrane that physically reconfigures and alters transparency according to the frequency of the electric field.

Space packs will generate a charged membrane that physically reconfigures and alters transparency according to the frequency of the electric field.

The electric field can retain heat, repel water particles and modulate temperature and light in much the same way as more physical barriers do. Its intangibility and environmental stability, however, liberate us from traditional methods of space-making, questioning the social economics of personalised space and city planning.

Available in different sizes from 'space-vending machines', space packs will generate a charged membrane that physically reconfigures and alters transparency according to the frequency of the electric field. The introduction of an external charge (such as from the nomadic service pod) will alter the equilibrium, thereby creating an endless spatial dialogue of rhythmic light and movement with the environment.

All that is needed is an electric socket. In this way, space-making will become the ultimate 21st-century 'throw-away' consumer product.

4

3

1 *Diagrams of virtual morphing* **2** *Cyber inhabitation* **3** *Cyber inhabitation in context* **4** *Sequence opening of device model* **5** *Plans and sections of virtual territories*

EPHEMERAL FIELDS

research project

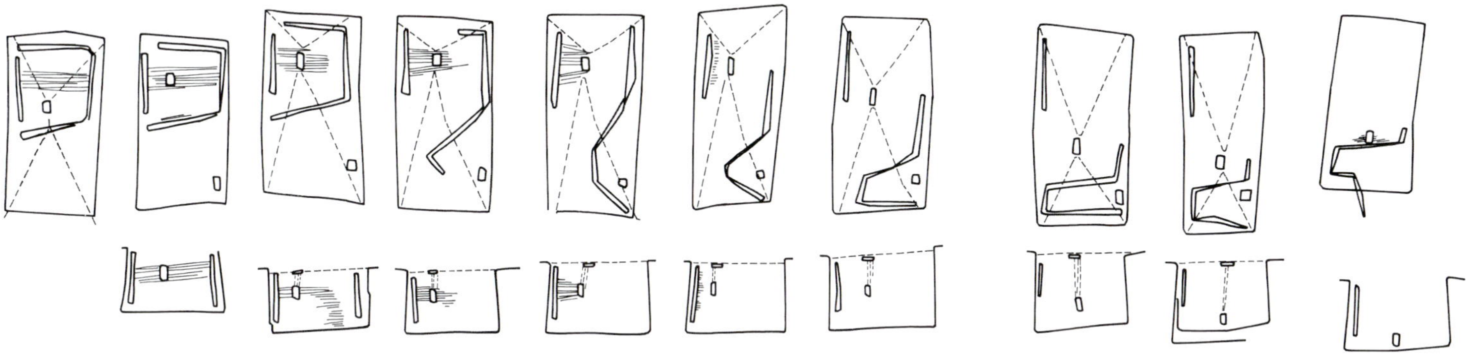

The role of the square and courtyard, which is crucial to the urban context of the Bloomsbury area, has been spatially reversed. The UCL Museum is an inhabitable void. The positive space has been shifted, fractured and sculpted into an internal courtyard housing all the exhibition spaces. UCLM is enclosed within four kinetic walls providing a perimeter for the site.

The blank south elevation of the Bloomsbury Theatre provides the north boundary to the site. The scale and presence of the wall has been utilised to maximum effect as a 'screen' on which to cast shadows. Shafts of light and shadow flood the complete length of the face. The wall is coated in a photo-reflective paint to highlight the most subtle changes.

The southern boundary to the site is formed by the end wall of the Victorian terrace. Light is projected through the building onto the flank wall, signposting the collections on each floor and is visible from the north of the site. During the day, when the projections can no longer be seen, the condition is reversed.

The west wall of the building forms the Temporary Display area for the Slade collection of contemporary art work which is exhibited running from top to bottom of the building.

The eastern façade and the public front of the building is an 'Interactive Façade' on Gordon Street. The glazed façade runs the full height of the building and is arranged in a vertical pattern of smaller panes. The outer layer is weather-proofed laminated glass, and the internal is liquid crystal laminate, which is transparent only when an electrical current is passed through it. Switches controlling the current are located in the floor of the main staircase and the information technology balconies, next to the corresponding panes of glass. When a movement triggers a switch, the glass becomes clear and the movement exposed to world outside. The transparency remains as long as the switch is activated. The façade is constantly and uniquely in a transient state; long traces can be left or just remote flickering.

The Slade Collection is split over two floors: a research study area and a

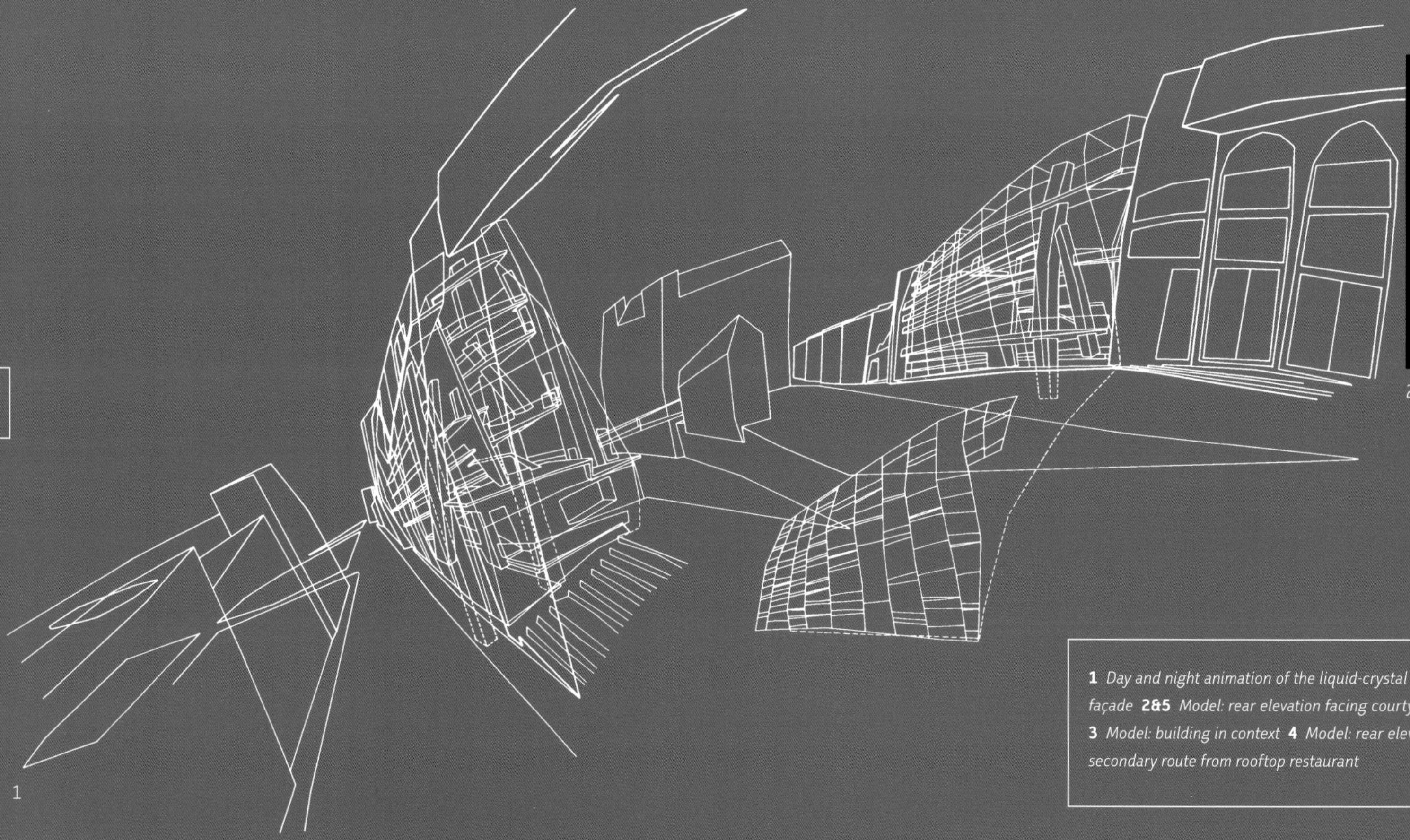

1

2

1 *Day and night animation of the liquid-crystal glass façade* **2&5** *Model: rear elevation facing courtyard* **3** *Model: building in context* **4** *Model: rear elevation secondary route from rooftop restaurant*

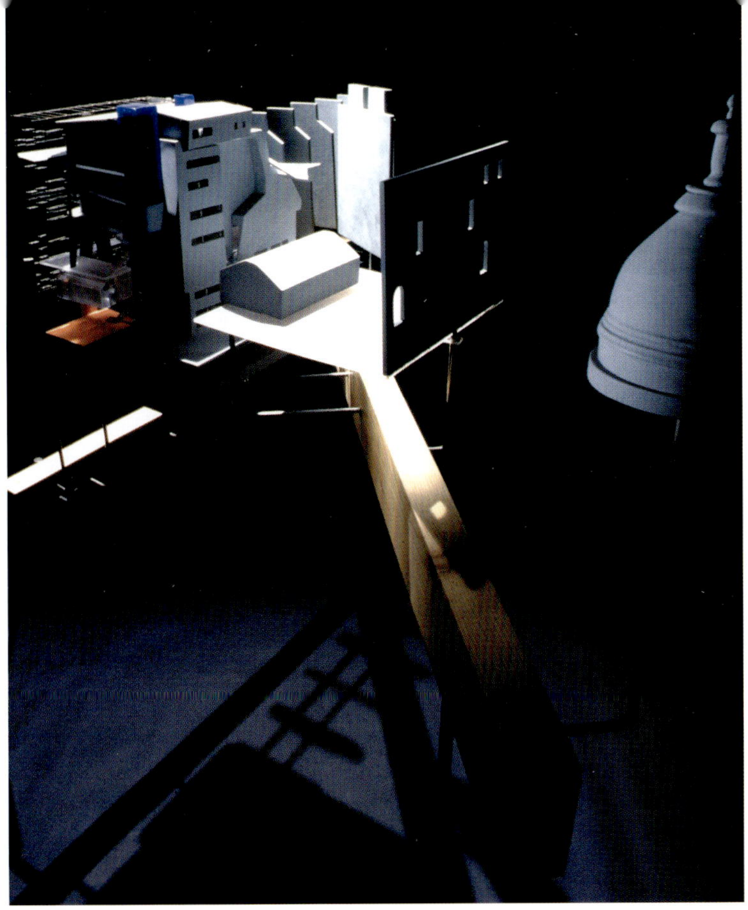

3

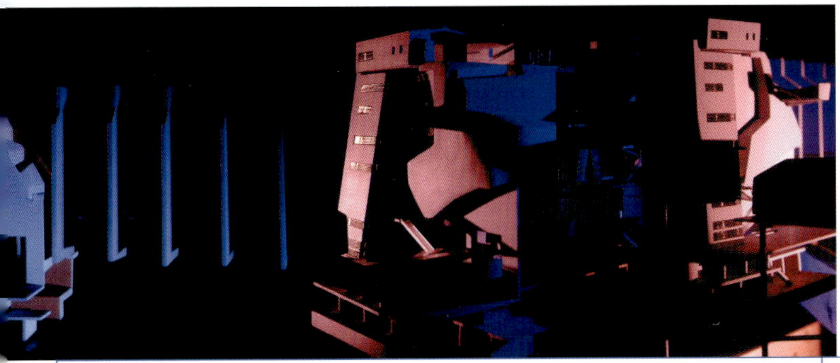

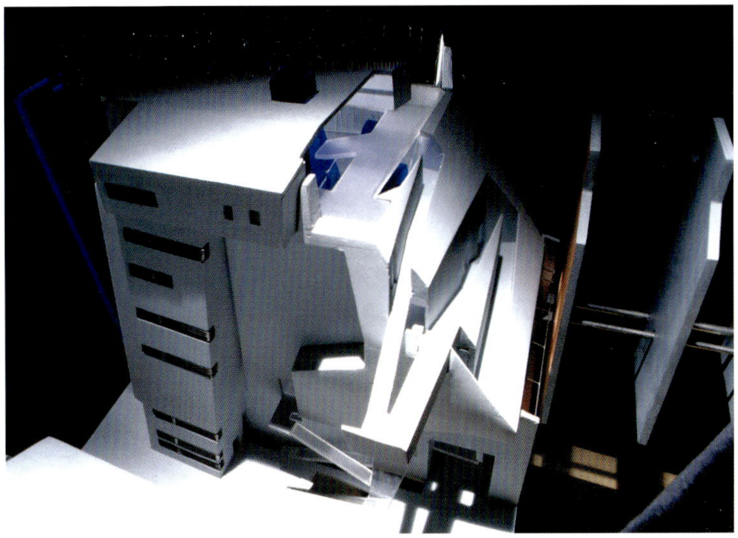

4

LONDON, UK

UNIVERSITY COLLEGE LONDON MUSEUM

competition entry

5

›››

dedicated exhibition area. An 'extended gallery' on the virtual reality balcony is also available.

The Strang Collection is sandwiched between the two Slade spaces. Study tables, exhibition and display cabinets occupy the majority of the floor area. An 'extended gallery' on the virtual reality balcony is also available.

The Petrie Collection is housed in the bottom floor, 10 metres below the lobby from where the larger exhibits can be viewed, together with a forest of display cabinets. Descent is required to the stepped basement for a closer inspection. The Flexible Exhibition Space has a 6-metre floor-to-ceiling clearance.

Arriving by lift at the restaurant, popping out of the top of the copper shroud, the visitor is presented with an unrestricted view of West London. Furthermore, in fair weather, the glazed panels on the south of the restaurant can be swung up to create a contrast from the internal, confined voids that make the exhibition spaces. On the Gordon Street side of the restaurant the interactive façade is still in operation at this level, reacting to the movements of the diners.

Undisplayed prints and paintings of the Strang and Slade Collections are housed in storage towers which penetrate the floor decks, visually creating vertical shafts running the depth of the building and connecting all levels. Light and humidity is kept under strict control providing a suitable environment for the storage of fine art. Images of all the works will be transferred to computer and can be examined on the virtual reality balconies. If closer inspection is required artwork can be chosen from the stored data and accessed from the storage towers at the appropriate level. An accurate record can be kept and viewing restriction imposed for the more fragile pieces in the collection.

6

7

8

9

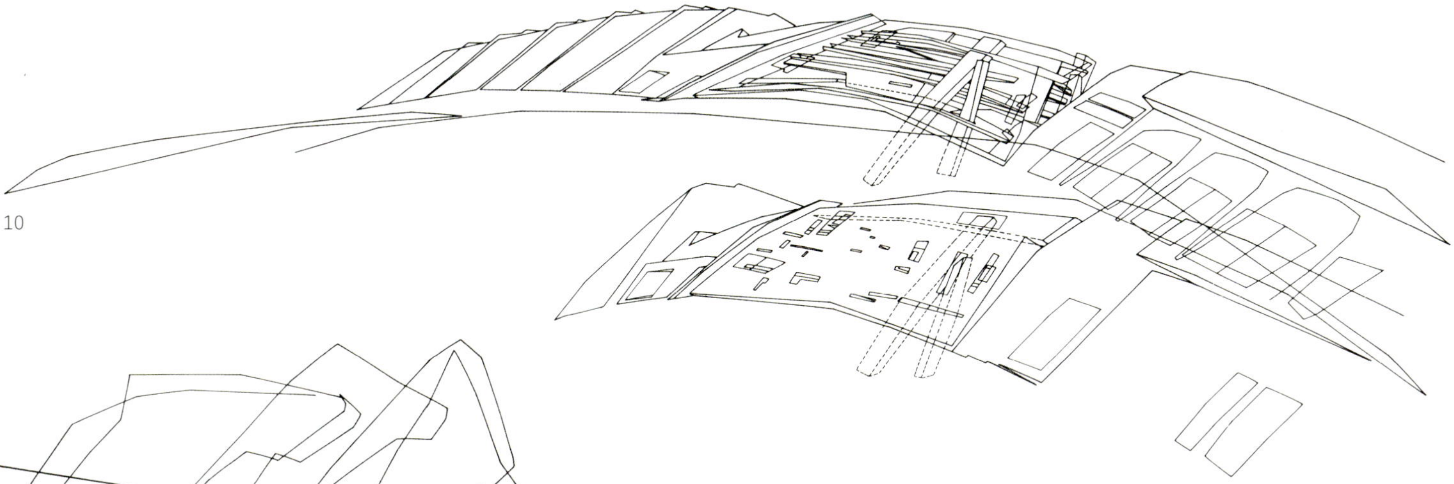

10

11

6,10,11 *Day and night animation of the liquid-crystal glass façade* **7–9,12,13** *Museum as the inhabitable void*

12

13

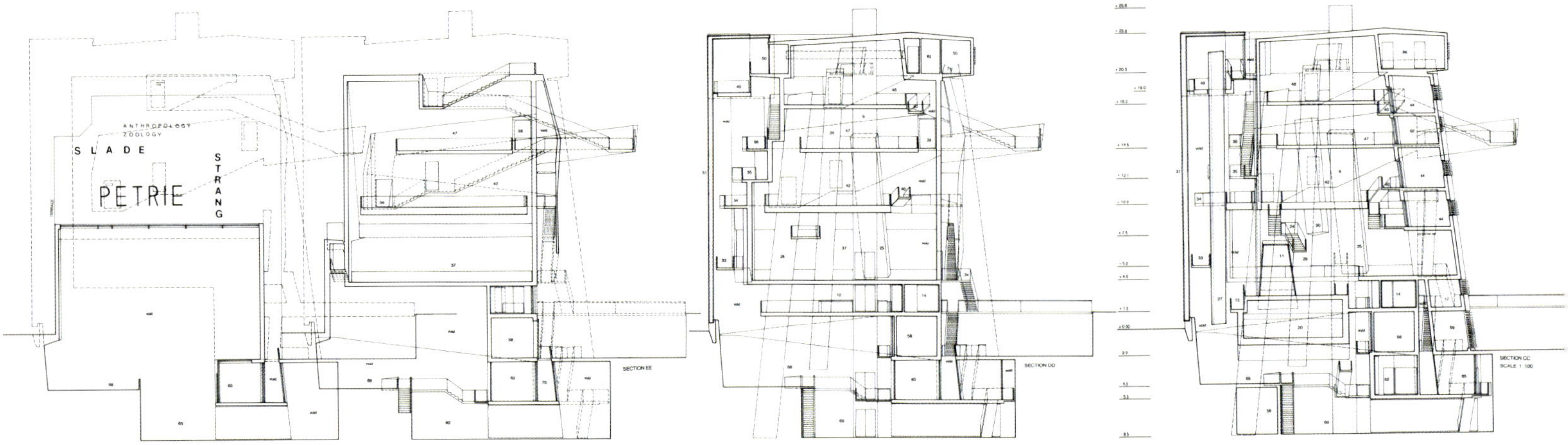

14

14&19 *Cross sections describing the layering of the building as an inhabitable void* **15&20** *Floor plans describing the inhabitable void* **16** *Model: front elevation liquid-crystal glass façade* **17&18** *Model: inhabitable void containing virtual reality balconies, storage towers, exhibition decks and auditorium*

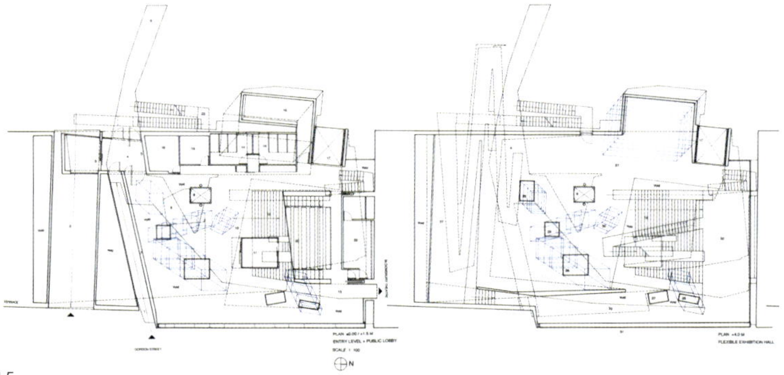

15

16

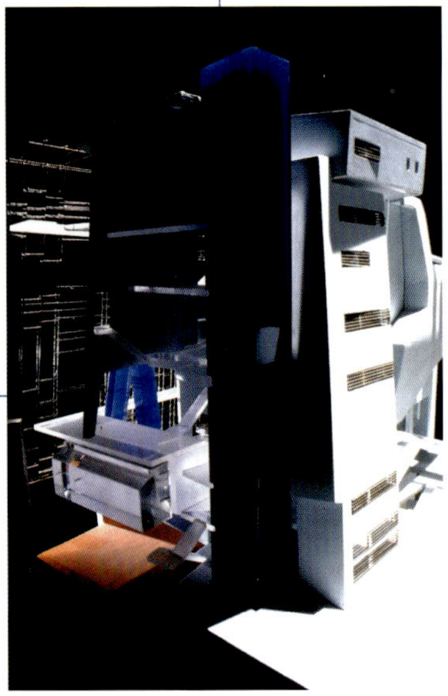

17

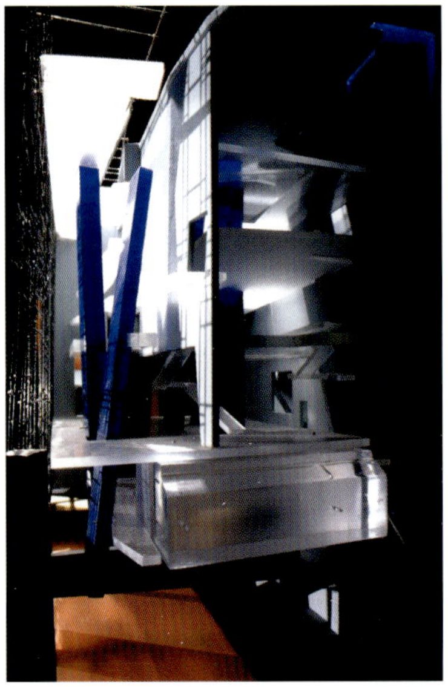

18

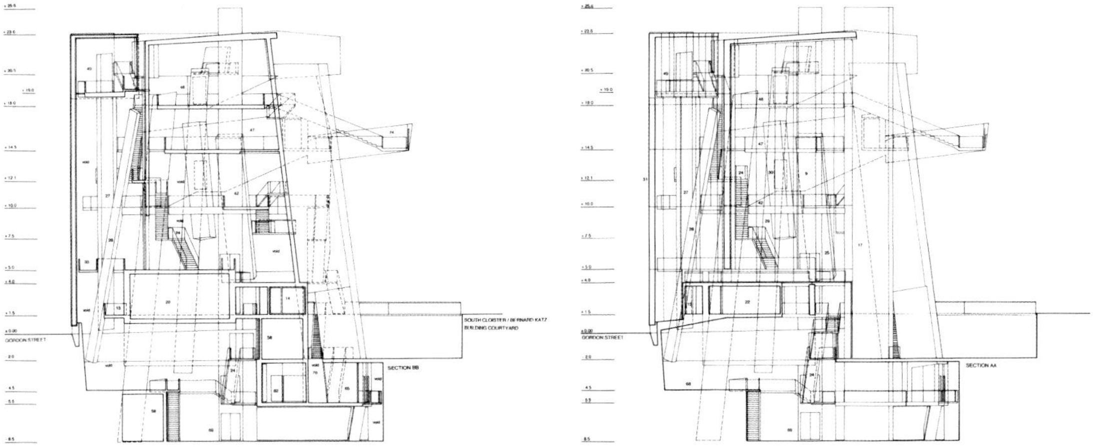
SOUTH CLOISTER / BERNARD KATZ
BUILDING COURTYARD
GORDON STREET
SECTION BB
GORDON STREET
SECTION AA

19

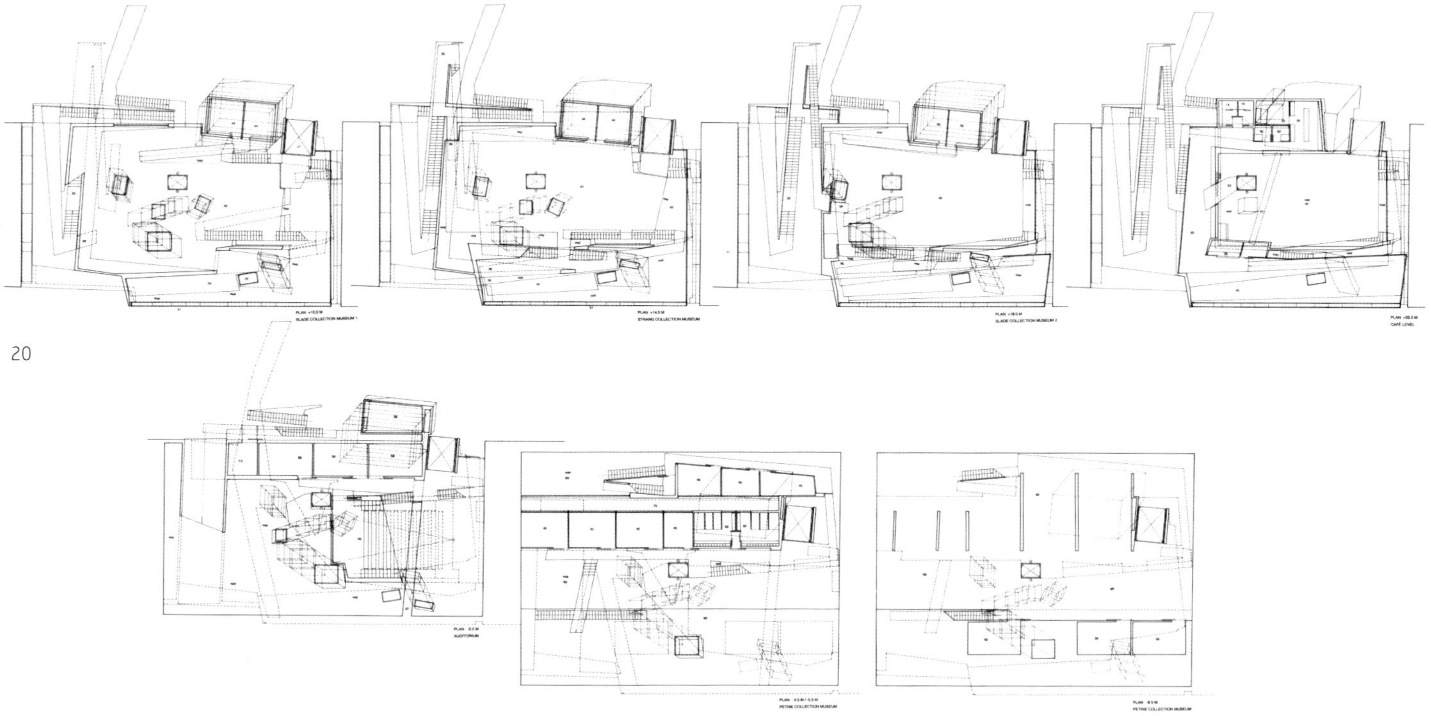

20

21

22

23

24

21&22 *Collection storage towers rotating around liquid-crystal glass façade* **23** *Composite painting of light study* **24&25** *Interior elements viewed through interactive liquid-crystal glass façade*

25

››› The Guest House exists only in an animated artificial and topographical landscape. The form is in direct relationship to the fluctuating host environment as the relocation of elements kinetically addresses any introduced circumstances.

The dialogue between the forms of the house and host can exist for only a few hours or for many months, oscillating between periods of dormancy and minute rapid fluctuations. The kinetic response is both aesthetic and functional but is dependant on both the internal programme provided by the occupants and the exterior environment (a multitude of ground surfaces, changing depths of water, reduced gravity fields or a combination of these conditions).

The architectonic pieces have many assembly permutations, haphazardly configured by infinite sequences of circumstances. Therefore, there are minimal formal boundaries and no resultant structure can be judged, aesthetically or formally, a success or failure. Only an oscillating dialogue between guest and host, constantly corrupted by the presence of the occupants, is definable.

The required bonding and shifting of the elements is powered by an electromagnetic force, presenting and splitting surfaces and contacts by harnessing the same energy that can lift scrap metal or even propel the Bullet Train. The house has a high degree of self-sufficiency: water collects in a balcony where it is filtered and stored. Degradable waste parcels are expelled into the host site and energy is stored in metal halide cells.

The boundary that exists between the host and the Guest House cannot be clearly defined. The fractured and dynamic landscape encroaches into the house blurring the boundary between the two. A door may become a floor, a canopy become a bed and then a wall. The traditional architecture of the house has become adaptive and responsive within a highly interactive dialogue.

1

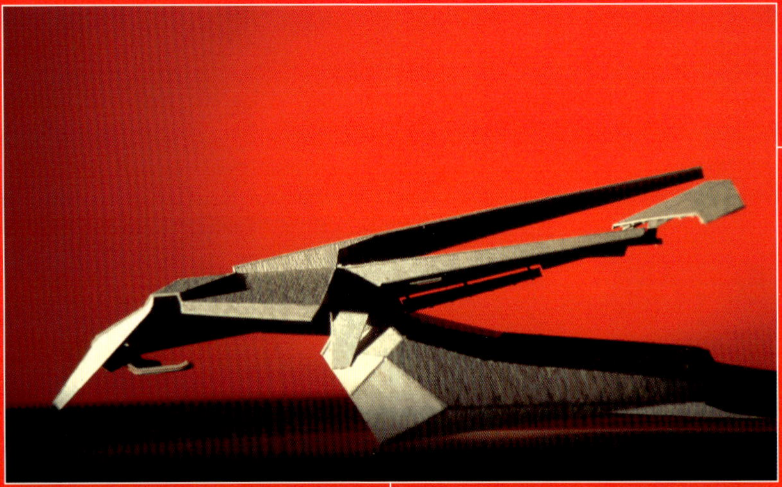

2

1 ***Time:*** *Day 7, evening*
Guest: *'If you sleep on the balcony you can hear the water resounding through the layers of the base'*
Position: *Vertical in tidal zone, water not to exceed 8 metres*
Altitude: *+ 5.0 m*
Climate: *Hot and humid, intermittent rain*
Special: *Unstable surface, caution to be exercised*

2 ***Time:*** *Day 2, evening*
Guest: *'At the top of the valley is a natural resting point. The house is arranged to our liking even though it's very exposed. We're still trying to configure the balconies in the soft ground; if there is a storm we don't want to lose the fun!'*
Position: *Unidirectional shelter, linear room configuration*
Altitude: *+ 15.0 metres*
Climate: *Storm warning, possible rain*
Special: *Partially anchored; storm may result in submergence and abrasive wear, suggested retraction of balconies*

3 *Guest House in sea condition*

4 ***Time:*** *Day 4, evening*
Guest: *'There's shelter from the rain in the lower bedroom; we'll reconfigure the house when we're stable'*
Position: *Elements reconfigured upon anchorage*
Altitude: *+ 20.0 metres*
Climate: *Storm conditions with intensifying rain*
Special: *House requires maintenance and inspection for possible damage*

5 ***Time:*** *Day 2, morning*
Guest: *'It's very slow moving over the dusty surface, but surprisingly quiet. We have now closed up to provide relief from the sun and to try and limit the amount of dust entering the house'*

The dialogue between the forms of the house and host can exist for only a few hours or for many months, oscillating between periods of dormancy and minute rapid fluctuations.

The dialogue between the forms of the house and host can exist for only a few hours or for many months, oscillating between periods of dormancy and minute rapid fluctuations.

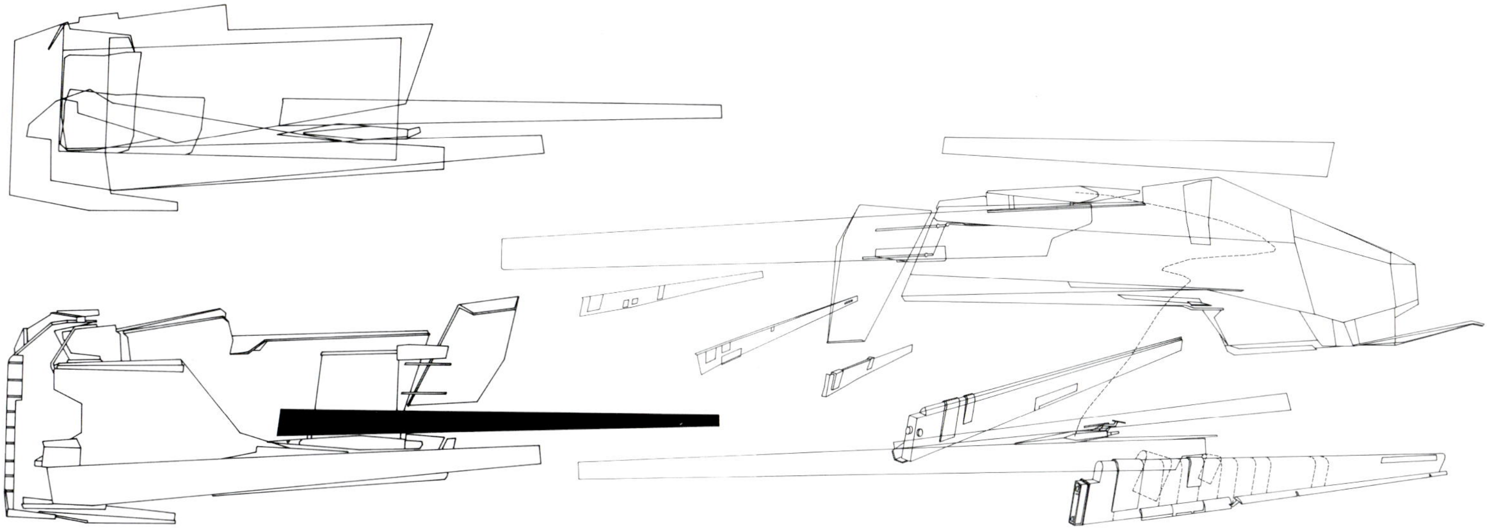

3

4

5

6

GUEST HOUSE

research project

Position: Horizon, compacted, tractor on
Altitude: + 2.0 metres
Climate: Calm, hot

6 *Time:* Day 6, evening
Guest: 'We've got time for dinner before we have to move'
Position: Positioned for rising within tidal zone
Altitude: 0.0 metres
Climate: Hot with intermittent rain
Special: Guest house has approximately four hours before tide returns

7

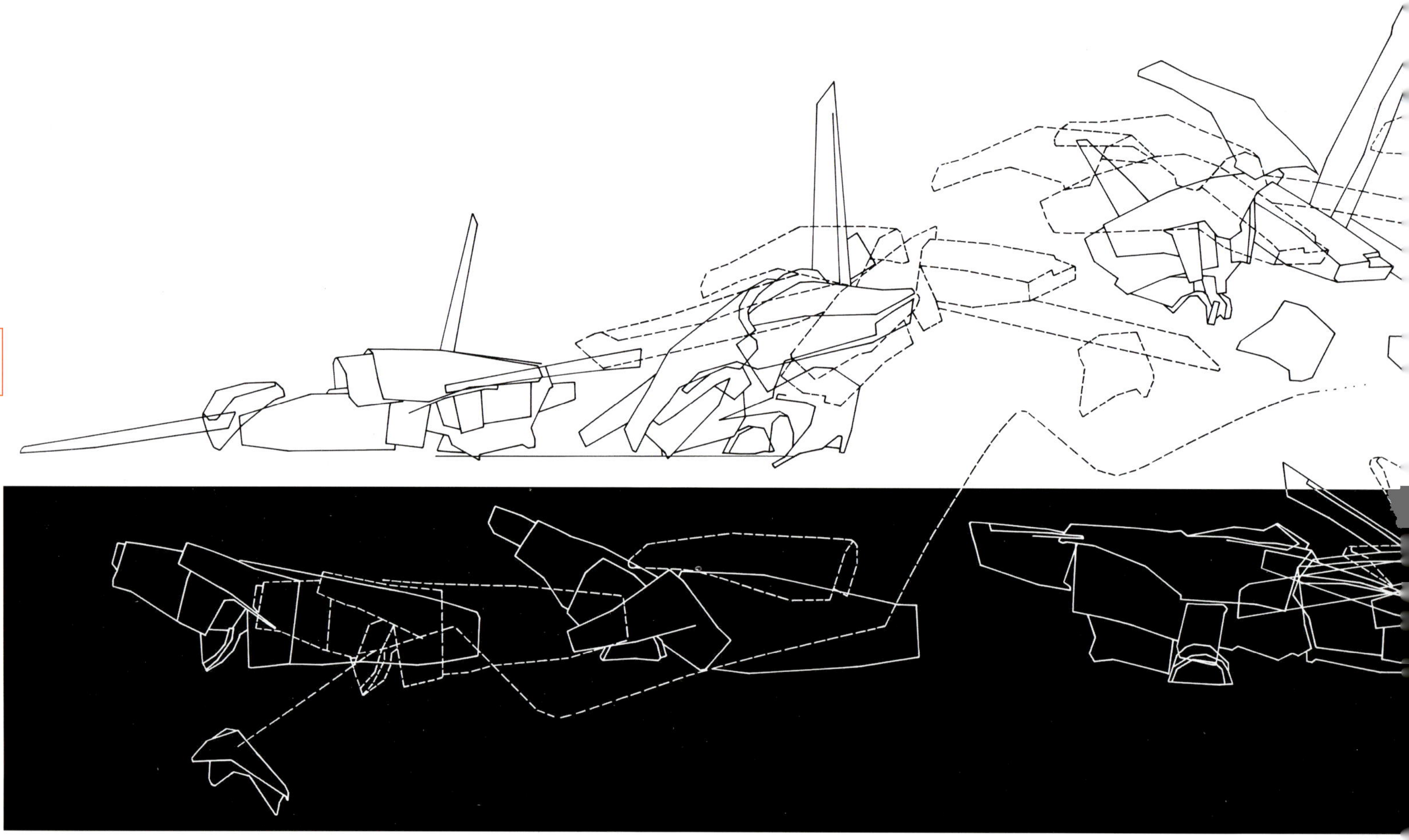

8

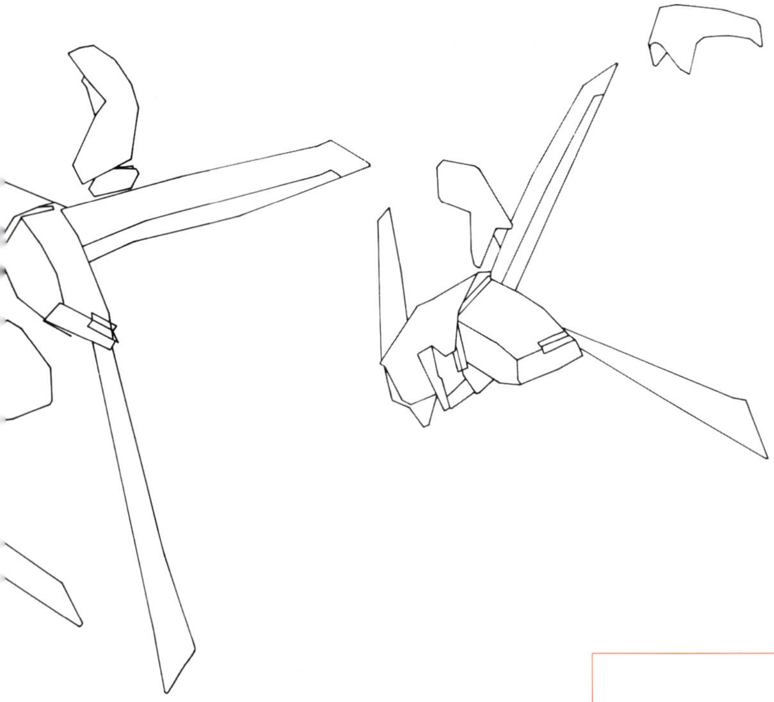

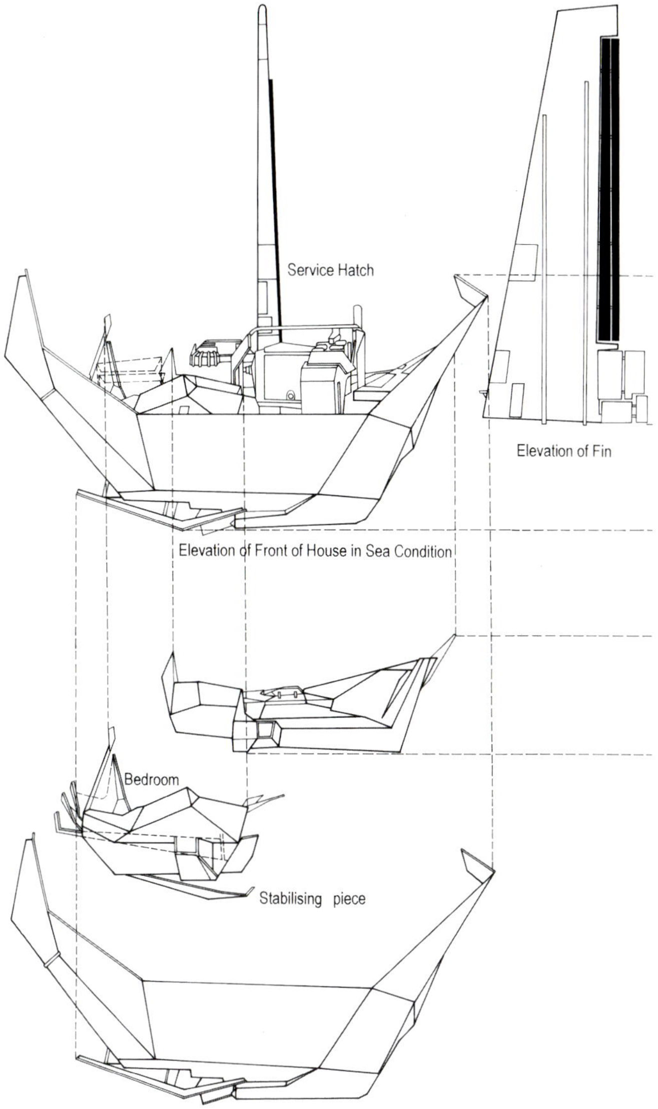

9

7 *Host conditions displaying varying contours and gravity fields, rainfall and tidal areas* **8** *Ground condition to sudden impact of strong winds* **9** *Elevation of front of house in sea condition*

The proposal for a new architectural centre is sited in a developing area close to the Newcastle riverfront. The 56-metre x 14-metre site is limited to three floors. A dedicated open-plan office is situated on the ground floor and the public spaces on the upper levels. The scheme provides a bookshop, exhibition hall, 200-seat lecture hall, café and ancillary services.

The simple enclosure is enhanced by two kinetic elements: a 'mobile cupboard' and 'flexible lecture hall', which provide a system of interactive volumes.

The 'flexible lecture hall' is suspended on rails that form the secondary structure of the double-volume exhibition space. A lightweight, rigid honeycomb construction enables the structure to fold and distort with the application of a simple hydraulic system. The lecture hall can travel within the length of the exhibition space and when not in use folds virtually flat into the ceiling. The folded volume, together with louvres on the southwest elevation, provides shade for the exhibition hall.
The 'mobile cupboard' extends the apparent boundary of the building and, in doing so, creates both internal and external lobbies. It is supported by a cushion of air, which facilitates ease of movement. The 'cupboard' accommodates a café on the first floor and a bookshop below while controlling the circulation throughout the building. Its position is most closely related to the occupancy of the exhibition hall and its fluctuating diurnal programme.

2

1

1 *Louvres choreographing the external façade*
2 *Sketch studies of modulating building* **3&4** *Building in context*

3

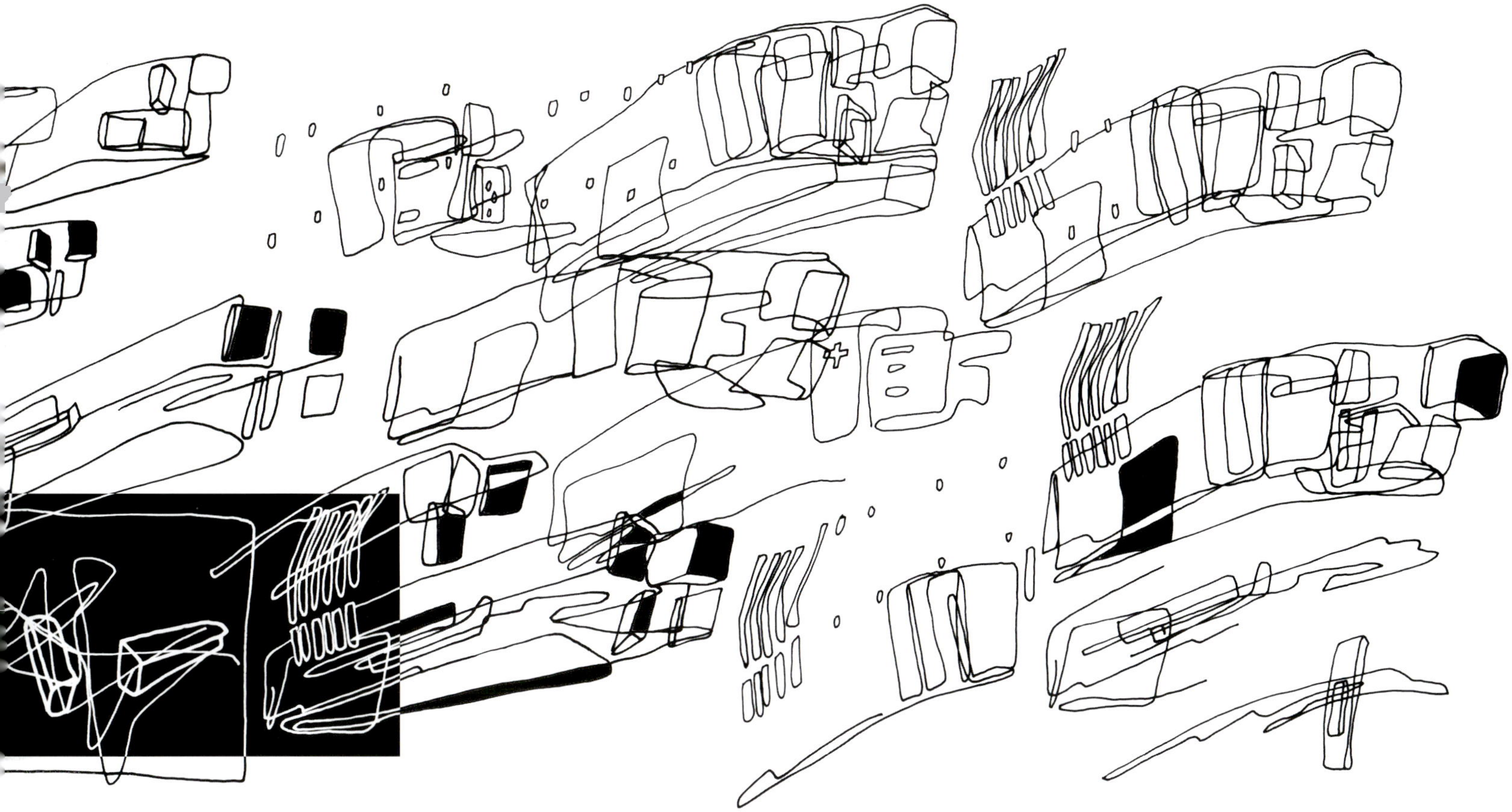

NEWCASTLE, UK

NEWCASTLE ARCHITECTURE CENTRE

competition entry

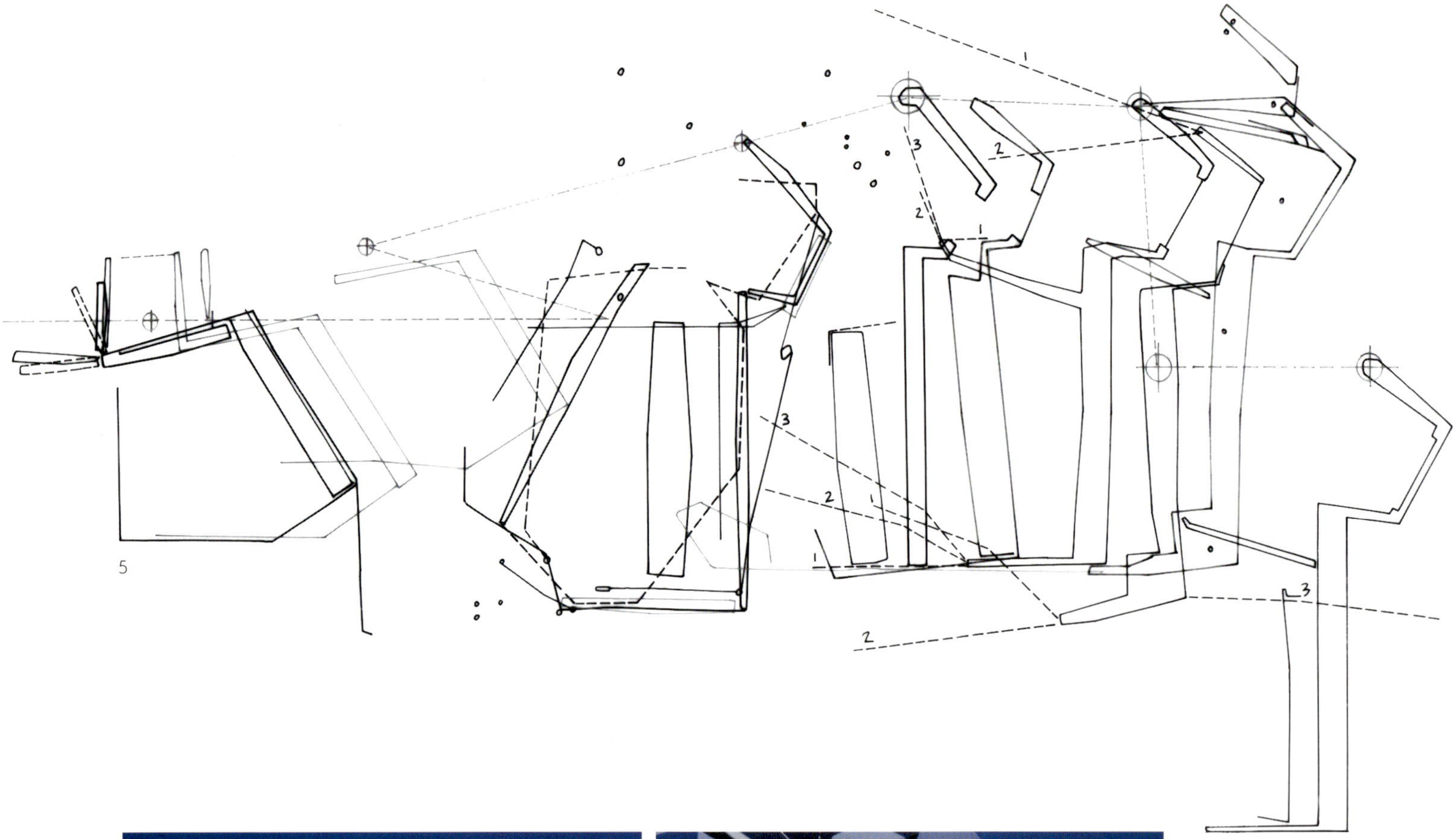

5

6

7

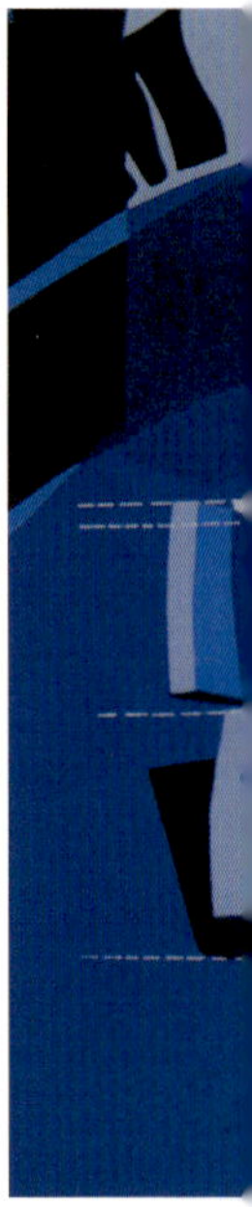
9

5&8 *Sketch studies of mobile cupboard in motion* **6** *Mobile cupboard in motion* **7** *Main entrance* **9** *Choreography of mobile cupboard* **10** *Light and shadow modulating main hall*

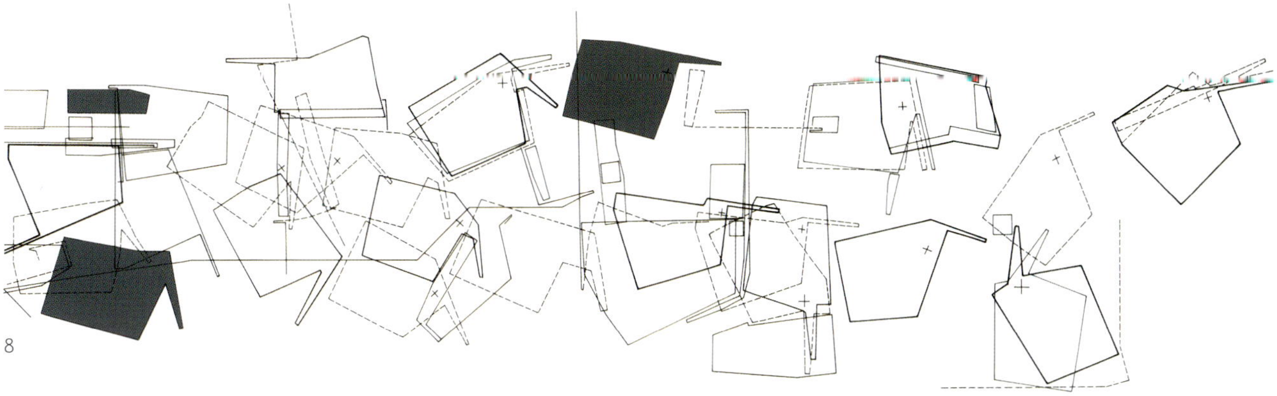

8

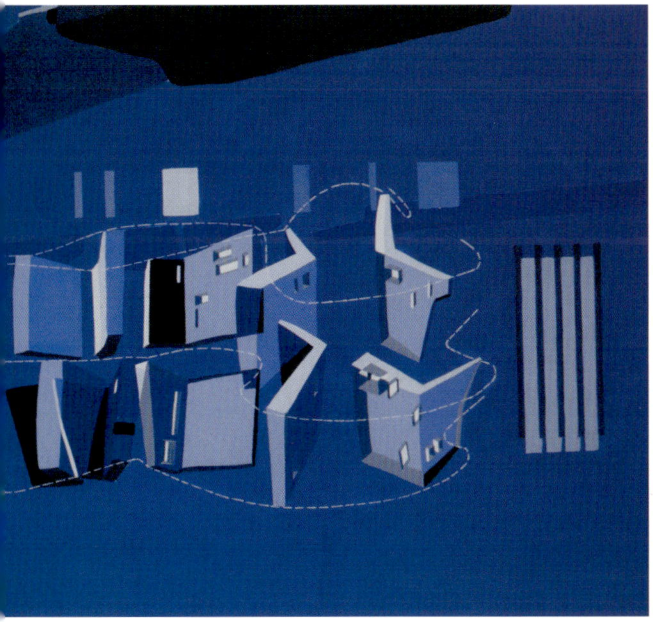

10

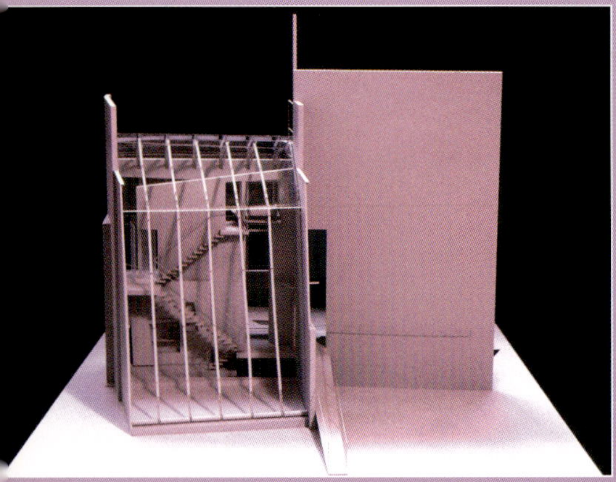

1

2

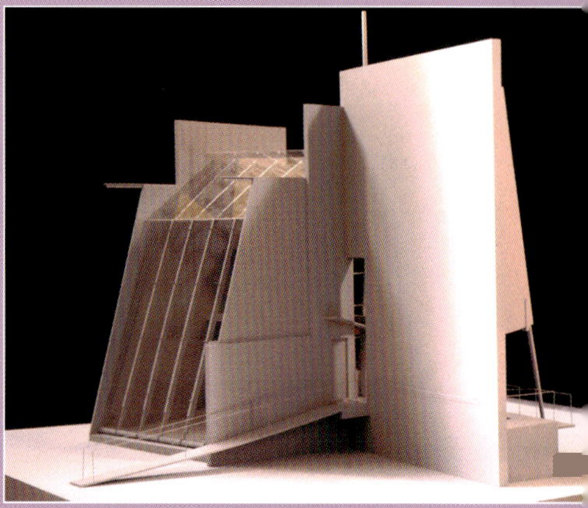

3

4

5

6

7

8

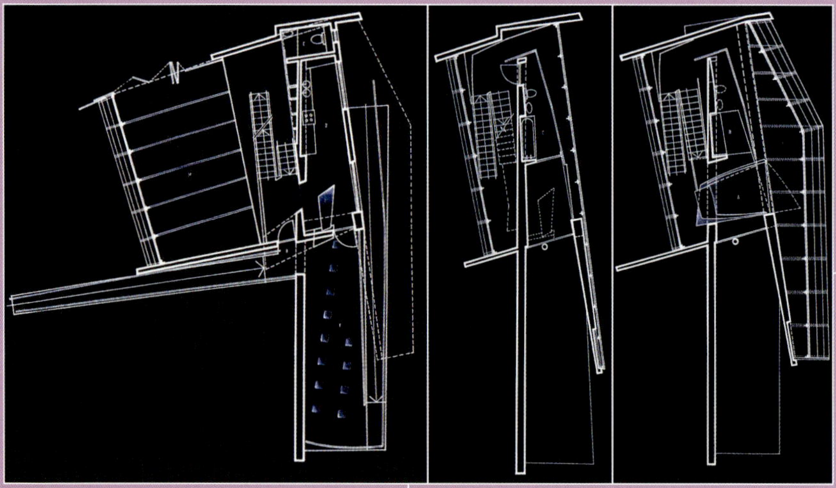

9

The transparency of the external glass skin compensates for the site's limitations by offering infinite panoramic views. The glass skin can be adjusted by manually pushing the mobile 'arms' mounted on rubber rollers on tracks.

This summer beach house in Whitstable is for a family of three. During their stay, the family would spend most of their time on the beach or in the water; a minimal amount of living space and furnishing is therefore required. The spaces included are for cooking, sleeping, washing, living and a dance studio. Spatial and visual links between the internal spaces are considered to be essential.

The house stands between the promenade on the north and the open beach and sea to the south. The constraints of the site (only 18.5 metres) and the idiosyncratic programme, inspire a piece of architecture with kinetic boundaries and volumes.

The site runs parallel to the sea and is subsequently divided into parallel zones. The concrete spine wall is the main structure of the house and is punctuated by a narrow slit to coincide with a main ramp leading to the entrance. This route offers a surprise glimpse of the sea when approaching the house. Storage, services, structures, furniture and circulation either exist within the inhabitable spine or are found clinging to it.

The transparency of the external glass skin compensates for the site's limitations by offering infinite panoramic views. The glass skin can be adjusted by manually pushing the mobile 'arms' mounted on rubber rollers on tracks. This enclosure adjustment provides a reciprocal relationship between the living room/conservatory and the dance studio.

With the dance studio 'opened' (daytime), the beach and sea act as the extended living space. The only reminder of the conservatory (closed by this time) would be the track marks on the sand 'carpet'.

At night, the family gathers in the 'opened' conservatory with the delicately lit townscape as backdrop. The structural system of the skin also allows the entire house to pack up like a suitcase when the family returns to the city.

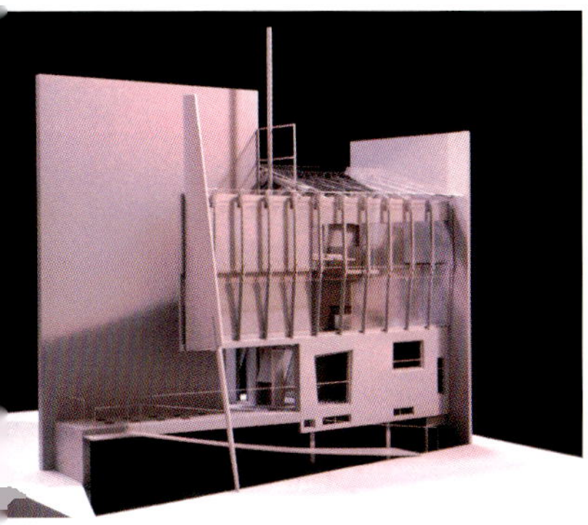

WHITSTABLE, UK

BEACH HOUSE

competition entry

1-4 *External views of house* **5** *Ramp from beach to patio* **6** *View from patio* **7** *Bird's-eye view of fireplace and glass membrane* **8** *Closeup of beach façade* **9** *Plan (left to right) ground, first floor and second floor* **10** *Beach façade*

The remaining spaces are seen as a continuous series of stage-sets with endless spatial theatre. An external patio extends from the viewing and eating areas (its triple-volume ceiling is the bed slab for the main bedrooms). A sleeping mezzanine overlooks a dark studio and the bathtub commands views down the length of the beach. The foundation 'box' structure provides subterranean playing and sleeping space for the child. Life is played out amongst the kinetic skin and the volumes of the building.

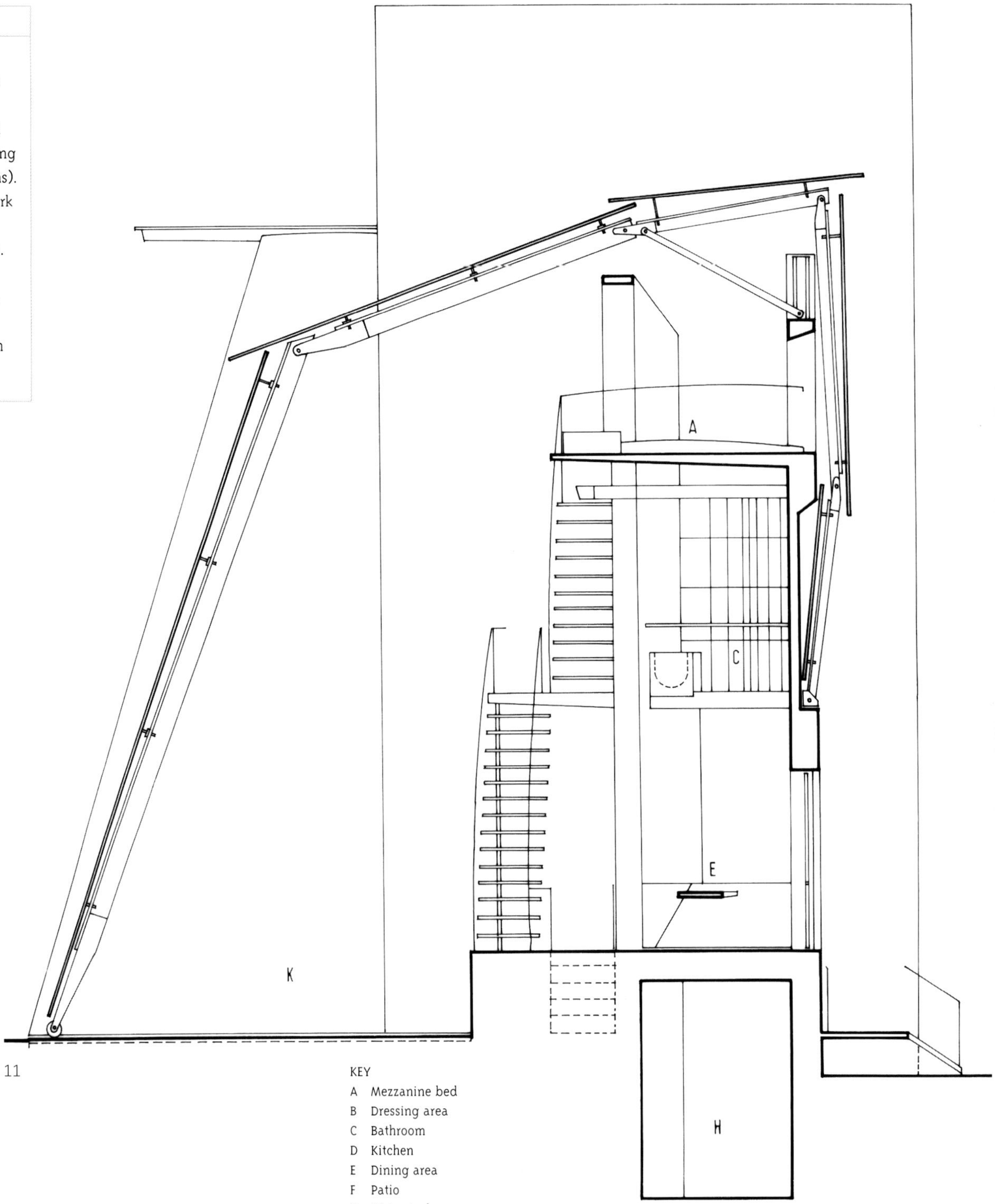

11

KEY

A Mezzanine bed
B Dressing area
C Bathroom
D Kitchen
E Dining area
F Patio
G Water tank
H Child's den
K Living room conservatory
L Dance studio

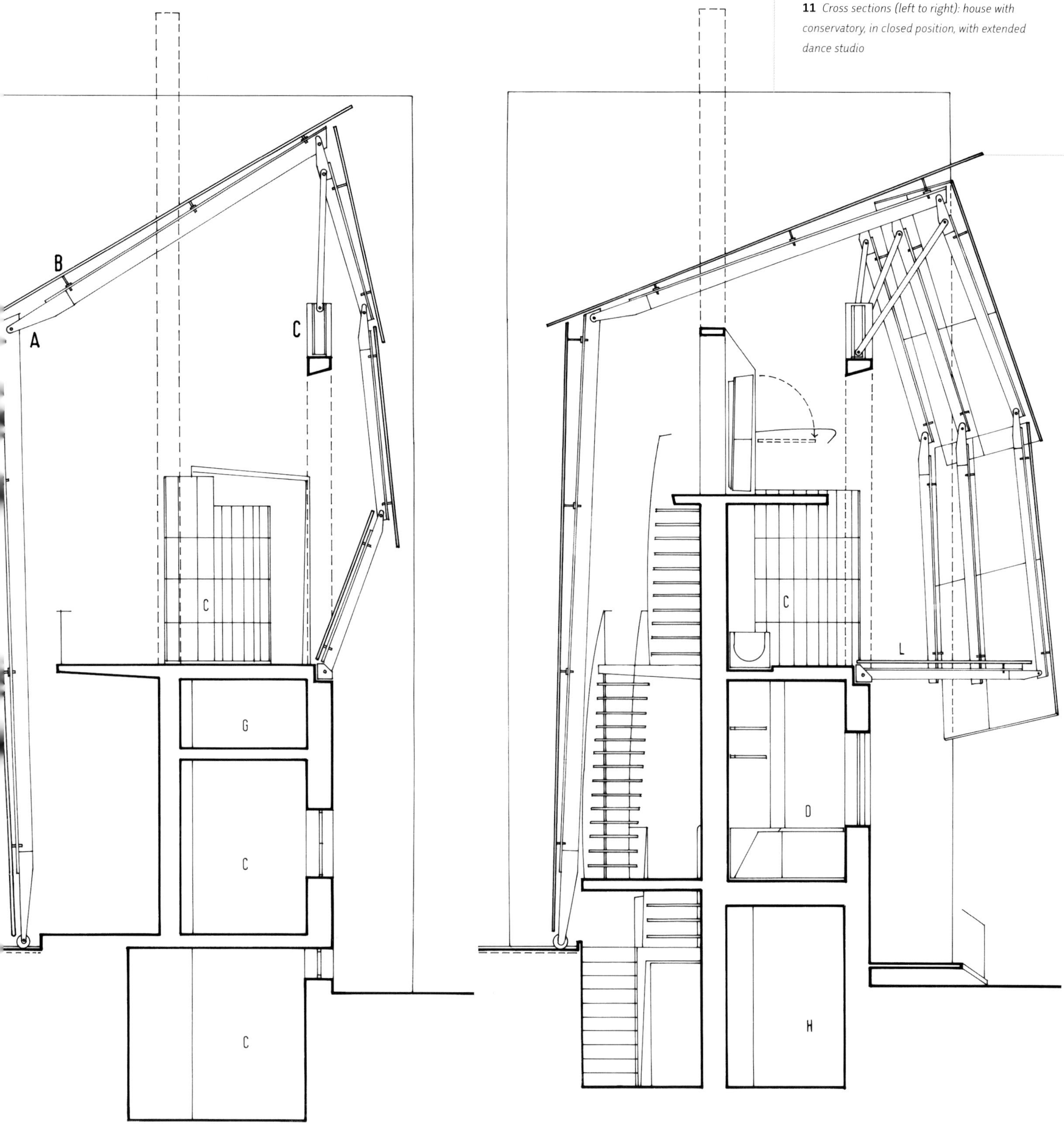

11 *Cross sections (left to right): house with conservatory, in closed position, with extended dance studio*

›››

2005

Royal Canal Linear Park International Competition, Ireland
Bonn Square Oxford International Competition, UK
Extension of the Kunsthalle Bremen International Competition, Germany
The United Cultures of Britain
Shaftesbury Avenue, London

2004

Virtually Venice
Olympic Paris 2012 Landmark, France

2003

Green Croft at NW6
Nam June Paik Museum International Competition, Korea

2002

Central Glass International Architectural Competition Japan: Restaurant in the Ruralscape
Sittingbourne Cultural International Competition, Kent, UK
New Tomohiro Museum Of Shi-Ga International Competition, Japan

2001

Aqua Centre International Competition, Aalborg, Denmark
3 Acres on the Lake: DuSable Park Proposal Project, Chicago
Central Glass International Architectural Competition Japan: GlassHouse
Accommodating Change – Circle 33 Innovation in Housing Competition 2001

2000

Sins: Kiss and Tell/Show Me the Money/You Talking to Me/Load of Bull/Twentyfourseven/Sodom and Gomorrah/Tonic
Palos Verdes Art Center, USA International Competition
15th Membrane Design International Competition, Japan: Public Urban Spaces
A Country House Competition, Lancashire, UK
Folkestone Seafood Stall Competition

1999

14th Membrane International Competition, Japan: Shoreline Membranes
Concepthouse 2000 (International) Ideal Home Exhibition: Clone House

1998

Ephemeral Fields
CO+CO Bar Prototype 1 + 2, London
Dreamfood Factory, London
96 Park St, London W1

1997

7th SXL Housing Design Competition, Japan
Lash, Roller Hockey Centre, London
Shinkenchiku Residential Competition, Japan: House Of Collaboration
Jyvaskyla Music/Arts Centre International Competition, Finland
Museum Costantini International Competition, Buenos Aires

1996

SW Sushi Bar, London

1995

UCL Cultural Centre International Competition
Nim-Ble
Guest House, Shinkenchiku Competition, Japan
56 Wardour Street, London
Northern Architecture Centre Competition
Nara/Toto World Architecture Triennale 1995: Wardour St & Compton St
Korean/American Museum of Arts and Cultural Centre International Design Competition, Los Angeles

1994

Landmark Competition for Museum of Moving Image, London
6th Shinkenchiku/Takiron Competition (Japan): City Threshold
Sunderland Glass Centre Competition

1993

Burgess Park Competition
Dance Partner I
Hamburg Bauforum 1993
Stereoscopic I

1992

Scottish Sports Council Hotel Swimming Pool Competition
Kent Design Initiative Competition
Conversations
Thames Path Bridge Competition

1990

The New Acropolis Museum Competition
Concours Architecture Textile, Nimes, France
Central Glass Co. (Japan) Competition: Glass House 2001
Dulwich Picture Gallery Competition
Freedom Square Competition, Entry no. 1 & 2

1989

A Chair for Joseph Competition
Central Glass Co. (Japan) Competition: A Terminal for a Linear Car

1987

Japanese/NCE Competition: An Image of the Bridge of the Future
Building Centre Trust Competition 'Housing: A Demonstration Project'

Olympic Paris 2012 Landmark
Project type: Competition entry
Date of completion: 2004
Location: Paris, France
Team: cj Lim, Yumi Saito, Maxwell Mutanda
Consultants: Matthew Wells/Techniker

Nam June Paik Museum
Project type: Competition entry
Date of completion: 2003
Location: Yong-In, Province of Kyonggi, Korea
Team: cj Lim, Christopher Wong, Matthew Thornley, Andrew Stanforth, JM Kong
Consultants: Matthew Wells/Techniker

Grasshopper Inn
Project type: Competition entry
Date of completion: 2002
Location: Hokkaido, Japan
Team: cj Lim, JM Kong

Sittingbourne Cultural Centre
Project type: Competition entry
Date of completion: 2001
Location: Kent, UK
Team: cj Lim, JM Kong, Ed Liu, Bartlett Architecture Lab
Consultants: Matthew Wells/Techniker

Park of Sand
Project type: Research project
Date of completion: 2001
Location: Chicago, USA
Team: cj Lim, JM Kong, Bartlett Architecture Lab
Consultants: Matthew Wells/Techniker

Hanging Gardens of Wanton Harmony
Project type: Research project
Date of completion: 2000
Location: London, UK
Team: cj Lim, Ed Liu, JM Kong

Urban Cowfarm
Project type: Research project
Date of completion: 2000
Location: London, UK
Team: cj Lim, Ed Liu, JM Kong

Jerry Springer Museum
Project type: Research project
Date of completion: 2000
Location: London, UK
Team: cj Lim, Ed Liu, JM Kong

Trafalgar Square
Project type: Research project
Date of completion: 2000
Location: London, UK
Team: cj Lim, Ed Liu, JM Kong

Country House
Project type: Competition entry
Date of completion: 2000
Location: Lancashire, UK
Team: cj Lim, Rhys Cannon, Bartlett Architecture Lab
Consultants: Matthew Wells/Techniker

Folkestone Seafood Pavilion
Project type: Competition entry
Date of completion: 2000
Location: Kent, UK
Team: cj Lim, JM Kong, Bartlett Architecture Lab
Consultants: Matthew Wells/Techniker

Clone House
Project type: Competition entry
Date of completion: 1999
Location: London, UK
Team: cj Lim, Ed Liu, Hans Drexler, JM Kong
Consultants: Matthew Wells/Techniker, Davis Langdon Everest

Ephemeral Fields
Project type: Research project
Date of completion: 1998
Team: cj Lim, Lee Harris
Consultants: Matthew Wells/Techniker

University College London Museum
Project type: Competition entry
Date of completion: 1995
Location: London, UK
Team: cj Lim, Mark Smout, Dominique Leutwyler, Rachel Calladine, Berthold Jungblut, Jens Rendecker, Alexander Franz, Mustafar Gur, Georg Stocker, Andrew Budd, Jane Houghton, James Mann, Andreas Charalambous, Mark Church, Jose Frojan
Consultants: Matthew Wells/Techniker, Crispin Matson/Rybka Battle

Guest House
Project type: Research project
Date of completion: 1995
Team: cj Lim, Mark Smout, Dominique Leutwyler, Georg Stocker, JM Kong

Newcastle Architecture Centre
Project type: Competition Entry
Date of completion: 1995
Location: Newcastle, UK
Team: cj Lim, Mark Smout, Dominique Leutwyler, Rachel Calladine, Berthold Jungblut, Andreas Charalambous,
Consultants: Matthew Wells/Techniker

Beach House
Project type: Competition entry
Date of completion: 1987
Location: Whitstable, UK
Team: cj Lim, Kevin Li
Consultants: Matthew Wells/Techniker

Company structure
Principal: cj Lim
Current and former staff: Ed Liu, JM Kong, Christopher Wong, Yumi Saito, Lawrence Wong, John Craske, Maxwell Mutanda, Pascal Bronner, Jacqueline Chak, Jenny Lam, Mark Smout, Lee Harris, Dominique Leutwyler, Rachel Calladine, Berthold Jungblut, Matthew Thornley, Andrew Stanforth, Hans Drexler, Kaoru Nakayama, Shuheng Huang, Phyllis Lam, Wing Tsai Tsui, Peter Wawra, Jason Pau, Jens Rendecker, Alexander Franz, Dirk Haertner, Mustafar Gur, Georg Stocker, James Mann, Andreas Charalambous, Mark Church, Jose Frojan, Winky Wong, Andrew Abdulezer, Andrew Budd, Jane Houghton

Studio 8 Architects Ltd was established in 1994. The practice consistently explores in parallel architecture, landscape and urban design possibilities through narratives, human behaviours and psychology, ethnicity and Victorian technological inventiveness.

The practice has won numerous international competitions, including Glass House Japan [2001], Ideal Home Concept House UK [1999], UCL Museum UK [1996], Bridge of the Future Japan [1987], Housing: a Demonstration Project UK [1987].

Other competition entries include museum and cultural buildings for Nam June Paik Museum Korea [2003], Sittingbourne Cultural Centre UK [2002], Tomohiro Museum of Shi-Ga Japan [2002], Palos Verdes Arts Centre USA [2000], Jyvaskyla Music and Art Centre Finland [1997], Museum Constantini Buenos Aires Argentina [1997], Newcastle Architecture Centre UK [1995], Korean American Arts and Cultural Centre Los Angeles USA [1995], and Glass Centre Sunderland UK [1994].

Designs for sports buildings comprise Aqua Centre Aalborg Denmark [2001] and LASH Roller Hockey Centre London UK [1997]. House and housing proposals include Accommodating Change Bow UK [2001], Country House Lancashire UK [2000], SXL Housing Japan [1997] and Guest House Japan [1995].

Landscape projects include Grasshopper Inn [2002], DuSable Park Chicago USA [2001], Urban Metazoo [1999] and Ephemeral Fields [1998]. Projects incorporating urban strategies are Virtually Venice [2004], Trafalgar Square London [2000], Water World China [1995] and Wardour St @ Old Compton St London [1994].

The projects have been widely published in international periodicals and newspapers. Monographs include *Sins + Other Spatial Relatives* [2001], *How Green is Your Garden?* [2003] and *Museums* [work in progress, 2004].

Drawings and models from this practice have won much acclaim within public and academic circles, and have formed part of the permanent architectural collection of the Victoria & Albert Museum London, Fonds Regional d'Art Contemporain du Centre [FRAC] France and the RIBA British Architectural Library London.

Major international exhibitions include Venice Architecture Biennale 04, British Pavilion [2004], Mackintosh Museum Glasgow [2004], ARCHILAB Fonds Regional d'Art Contemporain du Centre France [1999], RMIT Melbourne Australia [1996] and Stadelschule Frankfurt [1997].

Other group exhibitions include Mediatheque d'Orleans France [2002], Chicago Architecture Foundation USA [2001], Thread Waxing Gallery New York [2001], Storefront Gallery New York [2001], Gallery 312 Chicago USA [2001], Architecture Foundation London [2001], RIBA London [2000], Academie de France Rome [2000], CUBE Gallery Manchester [2000], Canadian Institute of Architecture Montreal [1998], Defence Corp Building Jyvaskyla Finland [1997], Nara World Architecture Triennale Japan [1995], Museo Nazionale Di Castel St Angelo Rome [1994], National Gallery Alexandros Soutzos Museum Athens [1990] and Dulwich Picture Gallery [1990].

cj Lim was born in Malaysia in 1964. Graduating from the Architectural Association London in 1987, he worked for several London firms before establishing his own practice, Studio 8 Architects Ltd in 1994.

In 2004, he was selected to represent the UK in the Venice Architecture Biennale 04 and was named as one of the 'New British Talents in Architecture' by the *Guardian* and *The Independent* newspapers. He is also listed in Debrett's *People of Today* and *The International Who's Who* for his architectural and academic contributions. In 1997, he was the first recipient of the Royal Institute of British Architects Award for Academic Contribution in Architectural Education. He received the award again in 1998 and 1999.

His academic work began in 1989 and he has since taught at the Architectural Association London, University of North London and University of East London. Currently, he is the Director, Bartlett Architecture Research Lab (1999– present), Director BSc Architecture Course (2001– present) and Diploma Unit Master (1993– present) at the Bartlett University College London. The Royal Institute of British Architects President's Medals in Education have consistently been awarded to his students: Bronze Medal runners-up [1992, 1995, 1996] and winner [1997, 1998]; Silver Medal winners [1993, 1994, 1995, 1998, 1999] and runners-up [1996, 1997].

He is a regular international visiting critic, RIBA External Examiner and Visiting Professor at Mackintosh School of Architecture, Glasgow (2001– present); Chiba Institute of Technology, Japan (2004); School of Architecture, Aarhus, Denmark (2002); Technological University, Lund, Sweden (2001 and 2003); Stadelschule, Frankfurt, Germany (1997 and 2000) and Curtin University, Perth, Australia (1996).

He has also edited architectural books including *Realms of Impossibility: AIR* [2002], *Realms of Impossibility: GROUND* [2002], *Realms of Impossibility: WATER* [2002], *Devices* [2005] and *Architectural Typologies* [2006].

PRINCIPAL BIOGRAPHY

2002	Central Glass International Architectural Competition Japan: Restaurant in the Ruralscape	Honourable Mention
2001	Central Glass International Architectural Competition Japan: Glass House	First Prize
2001	Accommodating Change – Circle 33 Innovation in Housing Competition	Commendation
2000	15th Membrane Design International Competition Japan: Public Urban Spaces	Shortlisted
1999	Concept House 2000 (International) Ideal Home Exhibition	Second Prize
1999	14th Membrane Design International Competition Japan: Shoreline Membrane	Honourable Mention
1997	Jyvaskyla Music/Arts Centre International Competition, Finland	Shortlisted
1997	7th SXL Housing Design Competition, Japan	Honourable Mention
1996	UCL Cultural Centre International Competition	First Prize
1995	NARA/TOTO World Architecture Triennale: Wardour St @ Compton St	Honourable Mention
1992	Scottish Sports Council Hotel Swimming Pool Competition: Crown Berger Colour Built Environment Awards	Commendation
1990	Dulwich Picture Gallery Competition	Shortlisted
1990	Freedom Square Competition, Entry No. 1 & 2	Shortlisted
1989	A Chair For Joseph Competition	Shortlisted
1987	Japanese/NCE Competition – An Image Of The Bridge Of The Future	Second Prize
1987	Building Centre Trust Competition 'Housing: A Demonstration Project'	First Prize

Books

Architectural Typologies, cj Lim (Ed), Lawrence King, 2006

Devices, cj Lim (Ed), Architectural Press, 2005

Museums [work in process], cj Lim, Glasgow School of Art Press, 2004

Nine Positions: British Pavilion, Peter Cook and Emily Campbell (Ed), 9th Venice Biennale of Architecture 2004, British Council, 2004

70 Years of Art and Architecture at the British Pavilion Venice, Sarah Gillet (Ed), British Council, 2004

Metamorph: Vectors, Trajectories, Focus, La Biennale di Venezia, Davide Croft (Ed), Marsilio, 2004

How Green is Your Garden?, cj Lim, Wiley-Academy, 2003

Architectures Experimentes 1950–2000, Marie-Ange Brayer and Frederic Migayrou (Ed), Fonds Regional D'Art Contemporain Du Centre, 2003

3 Acres on the Lake: Dusable Park Proposal Project, WhiteWalls Inc. supported by Illinois Arts Council, Graham Foundation, R Driehaus Foundation, Laurie Palmer (Ed), WhiteWalls, 2003

Realms of Impossibility: AIR, cj Lim and Ed Liu (Ed), Wiley-Academy, 2002

Realms of Impossibility: GROUND, cj Lim and Ed Liu (Ed), Wiley-Academy, 2002

Realms of Impossibility: WATER, cj Lim and Ed Liu (Ed), Wiley-Academy, 2002

Accomodating Change: Innovation in Housing, Hilary French (Ed), Circle 33 Housing Group, 2002

ARCHILAB: Radical Experiments in Global Architecture, Marie-Ange Brayer and Frederic Migayrou (Ed), Thames and Hudson, 2001

Sins + Other Spatial Relatives, cj Lim, Ind–E8 London, 2000

441/10...We'll Reconfigure the Space When You're Ready, cj Lim, Ind-E8 London, 1996

Periodicals and Newspapers

Articles by cj Lim or about the work of cj Lim/Studio 8 Architects have appeared in the following periodicals and newspapers:
AA Files (UK), *Abitare* (Italy), *A+U* (Japan), *Architects Journal* (UK), *Architecture Today* (UK), *Architectural Design* (UK), *Art-4D* (Thailand), *ArtPress* (France), *Bauwelt* (Germany), *Beaux Arts* (France), *Building Design* (UK), *Design Week* (UK), *Domus* (Italy), *GA Houses* (Japan), *Graphics International* (UK), *Japan Architect* (Japan), *Kenchiku-Bunka* (Japan), *Korea Architects* (Korea), *Monument* (Australia), *Shinkenchiku* (Japan), *Werk, Bauen + Wohnen* (Switzerland), the *Guardian* (UK), *The Herald* (UK), *The Independent* (UK), *The Sunday Times* (UK), *The Times* (UK).